The Musician's Guide to Pro Tools®

Second Edition

John Keane

New York   Chicago   San Francisco   Lisbon
London   Madrid   Mexico City   Milan   New Delhi
San Juan   Seoul   Singapore   Sydney   Toronto

The **McGraw·Hill** Companies

Cataloging-in-Publication Data is on file with the Library of Congress

McGraw-Hill books are available at special quantity discounts to use as premiums and sales promotions, or for use in corporate training programs. For more information, please write to the Director of Special Sales, Professional Publishing, McGraw-Hill, Two Penn Plaza, New York, NY 10121-2298. Or contact your local bookstore.

The Musician's Guide to Pro Tools,® Second Edition

1 2 3 4 5 6 7 8 9 0 DOC DOC 0 1 9 8 7

ISBN: Book p/n 978-0-07-154473-3 and CD p/n 978-0-07-154474-0
of set 978-0-07-149742-8

MHID: Book p/n 0-07-154473-9 and CD p/n 0-07-154474-7
of set 0-07-149742-0

Sponsoring Editor
Roger Stewart

Editorial Supervisor
Janet Walden

Project Manager
Aparna Shukla,
International Typesetting
and Composition

Acquisitions Coordinator
Carly Stapleton

Technical Editor
Rick Fowler

Copy Editor
Bill McManus

Proofreader
Nigel O' Brien

Indexer
Claire Splan

Production Supervisor
Jean Bodeaux

Composition
International Typesetting
and Composition

Illustration
International Typesetting
and Composition

Art Director, Cover
Jeff Weeks

Cover Designer
Pattie Lee

Cover Illustration
Ross Garcia

Contents at a Glance

This book is dedicated to the memory of Michael Houser,
friend and fellow musician.

About the Author

John Keane is a veteran producer, engineer, and musician who has been involved in many gold and multi-platinum records. He is best known for his work with R.E.M., Indigo Girls, Cowboy Junkies, and Widespread Panic. He owns his own studio in Athens, Georgia, and has been an avid Pro Tools user since 1991. A native of Athens, he began his recording career by making demos at home on a four track mounted in a shopping cart for portability. As his home studio progressed, he began recording projects for up-and-coming Athens bands such as Love Tractor, Pylon, and, of course, R.E.M. He no longer resides in his studio, as it has evolved into a full-featured recording facility. He continues to play live as a special guest with local bands such as Widespread Panic. He is also currently teaching a Pro Tools course for the Music Business Program at the University of Georgia. More information about the author's discography and his studio can be found at **www.johnkeanestudios.com**.

About the Technical Editor

Rick Fowler is a musician and an engineer/producer who has appeared on hundreds of recordings. He uses Pro Tools on a daily basis.

Contents

Foreword

by Peter Buck of R.E.M.

I've known John Keane for almost twenty-five years. When my band first worked with John, he had just made the huge technological leap from four-track to eight-track—analog, of course.

Over the next eighteen or nineteen years and seven or eight albums, I've watched John expand his studio from eight-track to sixteen-track to twenty-four track, and finally to forty-eight track digital. Every step of the way, John mastered the new equipment and squeezed the most sonically out of each format. Then along came Pro Tools.

I was doing a session with some band now lost in the mists of time when John unpacked the thing. My first question was, "Why would anyone want a television in the control room?" This prompted a twenty-minute explanation from John on the technology and uses of Pro Tools. Of course it was all over my head; I'd gotten lost somewhere between the switch from eight tracks to sixteen. I do remember, though, that John used the phrase "the wave of the future."

Over the course of the next year, I saw John work his way through the manual, and day by day, miracles occurred. As John became more and more familiar with Pro Tools, recording became easier and easier. Great takes that had one huge glitch were fixed; editing became instantaneous.

Over the years I've since worked with many Pro Tools operators, and I've got to say, John can make that thing do things that no one else can. I'd recommend this book to anybody, whether beginner or expert. As for myself, I'm almost ready to make the jump to sixteen tracks.

See ya,
Peter

Acknowledgments

I would like to express my thanks to the friends and colleagues who aided me in this endeavor: Chris, Joel, and Kelly Byron, Patrick "Tigger" Ferguson, Paul Lazzari, Randall Bramblett, Billy Field, Charles Driebe Esq., Wilson Sheldon, Vic Chesnutt, Mike Houser, Kai Riedl, Pat Priest, Rick Fowler, Terry Allen, Peter Buck, Pete Yandell, and Scott Sosebee. Many thanks to the folks at Digidesign: Johnny Andrews, Claudia Curcio, Thays Carvalho. For encouragement, support, and expert advice, I'd like to thank the crew at Atlanta Pro Audio: Chick Cusick, Troy Manning, Dean Klear, and Chris Neff.

Introduction

So you've succumbed to the allure of the magical world of hard-disk recording and plunked down your hard-earned cash on a Pro Tools system. Luckily for you, you've made a wise choice. Pro Tools is the de facto standard in professional digital recording. It is a rare recording studio, radio station, or film/video post production facility that doesn't use Pro Tools. If creating and recording music is your goal, I can assure you that the time spent learning this program will not be in vain. Aspiring audio engineers must learn Pro Tools if they intend to get any studio work. Even if you never become a Pro Tools wizard, if you're a musician, you need to know how Pro Tools works and what it can do.

"Overwhelming." This is the word I hear most often from people who are trying to get off the ground with Pro Tools. It's a lot to take in all at once.

When I bought my first Pro Tools system in 1991, I had no Pro Tools "guru" to go to for help, so I had to stumble through it on my own. There were no third-party books like this one, only a very large reference manual. To make matters worse,

I had no computer experience at all. For me, learning Pro Tools was a lot like learning to play a new musical instrument. I was very frustrated at first, and it was quite a while before I was able to do anything musical with it. Many times I was tempted to make a few sledgehammer adjustments. Of course, once I got the hang of it and realized what it could do, I was completely hooked.

At that time Pro Tools was a very new product. The software was version 1. It was primitive and clunky and slow as molasses. My computer, a brand-new 25-MHz Mac 2ci, puffed and wheezed and was barely able to keep up. It could only play back four tracks at a time, and since I didn't have a reliable way to sync it up to my 24-track tape machine, I didn't find it particularly useful except for editing 2-track mixes. Since I had never been interested in computers, I had resisted buying one until I was absolutely forced to by the need to be able to sequence my DAT mixes for mastering purposes.

I must admit that initially I rarely used Pro Tools to its full potential until I ran into a stumbling block that could only be solved by digital editing. While producing "Lay It Down" for the Cowboy Junkies, I needed to fly in a lead vocal from one version of a song to another, but the two versions were not at the same tempo. Pro Tools enabled me to make it work when nothing else could. It really opened my eyes to the potential of Pro Tools, and I have never looked back since. Today Pro Tools is much more stable and easier to use. It's also more complex.

Peripheral Gear: What Else Do You Need?

This book originally began as a collection of notes I gathered to help musician friends of mine who bought DIGI 001 systems for their home studios. The notes eventually evolved into this book as I came to realize that these inexpensive Pro Tools LE systems were about to take over the planet. The book was written mainly for musicians who want to record demos on their own at home, so I'm assuming you have a space set aside for recording, and you've bought a Pro Tools system, most likely using the LE version of the software. The various Pro Tools LE systems are so self-contained, you won't need much peripheral gear to complete the lessons. In addition to your Pro Tools interface and your computer, you will need the following items:

- Headphones and/or amplified speakers
- An instrument, such as a guitar or keyboard

It would also be helpful to have the following items on hand:

■ A keyboard with a USB port. If your keyboard only has a MIDI port, you also need a MIDI interface for systems such as the Mbox 2 Mini that don't include a MIDI input.

■ A MIDI-capable drum machine.

For those of you in a classroom or lab situation where it may not be feasible to have musicians playing and recording instruments, an academic version of Chapters 1 through 4 is included in PDF form on the Session Disc CD-ROM in the back of this book. In your case, you should complete the academic version of these four chapters and then return to the main part of the book for Chapters 5 through 13. The subject matter is the same in the academic version—the main difference is that instead of tracking and overdubbing with your own instruments, all sound files for the exercises are supplied on the Session Disc CD-ROM.

Before You Start: Skim That Pro Tools Manual!

You may have bought this book in the hopes that you wouldn't have to read the Pro Tools manual. Sorry! You still need to at least skim through it. *The Musician's Guide to Pro Tools*, Second Edition, is in no way intended to be a substitute for any of the Pro Tools documentation. As a longtime studio owner and admitted gear head, I've had to plow through countless manuals, and the Pro Tools manuals are some of the best I've seen.

This book assumes the following:

■ You have a basic understanding of how to operate your computer.

■ If you're using an LE system, you have read the *Getting Started* manual.

■ You have successfully installed and configured one of the Pro Tools— compatible interfaces and have familiarized yourself with the *Pro Tools Reference Guide*.

■ And now you wanna rock.

If you have installed Pro Tools LE or HD from the DVD installer disc, the appropriate reference documentation has already been placed on your hard drive. On a Mac the documents are located in the Applications folder. Look under Digidesign > Pro Tools > Release Notes & Documentation. On a Windows machine the path is as follows: C: > Program Files > Digidesign > Documentation. If you installed Pro Tools by downloading a web installer from Digidesign, you must also download and run the document installer for your version of Pro Tools.

The *Pro Tools Reference Guide* is included in these files and is accessible under the Help menu in an open Pro Tools session. A hard copy is provided with Pro Tools HD systems. The *Reference Guide* is several hundred pages long, and you should not confuse it with the thin volume, titled *Getting Started*, that comes with the LE systems.

When you're learning Pro Tools, it's handy to have a hard copy of the *Guide*. In my experience, switching back and forth between a Pro Tools window and a PDF file is tedious. If a hard copy did not come with your system, I strongly suggest you print out the *Reference Guide* and the *DigiRack Plug-Ins Guide* and bind them so that you can leaf through them at your leisure. I also suggest you print your Pro Tools serial number somewhere in the *Guide*. I usually also print it on the installation CD with a fine-point marker. I took my Pro Tools installation CD to a local copier and had these guides printed on quality paper and put in a sturdy binder. These guides can also be downloaded from the Digidesign web site (www.digidesign.com).

My advice to you is to skim the *Pro Tools Reference Guide* quickly, take a highlighter and mark the parts that interest you, and then revisit it after you have played around with the program awhile. Don't get bogged down in the advanced stuff. Unless you are some kind of genius, you can't digest the whole thing at once any more than you can eat a fifty-pound burrito.

You must read the installation section of *Getting Started* thoroughly and follow it to the letter. Truthfully, just about anybody with some patience can install a Pro Tools system. Just don't be in a hurry. If you bought an HD system and you're not comfortable popping the hood on your computer, ask a computer-savvy friend to help. If your Pro Tools dealer is worth his salt, he'll help you put your system together.

Pro Tools is a very deep and complex program. After more than a decade of working with Pro Tools, I'm still learning, and there are still many features I have never used. This book is not designed to take you into every last nook and cranny of Pro Tools. The trick to making Pro Tools work for you is to only go as deep as necessary to get the job done.

In the interests of flexibility, the designers of Pro Tools have provided a thousand ways to do every little thing. To the novice, it can seem like there are a thousand ways to screw up. Therefore, to avoid confusion, I'm just going to show you methods that have worked for me. Hopefully, you will be able to learn from my mistakes instead of making them yourself.

There will be times when you will make a wrong move and think that you have irretrievably lost part of your music. If you follow the procedures outlined in this book, this will rarely be the case. The beauty of hard-disk recording is that it is mostly nondestructive. What this means to you is that even when you've mangled your tracks to the point where they are either unrecognizable or they've disappeared from the screen altogether, you can almost always get back to where you were. The files are most likely still there on your hard drive unless you have purposefully deleted them.

Conventions Used in This Book

Initially Pro Tools was only available on the Macintosh platform. In recent years a Windows version has become available. The Windows version is almost identical; the main difference is in the keyboard commands. In most cases, the Mac COMMAND key (the one with the Apple logo and the ⌘ symbol) and the Windows CTRL key are the same, as are the Mac OPTION key and the Windows ALT key. The Mac RETURN key and the Windows ENTER key are the same. (To avoid confusion, the ENTER key on the numeric keypad on the right side of the keyboard will be referred to as NUMERIC ENTER.) The Windows keystroke equivalents will appear in parentheses. Aside from this, the conventions used in this manual are similar to the ones used in the Pro Tools manuals. For instance:

- ⌘+K means hold the COMMAND key and press the K key.

- CTRL+K means hold the CTRL key and press the K key.

- Display > Edit Window Shows > Sends View means look under the Display menu, choose Edit Window Shows, and then choose the Sends View submenu option.

- OPTION+click means hold the OPTION key and click with the mouse button.

- ALT+click means hold the ALT key and click with the mouse button.

- In general, when this book refers to a "button," it is in the Pro Tools window. When this book refers to a "key," it is referring to your computer's keyboard.

Most of the figures in this book are screen shots from the Macintosh LE version of Pro Tools. Some of the windows and dialogs may have a slightly different appearance in other versions.

About the Session Disc

The Session Disc is a CD-ROM with Pro Tools session files, plug-in demos, the academic versions of Chapters 1 through 4 in PDF form, and a PDF file of Appendix B, "Cheat Sheets and Function Key Labels," with printable function key labels and keyboard shortcut charts. If you don't have access to a printer, cutout versions are provided in Appendix B in the book. It is recommended that you label your keyboard's function keys and tape a Cheat Sheet to your monitor before you start the exercises.

The Session Disc is a CD-ROM; it cannot be played in a music CD player. The Pro Tools session files are specifically for use in certain exercises. The best course of action is to copy the entire contents of the CD to your audio drive from the beginning to save yourself the trouble of reinserting the Session Disc when the other session files are called for.

Copying the Session Disc to Your Hard Drive (Mac)

Remove the Session Disc CD-ROM from the back of the book and insert it into your computer's CD-ROM drive. When the Session Disc icon appears on the desktop, OPTION+drag the icon to your audio drive or main startup drive to copy the files and create a Session Disc folder at that location.

Once the files have been copied, place the Session Disc back in the sleeve in the back of the book.

Copying the Session Disc to Your Hard Drive (Windows)

Remove the Session Disc CD-ROM from the back of the book and insert it into your computer's CD-ROM drive. Then go to Start > My Computer and locate the Session Disc on your CD-ROM drive (usually the D drive). Right-click the Session Disc icon and choose Copy from the pop-up menu that appears. Right-click your audio drive or Desktop and select Paste to copy the files and create a Session Disc folder at that location.

Once the files have been copied, place the Session Disc back in the sleeve in the back of the book.

Part I

Making a Home Demo

Chapter 1

Getting Comfortable with Your Pro Tools System

I bought my first Pro Tools rig and my first computer on the same day, and I didn't even know how to turn the computer on. As a beginner, I would have found the information in this chapter invaluable. It was years before I figured out some of this stuff. If your computer is new to you, I encourage you to spend some time setting up your system before you start working your way through these exercises. It will go a long way toward alleviating the frustration and fatigue associated with plowing through the Pro Tools learning curve.

Display (Monitor) Resolution

Let's start with your computer monitor. You're going to be spending a lot of time staring at this screen, and the amount of space taken up by the various elements in the Pro Tools windows is going to become important to your workflow. You may not realize it, but it's easy to change the resolution settings for your monitor. Setting your display to a *higher* resolution will make everything on the screen a little smaller, but you will be able to view more items on the screen, and you'll do a lot less scrolling to find things. If your vision is not very good, a *lower* resolution might be better because everything will appear larger. Once you get the Pro Tools Edit window open, you should play with the settings and decide which resolution works best for you. You don't have to quit Pro Tools to do it. If you're not sure how to get to your display settings, consult Appendix A in the back of this book.

Get a Trackball

Many professional Pro Tools users prefer to use a trackball, rather than a standard mouse. My favorite is the Kensington Expert Mouse (about $100 at press time). This device has a scroll wheel and extra buttons that can easily be assigned to your favorite keyboard shortcuts.

Keyboard Shortcuts

Keyboard shortcuts are combinations of keys that enable you to select many of the commands without having to go to the Menu bar. Watch someone who can really fly in Pro Tools, and you'll realize that they've got the keyboard shortcuts down cold. Pro Tools has quite a few of them, and they usually involve pressing the COMMAND (CTRL) or OPTION (ALT) key and one other key. (Note that ⌘ is used to represent the COMMAND key throughout this book.)

If you look to the right of the commands in the menus, you will find shortcuts for most of them. These shortcuts are best learned a few at a time, as you need them. In the long run, they will speed things immensely and help prevent cramping in your mouse arm. Aching arm and shoulder muscles are a real problem among Pro Tools operators and can lead to serious injury. This can be alleviated to some degree by getting into the habit of using keyboard shortcuts, preferably with your nonmouse hand.

Cheat Sheets

In Appendix B at the back of this book, you will find Cheat Sheets like this one which you can cut out and tape to the edge of your monitor to use as a quick reference. If you have a printer, you can print them from the Cheat Sheets PDF file on the Session Disc CD-ROM included with this book. This will speed the memorization process and keep you from wasting time digging around in the book looking for them. Later exercises will have different Cheat Sheets with additional shortcuts.

Record & Play	⌘+SPACEBAR
Save Session	⌘+S
New Track	⌘+SHIFT+N
Zoom In	T
Zoom Out	R
Auto/Input	OPTION+K
Pre/Post-Roll	⌘+K
Crossfade	⌘+F
Separate Region	B
Heal Separation	⌘+H
Return to Start	RETURN key
Zoom to Fill Window	OPTION+F
Green Light	Input mode

Function Key Labels

It's also necessary to learn how to use the function keys on your keyboard to select the different tools and modes of operation in Pro Tools. To help speed the learning curve, Appendix B provides function key labels you can cut out and place across the top of your full-sized or Mac laptop keyboards. You can also print them from the Cheat Sheets PDF file on the Session Disc CD-ROM, if you don't want to cut up your book.

Since the publication of the first edition of *The Musician's Guide to Pro Tools,* Digidesign has introduced several upgrades to the program. This edition is written around Pro Tools 7.3.1. If you're using an older version of Pro Tools, some of the screen shots used in this book may not look exactly like what you see on your screen. The menus may have been rearranged, and some of the features mentioned in the lessons may not be present in older versions of Pro Tools. The different versions still work basically the same way, and most of these lessons will work on older systems.

Tips for Mac OS X Users

Which Programs Are Running?   Look at the Dock to see which icons have a black triangle under them.

Getting Icons off the Dock   There may be application icons on the Dock that you don't need and don't want to look at. With the exception of the Finder, you can get rid of these icons by simply dragging them onto the desktop, where they will vanish in a puff of smoke. These are only aliases, so the applications they refer to will not be disturbed.

Turn Off the Empty Trash Warning   If you hate this thing as much as I do, you can turn it off in the Finder Preferences (Finder > Preferences).

Asking Permission   You have to ask permission to do every little thing in OS X. You may find that you can't record on your audio drive without doing a "Get Info" on the drive and unlocking it. This is accomplished by selecting the drive in question, pressing ⌘+I to open the Get Info window, clicking Ownership & Permissions, clicking the padlock icon to unlock it, and then choosing Read & Write from the Access pop-up menu.

Dealing with the Dock (Mac OS X Only)

The *Dock* is the bar across the bottom of the screen with the different application icons. If this is not your first time starting Pro Tools, you may have noticed the Dock encroaching on your Pro Tools workspace. Unless you have a large display, you're going to need every inch of screen real estate you can get, so let's get the Dock out of the way before you start Pro Tools. Click the blue Apple icon in the upper-left corner of the screen to open the Apple menu. Choose System Preferences > Dock to open the Dock Preferences window, and choose Automatically Hide And Show The Dock. The Dock will disappear until you get close to the bottom of the screen with the mouse. This will help, but when you resize the Edit window to fill the screen, the Dock will still jump up in your way when you go for the horizontal scroll bar. In the Dock Preferences window, you can choose Position On Left. This will locate the Dock on the left side of the display, away from the scroll bars. You can also shrink the size of the Dock to make it less obtrusive.

A Word about Audio Drives

The care and feeding of hard drives is one of the least-understood aspects of recording in the Pro Tools environment, and it's a big source of problems. Many new users think they can buy a new FireWire or internal Advanced Technology Attachment (ATA) drive, and just plug it in and go. This is most definitely *not* the case.

Main Startup Drive

The main startup drive is the drive that was installed in the computer at the factory. On a desktop computer it's typically a 7200 rpm Serial-ATA drive that contains the computer's operating system and third-party applications, such as Pro Tools. A laptop computer will typically have a slower 5400 rpm drive. In most cases, Pro Tools sessions should *not* be recorded on the main startup drive of a computer. Digidesign does not support or recommend recording to the startup drive.

Of course, people ignore this warning and record on their startup drives all the time, especially laptop users who don't want to lug around extra hardware. I can tell you from experience that the main startup drive won't perform as well as a dedicated audio drive. It has its hands full running the computer's operating system (OS).

Internal Audio Drives

Most desktop computers can accommodate at least one extra internal drive. Digidesign qualifies most internal Serial-ATA drives for up to 32-track playback. Internal drives are usually cheaper (and quieter) because you're not paying for another enclosure, (noisy) fan, and power supply. Internal drives are also faster than FireWire drives. Adding an internal drive is a good option for those who record at home and don't plan to take their sessions elsewhere. They aren't difficult to install—just make sure you buy the right one for your particular computer. If the main drive is set to Master, make sure the jumpers on the second drive are set to Slave. If your system supports the Cable Select setting, then you can use that setting for both drives.

FireWire Drives

Most professional recording engineers use FireWire 400 or 800 drives to record audio in Pro Tools. They need that ability to take the drives with them when they leave the studio. A FireWire drive is basically a Serial-ATA drive with a chipset that enables it to send data through the FireWire interface. FireWire drives with the Oxford chipset have proven to work best with Pro Tools. Digidesign qualifies most FireWire drives for up to 24 tracks, but, in practice, FireWire drives will usually play back more than twice that number if there aren't a lot of edits in the song. I've seen sessions with well over 80 tracks play back from a single FireWire 400 drive.

USB Drives

USB drives are not currently supported or recommended by Digidesign for audio playback, but they can be used for backup and storage. However, some users have found that smaller Pro Tools sessions (less than 24 tracks) will play on a properly formatted USB Flash drive.

The Digidesign web site is the place to find up-to-date information about which drives are compatible with your Pro Tools system. The Digidesign User Conference (DUC) at http://duc.digidesign.com/ is a good place to find out which hardware people are using and how it is working for them.

Formatting Your Hard Drives for Pro Tools

I've found that it's a good idea to format audio drives periodically to sort of "wipe the slate clean" (after you've backed it up, of course). This will wipe out any corruption that may have accumulated in the drive's directories. This is a strong argument for using a dedicated audio drive. It's inconvenient to format your main startup drive, because doing so will wipe out your OS software and all of your applications. Also, if a separate audio drive starts having problems, chances are your main startup drive won't be affected. Of course, you already know all this because you read Digidesign's *Getting Started* manual, right? If you don't have access to a dedicated audio drive, the sessions included with the lessons in this book should run just fine on your startup drive, provided you have a couple of gigabytes of space available. When you start making important recordings that you want to keep, I recommend using a separate drive for audio. To learn more about preventative maintenance and dealing with hard drive problems, consult Appendix C in the back of this book.

Windows-formatted drives will not play and record on Macintosh Pro Tools systems.

Formatting Drives in Windows XP

The good news for Windows users is that most drives come from the factory preformatted with NTFS (New Technology File System) for use with PCs. The bad news is that you may need to reformat them anyway, depending on which format you want to use.

Windows XP users can use either NTFS or FAT32 formatting for Pro Tools. After Pro Tools 7.3.*x*, future versions of Pro Tools will not support FAT32 for recording. FAT32 (File Allocation Table, 32 bit) is the last incarnation of the FAT file system, which dates back to the beginning of DOS programming. As such, it was designed for much smaller disks. When used with Windows 2000 and Windows XP, volume (partition) size is limited to 32GB. This format is readable on Macs and older Windows machines. Readable and playable are two different things, however. A Windows Pro Tools session will have to be transferred to a Mac-formatted drive before it can be played on a Mac system.

NTFS is a much newer system that is "native" for Windows NT, Windows 2000, and Windows XP. NTFS achieves better performance on larger drives, and it has fewer corruption and fragmentation problems, but it's not readable on Macs without purchasing third-party software.

To format a drive in Windows XP:

1. You must use a user account that has administrative privileges. Sometimes Windows will detect an uninitialized volume, and you can simply follow the prompts. If it does not, go to Start > Control Panel > Performance and Maintenance > Administrative Tools > Computer Management > Disk Management. At the bottom of the Computer Management window, you should see a list of available drives, or volumes. Physical drives are in a column on the left, partitions are shown on the right.

NOTE

If the computer's Control Panel is set to Classic View, the interface skips the Performance and Maintenance screen listed in Step 1, so you can directly select Administrative Tools.

2. Choose your audio drive by right-clicking the partition space to the right of the physical drive label.

3. In the pop-up menu that appears, choose Format. When the Format window appears, choose the desired file system (NTFS or FAT) and click OK to format the drive. For drives larger than 32GB, Digidesign recommends formatting with NTFS or partitioning a FAT-formatted drive with a partitioning application such as PartitionMagic.

The Mac HFS+ Disk Support Option

The type of formatting used in Macintosh computers use is known as HFS+. Prior to Pro Tools 7.3, Windows XP Pro Tools systems could not record and play back on a Mac-formatted drive, but the Mac HFS+ Disk Support Option makes this possible. Windows users should be aware that if they install the Mac HFS+ Disk Support Option, these sessions won't play back on Windows XP Pro Tools systems prior to version 7.3. Also be aware that, while it is possible to format drives using the Format Mac Disk command that is installed with the Mac HFS+ Disk Support Option, Digidesign only officially supports playback and recording on drives that have been formatted on a Macintosh computer using Apple's Disk Utility.

Formatting Drives with Mac OS X

As mentioned in the previous section, most new hard drives are preformatted at the factory for Windows machines. Windows-formatted drives will not play and record on Macintosh Pro Tools systems. If you're using a Mac, you should format (erase) a new drive with the Apple Disk Utility before use. This handy application can be found in Applications > Utilities > Disk Utility. Simply open Disk Utility and select the new drive in the column on the left (be sure to select the drive itself, not the partition). Click the Erase tab, set the format to Mac OS Extended (Journaled), give the drive a new name, and then click the Erase button (do not choose the Case-Sensitive format option). If you plan to format a disk for use with OS 9, you must check the box titled Install OS 9 Drivers. I use the Disk Utility often, so I've dragged its icon into the Dock so I can access it more easily.

Plug and Play?

FireWire drives are convenient because they can be connected or disconnected while the computer is running. There are a few caveats, however:

■ You must quit Pro Tools before removing FireWire drives.

■ Removeable drives must be "unmounted" before you disconnect or power them down, or damage to the drivers and file directories may result. On a Mac, a drive can be unmounted either by dragging its icon into the Trash or by clicking its eject button in the Finder window. Windows XP users must take the following steps:

   1. In the System Tray (the area in the lower-right corner of the screen), click the Eject icon (usually a small green arrow).

   2. A list of ejectable items appears; choose the drive in question.

   3. A message appears, telling you it's safe to remove the device. You can then disconnect or power down the drive.

■ Several FireWire drives can be connected together in a "daisy chain." The data must pass through each drive on the way to the next one. The data cannot pass through a FireWire drive that is turned off; therefore, you can't unmount and unplug or power down just one of them, unless it's on the end of the chain. The safest thing to do is to unmount *all* the drives in the chain, and then reconnect the drives you want to use.

■ Up to 63 FireWire devices can be connected to a bus, with a maximum of 16 devices on one branch. Too many drives in the chain will slow the data transfer rate.

■ In a session with multiple drives, Digidesign does not recommend combining FireWire 400 and 800 drives.

Partitioning

Most computer users are familiar with *partitioning,* the process of dividing a hard drive into sections called *partitions,* which are treated as separate drives by the system. Each partition will have its own icon on the desktop. Some users may partition larger drives because it keeps the files associated with a particular session corralled into a smaller area, cutting down on the *seek time,* the time required for the drive to access the data. If you have a large session with more tracks than a single drive can handle, you may need to split up your tracks by allocating some of them to a second drive. It is not desirable, however, to allocate files for a session to different partitions *on the same drive*. This makes the drive work harder. The important thing to remember here is that you should split your tracks by allocating some of them to a second *drive,* not to a different partition on the same drive.

Chapter 2

Starting a New Session from Scratch

This chapter deals with the nuts and bolts of opening the session that you will use for the lessons that follow. As you go through these exercises, it's important to perform the steps exactly as they are outlined and in the order presented. If you strike out on your own, the remaining steps will not make sense, and you will get stuck. If you're not a beginner, be patient and plod along with the rest of us. If you want to experiment on your own, you can always open a separate session.

Trashing the Preferences

If this isn't the first time a Pro Tools session has been opened on your system, you've probably made some changes that your computer has stored in a Preference file. Or, you may have opened the Pro Tools Demo Session. For the purposes of this tutorial, Pro Tools must be reset to the factory defaults, or the exercises will not work correctly. The method for accomplishing this is known as "trashing the Prefs."

The Preferences are settings your operating system (OS) stores in a folder to keep track of the way you like to work. For reasons no one has ever been able to fully explain to me, they get corrupted every now and then, and they have to be trashed (especially after a crash). When you restart the program, new Preference files are automatically generated that are reset to the factory defaults. If Pro Tools is crashing on you, the first thing Digidesign Tech Support will tell you to do is trash all the Digidesign Preference files, and also the Digidesign Database files that Pro Tools puts on every audio drive. Therefore, you might as well learn how to do it. Hopefully, it's not something you will need to do very often. It's a relatively harmless procedure—you won't lose any sessions or plug-ins.

Trashing the Prefs in Mac OS X

To reset Pro Tools to the factory defaults in OS X, quit Pro Tools if it is running. With the Finder running, press ⌘+N to open a new Finder window. In the column on the left, click the Home icon (a picture of a house), and then go to Library > Preferences. In the Preferences Folder, you will find three or four different sets of Digidesign Prefs depending on which system you have:

- ■ DAE Prefs

- ■ DigiSetup OS X Prefs

- ■ Pro Tools Prefs

- ■ Com.digidesign.ProToolsLE.plist

They will not necessarily be listed together. When your Pro Tools system is having problems, you will want to drag all of these into the Trash. Because we just want to get back to the factory default settings for the Edit window, we only need to trash the Pro Tools Prefs. Drag the Pro Tools Prefs icon into the Trash. If you've been fooling around with Reason Adapted for Digidesign, trash the Prefs for that as well. (If you don't know how to drag something into the Trash, you need to go through the Mac Tutorial under the Help menu.) Then, be sure to empty the Trash by choosing Finder > Empty Trash. If you did it correctly, the trashcan will appear to be empty.

Trashing the Prefs in Windows XP

To reset Pro Tools to the factory defaults, quit Pro Tools if it is running. There are two Preference files in different locations that must be deleted.

1. Go to Start > My Computer > Local Disk (usually the C drive) > Program Files > Common Files > Digidesign > DAE > DAE Prefs. Drag the DAE Prefs Folder into the Recycle Bin (or right-click the folder and choose Delete).

2. Go to Start > My Computer > Local Disk (usually the C drive) > Documents and Settings, and then open the current User Folder. If the Application Data Folder is not showing, go to the Menu bar, choose Tools > Folder Options > View > Hidden Files and Folders, select the Show Hidden Files And Folders radio button, and then click Apply. Then continue: Application Data > Digidesign. In the Digidesign Folder, locate the Pro Tools Preferences file and drag it into the Recycle Bin (or right-click the file and choose Delete). Close the Digidesign Folder. Right-click the Recycle Bin on the Desktop, choose Empty Recycling Bin, then confirm.

3. Relaunch Pro Tools.

Making the Preference Folder More Accessible

The path to the Preferences Folder isn't that easy to remember, so let's put an alias of it where we can find it more easily. Mac users: Simply drag the folder to the bottom of the column on the left side of the Finder window, and then relaunch Pro Tools. Windows users can create a shortcut for the Preferences Folder and put it on the Desktop. In Windows Explorer, right-click the Preferences Folder and choose Create Shortcut. Right-click the shortcut and choose Send To > Desktop.

Start Your Engines

For Mac users: Double-click the Pro Tools icon on the Dock to start Pro Tools. Choose Quit for any plug-in demo windows that appear. Once Pro Tools is running, choose File > New Session.

For Windows users: Double-click the Pro Tools icon on the Desktop to start Pro Tools. Choose Quit for any plug-in demo windows that appear. Once Pro Tools is running, choose File > New Session.

The New Session Dialog

The New Session dialog, shown in Figure 2-1, is the first thing you see when you open a new session. Some crucial decisions must be made here. At the top you are

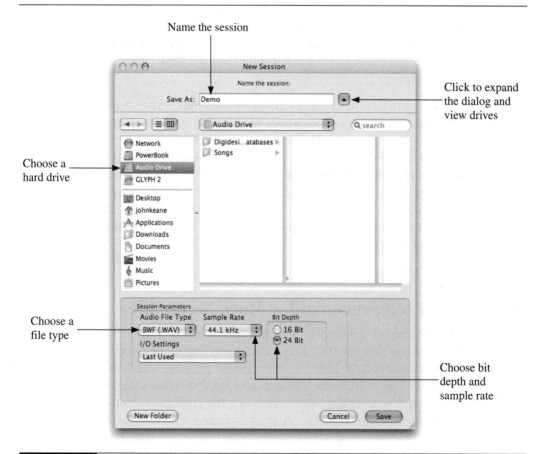

FIGURE 2-1   Many crucial decisions are made in the New Session dialog.

prompted to type in a name for the session, which would normally be the title of the song. For this lesson, type **Demo**.

Next you must choose the hard drive where the session will be stored. If necessary, click the pop-up menu shown in Figure 2-1 to expand the dialog, so that the center of the window shows a list of available drives. Select your audio drive if you have one. If not, just save the session to the Desktop or the main startup drive.

Choosing the Audio File Type

Mac users have a choice of three audio file types: BWF (.wav), AIFF, or SD II (Sound Designer II). Windows users can choose either BWF (.wav) or AIFF. The seldom-used Sound Designer II is an older format originally introduced by Digidesign, and is not supported by Windows XP machines. There is no difference in sound quality between these three file types. AIFF (Audio Interchange File Format) was codeveloped by Apple. The more commonly used BWF (.wav; pronounced "wave") format is a Microsoft and IBM audio file format. Choose BWF (.wav) for this session.

Choosing a Sample Rate and Bit Depth

The sample rate and bit depth are the two main specifications that determine the audio quality for the session. The sample rate refers to the number of times per second the incoming audio is sampled, and bit depth refers to the size of the digital word that describes each sample. Higher sample rates and bit depths result in better audio quality, but take up more hard drive space. Choosing higher sample rates may reduce the number of available voices, which determines how many tracks can play at once. For this session, we'll choose 44.1 kHz. Pro Tools lets you record at either 16 or 24 bits. For this exercise, choose 24 bits. This bit depth takes up 50 percent more space on the hard drive, but sounds noticeably better because of the increased resolution.

Many professionals prefer to work at 44.1 kHz or a multiple of that number, such as 88.2 kHz. At 24 bits, the difference in sound quality between 44.1 kHz and 48 kHz is undetectable by most people, but if you plan on burning a mix of a session onto a CD, recording at 44.1 kHz will save you the trouble and sound quality loss of converting from 48 kHz to 44.1 kHz. (Standard audio CDs are 44.1 kHz only.) Once you record audio in a session, you've made a commitment. You cannot mix sample rates within a session.

Leave I/O Settings at the default setting. After you have entered all of these items, click Save or press RETURN (ENTER). Pro Tools will create a folder on the selected hard drive titled Demo. The next time you want to open Demo, you'll open this folder and double-click the Pro Tools Demo session icon within.

The Edit Window

The two main windows in Pro Tools are the Edit window and the Mix window. Only one of these can be active at a time. The first time you open a new session after trashing the Prefs, the Edit and Mix windows will usually be shown side by side, with the Edit window active and located on the left side of the display.

The Edit window is where you will spend most of your time during these exercises, and you'll probably want it to fill up the whole screen. Chances are, however, that it will only cover a portion of the screen when you open your first session. If so, you should resize the window. On a Mac, there's a round green button near the upper-left corner that will resize the window. On a Windows machine, the resize button is a blue square in the upper-right corner. Click this button now. If you Mac users have moved the Dock out of the way, the Edit window will fill the entire screen, obscuring the Mix window, as shown in Figure 2-2.

I like to keep the Edit window as uncluttered as possible so I can see more audio. We don't need some of the items in this window right now, so let's hide them. Locate the multicolored ruler bars across the upper portion of the Edit

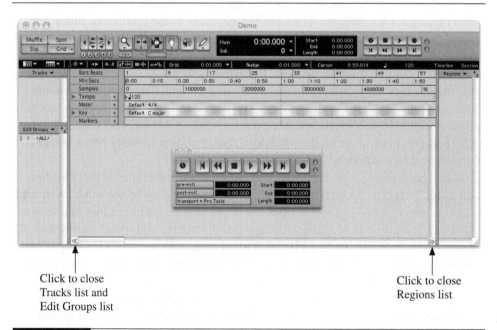

Click to close
Tracks list and
Edit Groups list

Click to close
Regions list

FIGURE 2-2   The default Edit window shows all the rulers and lists.

window labeled Bars:Beats, Min:Secs, Samples, and so forth. These can be hidden individually or all at once.

1. On the Menu bar, go to View > Rulers and select None. This leaves only the Main Time Scale in the Ruler display. It is currently at the default setting of Minutes and Seconds.

2. On the left side of the Edit window, you will see a vertical scrolling window titled Tracks. This is the Tracks list, which is used for choosing which tracks will be visible in the Edit window. Below it, you'll find another list titled Edit Groups. These lists will come in handy later, but you don't need them right now. Close the lists by clicking the double-arrow symbol (<<) at the bottom of the column, as shown in Figure 2-2.

3. On the right side of the Edit window, you will see a similar list titled Regions. This is the Regions list. It will show a list of your audio and MIDI files once they have been recorded. It also displays region groups. Close the list by clicking the double-arrow symbol (>>) at the bottom of the column.

4. Depending on which system you have, one or more Views columns may be showing. Go to View > Edit Window and make sure only Track Color and Transport are checked.

Now that we have uncluttered the Edit window, it should resemble the one in Figure 2-3. This looks a lot less daunting now, doesn't it?

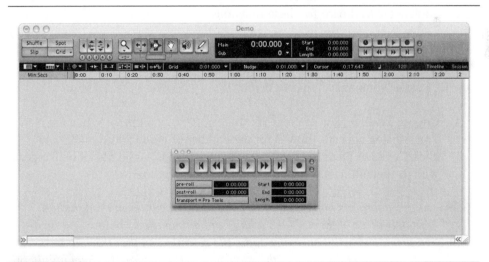

FIGURE 2-3   Uncluttering the Edit window creates more space for audio tracks.

The Transport Window

The Transport window is the small floating window on your screen that contains buttons analogous to those found on a tape machine transport. The Record button on the far right is the one you'll use most often. This window displays important information and should be kept in view most of the time. Note that the transport buttons also appear in the toolbar. The Transport window can be expanded to show MIDI controls. Go to View > Transport and select MIDI Controls. The Transport window should appear as shown here:

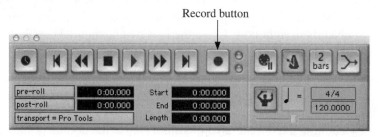

Record button

If the button labeled 2 Bars is illuminated, click it to turn off this feature. It causes an irritating 4-second lag when trying to record on a track. Then go back to View > Transport and uncheck MIDI Controls.

Forget about using those cute little Play, Record, and Stop buttons in the Transport window. I never use them, and neither does anyone else I know. You'll be tapping the SPACEBAR to start and stop the playback. Use F12 or ⌘+SPACEBAR (CTRL+SPACEBAR) to put Pro Tools into Record/Play. Pretty soon, you won't even have to look at the keyboard for these functions.

Creating New Tracks

Now let's create some tracks for our demo.

1. Choose Track > New or press ⌘+SHIFT+N (CTRL+SHIFT+N). When the New Track dialog appears, enter **3** for the number of mono audio tracks and click Create or press RETURN (ENTER). Three mono audio tracks will appear with the default names Audio 1, Audio 2, and Audio 3.

TIP *At this point, it's important to rename these tracks, even though there are only three of them. Make a habit of naming tracks before you record on them. This will cause any audio file recorded on that track to be automatically labeled with the same name. This will make them infinitely easier to find if they get misplaced.*

2. Rename the first track by double-clicking Audio 1. The Track Naming/ Comments dialog appears. Type the word **DRUMS** (I like to use capital letters because I can read them from a distance more easily).

3. Click Next. Label the next track **RHYTHM,** click Next, and label the next track **LEAD**.

4. Press RETURN (ENTER) to close the Track Naming dialog. Press ⌘+S (CTRL+S) to save your session. You can vary the height of the audio tracks in a variety of ways. Your tracks should currently be set to the default Medium setting, as shown in Figure 2-4. The Track Height can be changed by clicking in the area shown in this figure. A pop-up menu will appear with eight different height settings. Choose the different settings and note that the various buttons are easier to read on the larger settings. For the purposes of this lesson, we'll use the Medium setting.

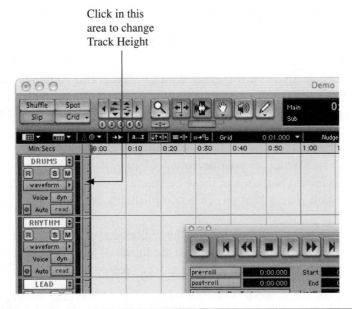

FIGURE 2-4   Changing the Track Height

NOTE

You can change the Track Height in other ways. With the Track Height set to Medium, notice the small arrow button next to the word "waveform." Clicking this arrow will also bring up the Track Height pop-up menu. New in Pro Tools 7.3, Track Heights can be varied incrementally by clicking and dragging along the bottom line of the track in the track column. They can be varied continuously by ⌘+SHIFT+clicking (CTRL+SHIFT+clicking) on this same line.

5. Hold down the OPTION (ALT) key and set the height of one of the tracks to Large. Note that all the tracks are expanded. This is a recurring theme in Pro Tools: OPTION+clicking (ALT+clicking) a command usually affects *all* the tracks in the window. Return all the tracks to Medium height.

Relabeling the Inputs and Outputs

On a tape machine the audio inputs and outputs for each track are fixed, but in Pro Tools any input or output on the interface can be routed to any track. In Pro Tools, the inputs and outputs are displayed in the I/O View. To display the I/O View, go to View > Edit Window > I/O. Note that a new display labeled I/O shows up in the Edit window. I like to keep the I/O View displayed all the time, unless I'm using a small monitor and need the space.

If you open a session that was created on a different Pro Tools system, the I/O Setup from that system will be imported as well, and it may not match the current system. The purpose of this exercise is to show you how to change the I/O Setup to match the current system.

The default labels for your I/O column will vary according to the type of interface you have. Whatever your defaults look like, you need to change some of your I/O labels for the purposes of these exercises. You can always change them back to the default setting later on. To accomplish this, take the following steps:

1. Go to Setup > I/O. When the I/O Setup dialog appears, click the Input tab at the top. The dialog now displays the inputs of your particular interface in stereo pairs. That's because tracks can be created in either stereo or mono.

2. Locate the first stereo I/O label (it might be titled Mic/Line 1-2 in a Digi 002, or 1-2 on some Mbox systems). Click the right-pointing arrow next to the label so that it points down. It will open to reveal the individual mono I/O labels for inputs 1 and 2, like the Mbox example in Figure 2-5. If you have more than two inputs, do the same for 3-4, 5-6, and 7-8, until all eight stereo and mono analog input labels are visible, as in Figure 2-6. If you see ADAT inputs, leave them closed.

Click this arrow to reveal mono I/O labels

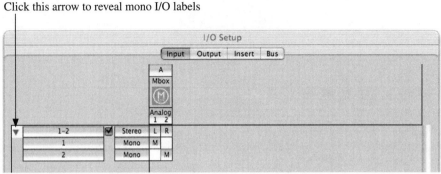

FIGURE 2-5   Mbox I/O Setup dialog (inputs)

3. Double-click the first I/O label and rename it **IN 1-2.**

4. Tab down to the next Mono label and rename it **IN 1**. Label the next one **IN 2.**

5. If your system has more than two inputs, tab on down the line until you've renamed all the I/Os for channels 1 through 8, as in Figure 2-6.

6. At the top of the I/O Setup dialog, click the Output tab and rename the outputs the same way (**OUT 1-2**, **OUT 1**, **OUT 2,** and so forth). Click OK to close the I/O dialog when you finish, and notice that the I/Os in the Edit window are now displaying the new labels.

7. Now that your inputs and outputs are in view, check to make sure that the outputs of all three tracks are set to OUT 1-2. This is the Pro Tools default setting for outputs, because most people use channels 1 and 2 for their stereo mix. To change the input or output of a track, simply click its label, such as OUT 1-2, and select a different input or output from the pop-up menu that appears. If you have more than two outputs, go ahead and change a few outputs to get the hang of it. Just make sure to change them back to 1 and 2 when you're done.

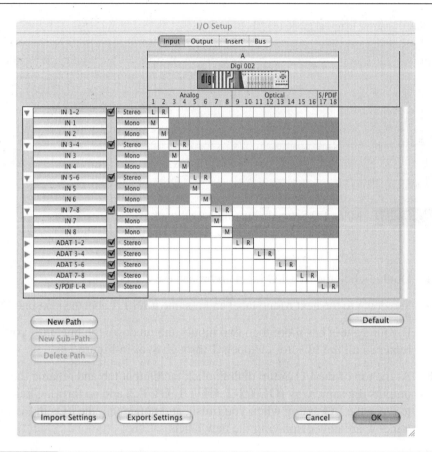

FIGURE 2-6   Digi 002 I/O Setup dialog (inputs)

The Digi 002 and 003 Systems
Are Expandable to 18 Channels

You might look at the I/O Setup dialog in a Digi 002 or 003 system and think, "Hey, I've got 18 ins and outs here." Well, sort of. What you have are eight analog inputs and outputs and eight additional digital inputs and outputs via the optical connectors on the back of the interface. The stereo S/P-DIF digital input brings the total to 18. This makes it possible to expand your system by adding another eight analog I/Os with an optical lightpipe device such as the Presonus Digimax. Pretty cool, huh?

Labeling the Function Keys

In the interest of reducing frustration and speeding the learning process, label the function keys across the top of your keyboard. In Appendix B of this book, you will find function key labels that can be cut out and placed above the function keys to your keyboard. The Session Disc CD-ROM in the back of this book also includes printable function key labels in the form of PDF files.

The various tools you need for editing can be accessed easily with the function keys, as opposed to clicking their icons in the Edit window. The Pro Tools HD packages come with nifty stickers to put directly on the keys, but the LE systems don't. These stickers can be purchased online at Digidesign's web site.

Press the different function keys (F1 through F10) and you can see the different tool icons light up in the Edit window. Press F2 to get back into the Slip mode, where we will spend most of our time. Press F7 to choose the Selector tool, which is one of the most often used tools. You can also scroll through the tools by pressing the ESC key.

For the remainder of this book, when the directions say Play or Stop, do so by tapping the SPACEBAR. When the directions say Record, press F12 or ⌘+SPACEBAR (CTRL+SPACEBAR).

Now, at last, you have a blank session set up and ready to record. Take heart! You only have to do most of this stuff once. Pro Tools will remember most of these settings for future sessions.

Saving Your Sessions

Go to File > Save As and type **Demo 1blank**. This creates a new and separate session. Pro Tools will assume correctly that you want to put this new version of your session in the same folder as the old one. Click Save. Note the new title at the top of the Edit window. You are now in a *new* session titled Demo 1blank, which, at the moment, is an exact copy of Demo. As you will learn, using the Save Session As command is a procedure that is going to keep you out of trouble.

Now we're going to "hide" Pro Tools and look in your Demo Session Folder to see what's happening.

Hide Pro Tools

Mac (OS X)   Go to Pro Tools > Hide Pro Tools. This is a good way to get the Pro Tools windows out of the way without closing the session.

Windows   Near the upper-right corner of the screen, you will see two sets of buttons. Click the Minimize button in the upper set to hide Pro Tools and view the Desktop.

Look on the drive where the current session is located. Pro Tools has created a folder titled Demo that contains the elements of your session. Inside, you will find two session icons (labeled Demo and Demo 1blank), an Audio Files Folder, a Fade Files Folder, a Region Groups Folder, and possibly a Session File Backups Folder.

These session icons represent files containing the session data. All of your edits, track assignments, automation, and so forth will be stored here. The exercises in this book are designed to get you into the habit of saving updated versions of a session, just as you would save updated versions of a document. Changes made to the new session will not show up in the previous sessions. After you get some tracks recorded and saved, you'll use the Save Session As command to create a new session titled Demo 2tracking. You'll do an overdub, get something that works, and save that as Demo 3overdub. After some punching on the RHYTHM track, you'll save it as Demo 4rhythm, and so on. Pro Tools will automatically keep putting these new versions in the same folder and will continue to do so unless you instruct it otherwise.

NOTE *I use the Save As command often but, like most applications, Pro Tools does not have a keyboard shortcut for it. Mac users can create one in the System Preferences, however. Here's how: Click the blue Apple icon in the upper-left corner of the screen and go to System Preferences > Keyboard and Mouse. Click the Keyboard Shortcuts tab and then click the plus-sign icon in the lower-left corner of the dialog. A pane with an Application drop-down menu will appear. Navigate to the Pro Tools application to add it to the Application field and type **Save As…** in the Menu Title field (you must type in the three periods after As). In the Keyboard Shortcut field, enter a key combination that is not already being used by Pro Tools, such as COMMAND+OPTION+S, and click Add. Pro Tools must be restarted before the new shortcut will work.*

It's important to keep all versions of a session *in the same original folder.* This way, if you screw up a session (and you will), you can close the mangled session, open an earlier version, and start over from there, instead of starting from scratch.

Demo is our song title. Putting a number after each version helps keep things in chronological order in the Session Folder. After the version number, a description (blank, tracking, edits, and so forth) reminds us of what we were doing at that point. I often end up with 20 or 30 of these per song. They don't take up much space, and you can always toss the ones you don't need into the Trash when you're done. If a session becomes corrupted or mangled due to operator error, you can go back to an earlier session and start over at the point at which it was last saved. This is how many of the pros work. This procedure will add years to your life and possibly prevent angry musicians from beating you to a pulp with a mic stand.

TIP *Pro Tools has an Auto Backup feature that is set by default to automatically back up your session every 5 minutes. While it's a wonderful thing, don't think it makes the procedure outlined above unnecessary. Auto Backup only keeps a predetermined number of sessions at a time and it has no way to label them descriptively except to number them sequentially and display the date and time they were created.*

Never, ever drag one of these session icons from the Session Folder and put it somewhere else, such as the Desktop, to try to get to it more conveniently. I tried this once, and quickly descended into Pro Tools Hell. Believe me, you don't want to go there. Scattering elements of your session all over the place is the worst thing you can do in Pro Tools. If you want to be able to open a session from the Desktop, make an alias (or shortcut) of the session icon (on a Mac, OPTION+⌘+click and drag to the new location; on a Windows PC, right-click and select Create Shortcut) and put the alias wherever you like. Double-clicking the alias will open the original session. Any changes you make to the session will be saved in the original Session Folder.

CAUTION *Never, ever drag a session icon from the Session Folder and put it somewhere else.*

Any audio you record into your session will be placed in the Audio Files Folder. When you have performed some crossfades, they will be placed in the Fade Files Folder. Sessions that have been backed up by Auto Backup reside in the Session File Backups Folder. If your computer crashes, you would normally go to this folder and open the most recent backup.

Enough preaching for now—let's get to the fun part.

Unhide Pro Tools

Mac (OS X)   To get your session back onscreen, click the Pro Tools icon in the Dock.

Windows   Click the Pro Tools icon on the taskbar at the bottom of the screen to bring the Edit window back into view.

Chapter 3

Tracking and Overdubbing

In this chapter, you will create a rhythm track for your demo, preferably by using a repeating drum-machine pattern. If you don't have a drum machine, you can plug in a mic and tap your feet, snap your fingers, or beat on a cardboard box; it really doesn't matter. The music you record for these exercises should be completely disposable. You're just trying to learn the program, not create art. If you don't play any instruments, ask a friend to come over and lay down some tracks (pick someone patient). A short, mindless, throwaway jam is best, and anyone you recruit to play on it needs to understand what you're trying to do. If you go this route, get someone who is competent, but not a perfectionist, or they'll drive you nuts. If you're worrying about the performance, the sound quality, or the song structure, you'll get completely bogged down and distracted from the task of learning the program. Keep the tune well under two minutes. Anything longer will be a waste of your time. Put the parts down fast and dirty in one or two takes, and leave the mistakes in. Part of the tutorial will be fixing those mistakes. Now would be a good time to cut out the Cheat Sheet for Chapters 1–5 and tape it to your monitor if you haven't done so already.

Laying Down the Drum Track

Setting levels is a crucial step when preparing to record. It's important to realize that the gain, or volume level, of the signal must be adjusted *before* it goes into the computer. Most interfaces designed for use with Pro Tools LE make this step simple because they come with built-in preamps and gain controls for setting levels. Interfaces that don't have microphone inputs require an external mixer or mic preamp to achieve the proper level.

In general, record levels should be set as high as possible without clipping, but don't drive yourself nuts trying to get it *just perfect*. At 24-bit resolution you can afford to leave yourself some headroom without sacrificing audio quality, so there's really no need to ever clip the meters in Pro Tools unless you enjoy the sound of digital clipping. Some engineers like to slam every meter. In my opinion, that technique does not work well in Pro Tools.

In the following exercise, we'll set the record level and record our drum sound on the DRUMS track. Setting the record level basically consists of bringing up the Input level until clipping occurs, then backing it down until it doesn't clip anymore.

1. Connect your drum machine or drum mic to Input 1 (or the left input) of your interface. If you're not sure how this works, the *Getting Started* manual does a good job of explaining how to connect your system.

2. Record-enable the DRUMS track by clicking its R (record) button, which is located under its track name. The DRUMS track's input should be set to IN 1.

3. Drum machine users: If your interface has a Mic/DI or Mic/Line switch, it should be set to DI or Line. If there is a Pad button, it should be enabled as well (the purpose of the Pad is to reduce levels that are too high for the input). If you're using a microphone, set the switch to Mic. Start with the interface's Input 1 knob set to minimum.

4. Start up your beat. If your system is connected correctly, you should see some movement on the DRUMS track meter and hear sound from Outputs 1-2. Bring up the Input level control until the red clip indicator at the top of the meter lights. The *clip indicator* tells when the gain is set too high, which will result in "clipped" waveforms and nasty digital distortion. If you can't get the Input level high enough to light the clip indicator, you need to turn off the interface's Pad. Click the clip indicator to turn it off, and back off the gain until it stops clipping. The outputs of all three tracks should be set to OUT 1-2, and the pan should be at >0<, which puts the sound in the center of your speakers. Your monitoring system should be set up to listen to the output of 1-2 in stereo, with 1 to the left and 2 to the right. If it's connected correctly, when you click the Pan control and move it from left to right, the sound will move accordingly. OPTION+clicking (ALT+clicking) the Pan control will return it to the center position.

5. Press RETURN (ENTER) on your keyboard to "rewind" to the beginning of the session, and stop the beat.

6. Press F12 or ⌘+SPACEBAR (CTRL+SPACEBAR) to put Pro Tools into Record, and then start the drum beat. Notice that the record light in the Transport window glows red. The vertical line moving across the screen is called the Playback cursor.

7. Let it run for two minutes; then stop the beat.

8. Press the SPACEBAR to stop the transport. There is no need to rewind; Pro Tools should automatically go back to the beginning of your recording.

9. Click the DRUMS track's R button to take it out of Record. Notice that the audio you have just recorded is now displayed as a waveform in the Edit window. This waveform is a graphic representation of an audio file that now resides on your hard drive in the Audio Files Folder. An audio file can

be nondestructively divided into separate pieces called regions (more on this in Chapter 4).

10. Save your session (⌘+S / CTRL+S). Because this might be a good point to return to if you mangle something while tracking, save it again using the Save As command (under the File menu, remember?) and name the new session **Demo 2tracking**. Throughout this book, any time you reach a milestone in a session, you'll save the session, and then save it again under a new name, using Save As before continuing.

Basic Zooming with the Commands Focus Feature

Zooming performs a function similar to that of a zoom lens on a camera. In Pro Tools, waveforms can be zoomed both horizontally and vertically. In these lessons, we are mainly concerned with horizontal zooming, which can be accomplished in a number of ways. The most obvious way to zoom horizontally is by using the Zoom buttons shown in Figure 3-1. It's definitely not the best method for zooming, however. We can zoom much faster by enabling the Commands Focus feature.

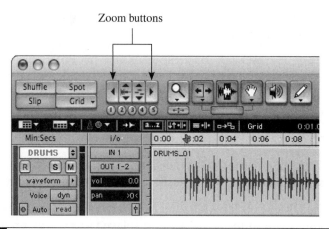

FIGURE 3-1   Horizontal zooming

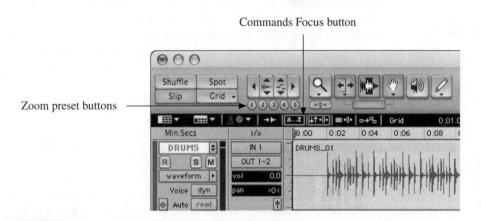

Commands Focus button

Zoom preset buttons

FIGURE 3-2   Enabling Commands Focus

Commands Focus

Commands Focus is a useful feature that we will use for the remainder of this book. It enables a host of keyboard shortcuts that can be implemented by pressing a single key. When Commands Focus is enabled, the R and T keys will zoom the waveform horizontally. This is one of my favorite ways to zoom in and out, because I can do it with my left hand with a single keystroke. Click the a...z button, as shown in Figure 3-2, to enable Commands Focus.

NOTE   *A blue border appears around the a...z button to show it is active.*

Setting the Zoom Presets

Look for the Zoom preset buttons labeled 1 through 5 near the upper-left corner of the Edit window, as shown in Figure 3-2. Click them to recall the default zoom settings. For the purposes of this lesson, we need to enter our own specific preset values. Of course, the results of the following steps will vary, depending on the size of your display and the resolution setting.

1. Press F8 to select the Grabber (more on this tool later in the chapter). The cursor changes to a hand.

NOTE

Mac laptop users: If pressing F8 does not select the Grabber, you may need to change a System Preference. Click the blue Apple icon in the upper-left corner and choose System Preferences > Keyboard and Mouse. Click the box labeled Use The F1-F12 Keys To Control Software Features, and then close the dialog.

2. Click the audio file in the DRUMS track to select it. It will become highlighted.

3. Holding the OPTION (ALT) key, press the F key. This is the Zoom to Fill Window command.

4. Press ⌘ (CTRL) and click preset button 1. It will blink to indicate that a new setting has been stored. From now on, you can get back to this zoom setting by clicking this button or by typing 1 on the alpha keyboard (these are the number keys above the letter keys on your keyboard, not to be confused with the numeric keys on the right side of a full-sized keyboard).

5. Zoom in by tapping the T key twice. Use the method in the previous step to store this setting as Zoom preset 2.

6. Zoom in two more clicks of the T key and make that Zoom preset 3.

7. Zoom in two more clicks. Make that Zoom preset 4.

8. Zoom in two more clicks and make that Zoom preset 5.

9. Return to Zoom preset 1 by pressing **1**.

Now your personal zoom settings are stored, and you can access them by simply pressing the number keys 1 through 5 on your keyboard. Go ahead and try it. As you can see, it's much faster than clicking the Horizontal Zoom buttons with the mouse. Like all computer programs, the scroll bars in the Edit and Mix windows enable you to scroll horizontally and vertically to get around in your session. Pro Tools provides many other zooming methods that we won't get into now. If you have an unquenchable thirst for knowledge, check the *Reference Guide* for more zooming details.

Using Monitor Modes During Overdubbing

Overdubbing is the process of adding new tracks while listening to previously recorded material. *Punching in* is the process of replacing part of a recorded performance. To accomplish these tasks, you need to have a clear understanding of how the Monitor modes work.

When overdubbing in Pro Tools, you will be constantly changing back and forth between the two Monitor modes: Input Only and Auto Input. From now on, I'll refer to these two modes as Input and Auto, respectively. These modes will be familiar to anyone who has operated a multitrack recorder, as they are a basic necessity for overdubbing.

These modes can be toggled from one to the other in the Track menu or by pressing OPTION+K (ALT+K). In Pro Tools HD, Input mode can be selected individually for each track by clicking its Input button (next to the Record button). Here is a brief explanation of the differences between the two.

Input To rehearse your part during playback prior to recording, the track you want to record on should be in Record-Ready (the R button is blinking red) and you should be in Input mode (the I button is illuminated), or you won't be able to hear yourself. In Pro Tools LE, you'll know you are in Input mode because the green Input mode indicator in the Transport window will be illuminated. In Pro Tools HD the track's Input button will glow green.

Auto Once you record something and you want to listen back, you have to toggle to Auto to hear the playback. The green Input indicators go back to their usual gray color. The Auto Input mode gets its name from the fact that it automatically switches to Input when you punch in. This way, you'll hear the playback of the previous performance up to the punch in point. It also switches to Input when the transport is stopped.

These modes typically affect only the tracks that have been placed in Record-Ready. So, to recap:

- In *Input,* you only hear the track's input. You can't hear what you've recorded.

- In *Auto,* during playback you hear what you have previously recorded until you either punch in or stop the transport.

During overdubbing, you will find yourself switching back and forth between these two modes fairly often. It's far too time consuming to go to the Track menu every time you want to switch modes. Learn to toggle from Auto to Input by pressing OPTION+K (ALT+K), which is a vast improvement. Going to the menus for often-used commands like this is a bad habit that will wear out your mouse arm and slow your workflow to a crawl. If possible, get used to invoking this shortcut with your left hand. You can label the K on your keyboard with a small, green-colored piece of tape until you get to the point where you can do it without looking. Your right forearm will thank you. I use this command so often I have one of the extra buttons on my trackball programmed to toggle it.

You'll need to get into the habit of watching for the green Input indicators as you toggle back and forth between Auto and Input. That's why GREEN LIGHT = INPUT MODE is included on your cheat sheet.

NOTE   *Speakers should be muted or kept at a low level when using a microphone to record quiet sounds such as vocals. This will prevent feedback and keep the mic from picking up sound from the speakers. Headphones usually work best for this application. Also, be sure either to mute the mic or take the track out of Record-Ready before you crank up the speakers for playback.*

Pre-roll and Post-roll

When recording by yourself, you will need to use pre-roll and post-roll. This makes it possible to punch in and out automatically so your hands will be free to play your instrument. The most common use of pre-roll is to give yourself a few seconds to get in the groove with the music before punching in. Pre-roll and post-roll can be toggled on and off by clicking their buttons in the Transport window, but of course, I don't want you to do that because it takes too long. ⌘+K (CTRL+K) is the shortcut for this command. This is the other command that I have programmed to one of my trackball buttons. Think of it this way: Commander K is the guy who toggles the pre-roll/post-roll on and off. (Silly, I know, but it helps me remember the shortcut.) To demonstrate how this works:

1. Watch the Transport window as you press ⌘+K (CTRL+K). Note how the pre-roll and post-roll indicators light up to show they are active. They can be toggled separately by clicking the buttons in the Transport window. In the numerical display next to the pre-roll indicator, you will see digits representing minutes, seconds, and milliseconds. Leave pre-roll and post-roll off for now.

2. Make sure you are still on Zoom preset 1, where you can see the entire song. Using the Selector tool (F7), click the DRUMS track somewhere in the middle of the waveform. Note that when you use the Selector, the cursor turns into an I-beam, like the cursor in a word processor. A separate blinking Playback cursor appears at the location you selected.

3. Press Play (SPACEBAR). Note that playback starts from the spot you selected. Stop and start again. Playback should start from the same place every time.

NOTE

If playback doesn't start from the same place every time, you have accidentally changed the Preference known as Timeline Insertion/Play Start Marker Follows Playback by brushing against the N key. Reset it by pressing the N key again.

4. Select different spots in the song and press Play. This is a good way to hop around to different locations in a song.

5. In the Transport window, click the middle two zeroes in the pre-roll field, as shown here:

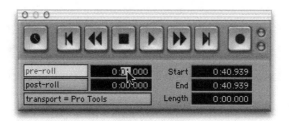

6. These middle digits represent seconds of pre-roll. They will light up, indicating that they are ready to have a value entered. Type in a **1** and press RETURN (ENTER). You have just entered a one-second pre-roll. To the left of this display is the pre-roll button, which lights when pre-roll is activated. Click this button if it is not illuminated.

7. Press Play. Note that playback now starts one second before the selection.

8. Using the Selector, click somewhere in the middle of the region on the DRUMS track and drag the cursor an inch or so to the left or right, as if you were highlighting a phrase in a document.

9. Press Play. Note that the transport starts one second before the highlighted area, and then plays through the selection and stops precisely at the end of the selection.

10. In the post-roll numerical display, enter a one-second post-roll, as shown next, and press RETURN (ENTER). Press Play and note that playback now continues for one second after the selection. On the right side of the

Transport window, a display indicates the exact location of the start and end, and also the length of your selection.

Now that you have entered pre-roll and post-roll values, two little green flags will appear in the Timeline, as shown here:

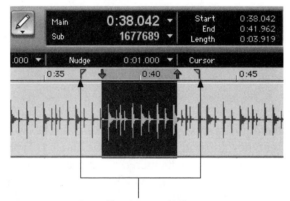

Pre-roll and post-roll flags

When pre/post-roll is disabled, the flags will turn gray. You can drag these flags to the left or right to change the pre-roll and post-roll values, a method you may find easier than typing them into the pre/post-roll fields. Save your session.

Latency Issues

During overdubbing, you may experience a phenomenon known as *latency*. Latency is the lag time audio experiences when entering and leaving the computer. Every digital recording system has a certain amount of latency. The latency of HD systems is so miniscule that it's not usually an issue, but with host-based systems running Pro Tools LE, latency can be a problem. When you have a track in Record and you're monitoring it through Pro Tools, you may hear a noticeable delay in the notes you play. This latency can be reduced by lowering the H/W (Hardware) buffer size. The path to this setting is Setup > Playback Engine > H/W Buffer Size. Lowering this buffer will also reduce the number of tracks and plug-ins allowed, so a lower setting is best for overdubbing, and a higher setting is best for mixing.

Digi 002, 003, and Mbox 2 Pro systems have the option of selecting Low Latency Monitoring under the Options menu. This option allows you to monitor the sound at the interface before it goes through the computer. Other Mbox systems, like the Mbox Mini, accomplish the same thing by providing a Mix control on the interface that allows the user to balance between the sound at the interface's input and the recorded tracks. Be aware that when the knob is set to Input, you will not hear the effect of any plug-ins you may have inserted on the input of your overdub track until you take it out of Record.

Overdubbing on the Rhythm Track

Once you understand how to switch Monitor modes, adjust pre-roll and post-roll, and make any necessary latency adjustments, you're ready to overdub your rhythm instrument.

1. Plug a guitar, keyboard, or other instrument into Input 1 of your interface and put the RHYTHM track (the second track we labeled earlier) into Record via the R button.

2. Set the RHYTHM track's input to IN-1 (Mono).

3. Play your rhythm instrument and adjust the interface's level control to get a good healthy level without clipping.

4. Watching the Transport window for visual confirmation, turn off the pre-roll (⌘+K / CTRL+K) and select Input mode (OPTION+K / ALT+K).

5. Press RETURN (ENTER) to get back to the start of your session. Note that the area you had highlighted on the DRUMS track is now deselected.

6. While playing along with the drums, adjust the RHYTHM track's Volume and Pan controls in the Edit window until you are comfortable with the balance between the DRUMS and the RHYTHM track. Realize that adjusting the Volume control on the screen will not affect the record level, it only affects what you're hearing.

7. Go back to the start and begin recording by pressing the F12 function key. When you record this track, be sure to include a mistake or two, so you'll have something to go back and fix. Keep it simple; don't waste time doing a bunch of takes. Try to keep the first pass. If you are in the middle of a take and want to abort, press ⌘+. (CTRL+.). The audio will not be saved to the hard drive. If you've just finished a take and want to get rid of it, press the Undo command keys (⌘+Z / CTRL+Z).

8. When you're finished, take the RHYTHM track out of record by clicking its R button and do a Save As with the name **Demo 3overdub**.

Destructive and Nondestructive Recording

Before you start punching in to correct mistakes, make sure you are in Nondestructive Record mode, which is normally the default setting. CONTROL+click (START+click or right-click) the red record light in the middle of the Record button in the Transport window to cycle through the various Record modes. Different symbols will appear in the center of the Record button. Here's what they mean:

No symbol	Nondestructive Recording
D	Destructive Recording
Circular arrow	Loop Recording
P	Quick Punch
T	Track Punch (HD only)

Most people stay in one of the nondestructive modes most of the time. I won't get into a complete explanation of each mode at this time. You can look it up in the *Reference Guide* in your spare time if you're curious. I just want to briefly explain some pros and cons associated with destructive and nondestructive recording because a lot of people get confused about this.

Destructive Record Mode

In *Destructive Record* mode, Pro Tools records like a tape machine. If you record over an existing audio file, the old audio will be erased and cannot be recovered. It's one way to get rid of stuff you're sure you don't want.

Advantages

When punching in or recording over an existing track, you are erasing the previous take. In other words, you aren't piling up a bunch of outtakes on your hard drive that you have to go back and delete later. I often use Destructive Record mode during tracking sessions to record over takes I'm sure I don't want to keep. Hard drives can fill up quickly when recording 24 tracks at a time, and I don't relish the task of deleting the outtakes. I've found that it's good practice to make immediate decisions about whether or not something is worth keeping. Keeping all your options open can make you crazy later on and clog up your hard drive (and your brain) with a bunch of useless junk. I've seen many a Pro Tools user fall into this trap. You can waste hours of your valuable time trying to sift through it all at the end of the project.

Disadvantages

During overdubbing you will often be punching in on existing tracks to fix mistakes. Punching in and out using Destructive Record mode will sometimes result in pops and clicks at the in and out points, which are time consuming to remove. This is why I rarely use this mode when overdubbing.

Nondestructive Record Mode

In this mode, Pro Tools keeps everything you record. When you record over a track, the original material is not erased.

Advantages

When explaining nondestructive recording to people who are used to tape machines, I often use this analogy: In your mind, visualize a vocal performance recorded on a piece of analog tape. Let's say you want to sing the second verse again without erasing the original. Theoretically (of course), you paste a new strip of blank tape over the vocal track in the second verse, and record another verse on the new tape. You want to try a few more times, so you keep adding layers of tape over the same verse and recording new takes on them. Then you decide that the performance on the third layer was the best, so you peel off the layers until you're back to the third take.

The next day, you decide that the original take was better in the first half of the verse. You peel off the strip of tape covering the first half of the verse and snip it with a pair of scissors. Voila! You have fixed the second verse without destroying anything. Of course, you can't really do that with a tape machine, but when you punch in repeatedly on a track in Pro Tools using Nondestructive Record mode, in effect, that's what you're doing. You can only see the most recent take, but the others are still there on your hard drive, and you can get them back whenever you want. They are numbered sequentially and listed in the Regions list (the window on the right side of the Edit window that we closed earlier). As you can imagine, this can be a tremendous advantage over Destructive Record mode. Also, pops and clicks at the punch-in points can be quickly and easily dealt with, as you'll see.

Disadvantages

Keeping everything can be a disadvantage if you don't take out the trash once in a while. After days of recording multiple passes on various tracks in a session, you can accumulate a large number of useless audio files on your hard drive. Packrats will eventually find themselves up to their eyeballs in outtakes. I worked on one Pro Tools session for a major-label artist that was so out of hand, one four-minute, 16-bit song completely filled up a large hard drive. Dozens of outtakes that should have been dumped were preserved in all their glory, because the producer refused to make any decisions. The hard drive became more and more sluggish as it filled up. (To avoid this scenario, I'll show you some ways to get rid of unused audio in Chapter 4.)

The Selector, the Grabber, and the Trimmer

Now is the time to get your scissors and cut out the Function Key Labels in Appendix B if you haven't done it yet, and place them above the function keys on your keyboard. You can also print them out from the PDF files on the Session Disc (glossy photo paper holds up well). This will speed up the learning process considerably.

Like most software programs, Pro Tools has a variety of tools for different tasks. Any of these tools can be selected by clicking its icon, but it's much faster to use the function keys. The Selector, Grabber, and Trimmer are the three most commonly used tools. You'll have to know their basic functions to accomplish punching in and editing. If you look closely at the tool icons in the Edit window, you'll notice that some of them have little arrows at the bottom. These tools have alternate versions that you may encounter when pressing the function keys. For instance, click and hold on the Grabber icon (it looks like a hand) and a drop-down menu will reveal the different versions. The icons for the alternate versions have a slightly different appearance. Pressing a tool's function key repeatedly will cycle through the different versions of the tool, so it's easy to select them by accident.

The one to watch out for is the TCE Trimmer tool (with the little clock in the icon). You can do some serious damage with that one. For this exercise, we will be using the plain version of each tool.

The Selector (F7) is usually used to make a selection *within* a region, but it can be used to make a selection anywhere in the Edit window. To demonstrate, place the Selector anywhere in the DRUMS track's audio region and click. The vertical line that appears is the Playback cursor. Now click somewhere in the DRUMS track region with the Selector and hold, dragging a few inches to the left or right, and then release the mouse. In this book, this action is referred to as "making a selection." The audio that is highlighted has been selected. This is the method you will use to select an area you want to punch in on.

TIP   *Remember that you can always click elsewhere in the Edit window to cancel the selection.*

You choose the Grabber by pressing the F8 function key. The *Grabber* is usually used for selecting an *entire* region. To demonstrate, place the Grabber anywhere within the audio region on the DRUMS track. Click once on the region and note that the whole region changes color, and the background turns black. This is referred to as "selecting a region." As long as the region remains highlighted, it is considered selected. Whenever you want to select an entire region, you'll use the Grabber. You'll also use the Grabber when you want to drag a region to another location. To deselect a region with the Grabber, click any empty space in the Edit window that doesn't contain audio. Click twice on a region, and a dialog will pop up that enables you to rename the region.

You choose the Trimmer by pressing the F6 function key. The *Trimmer* is primarily used to change the length of a region by trimming off the beginning or end. This is the tool that really gets people cursing when they're learning how to use it. Accidentally clicking in the middle of a region with the Trimmer will most likely cause a large chunk of it to disappear. When this happens, stay calm and use the Undo Command (⌘+Z / CTRL+Z). The following steps demonstrate how the Trimmer works.

1. You should still be at Zoom preset 1. Choose the Trimmer (F6) and position it over the middle of the audio region on the DRUMS track, *but don't click yet!*

2. Move the Trimmer from left to right over the region and note the way the icon changes direction when it crosses the middle of the region. The direction it faces tells you which end of the region is about to be trimmed.

3. Press the OPTION (ALT) key and note that the Trimmer icon changes direction. Clicking outside of a region with the Trimmer will have no effect.

4. With the Trimmer still selected, click the region near the end of the song and drag to the left a few inches. You have now shortened the region by trimming off the end. The audio is still there; all you've done is tell the computer where to stop playing that particular region.

5. Click within the region (near the end again) and drag the Trimmer to the right until the region stops expanding, and then release the mouse. The DRUMS tracks audio region has now been restored to its original length.

6. Press RETURN (ENTER) to get back to the start of your session.

NOTE

Pressing F6 when the Trimmer is already selected results in the selection of other Trimmer tools. If this happens, Press F6 until you get back to the standard Trimmer.

Important!

For the remainder of this book, when you see the phrase "select the region," click the region with the Grabber to select the *entire* region. When you see the phrase "make a selection," drag the Selector across *part* of a region.

Chapter 4

Basic Editing Techniques

In this chapter, you will use your demo session to learn the basics of punching in, editing regions, crossfading, and comping tracks. You will also learn techniques for clearing unwanted audio from your session.

Auto-Punching on the Rhythm Track

As I mentioned in Chapter 3, *punching in* is the process of recording over part of a track to fix a mistake. Anyone who has operated a multitrack tape recorder knows that punching in on an existing track can be a hit-or-miss proposition. You have to try to punch in and out near rests or gaps in the audio. With a tape machine, once you punch in on a track, the original material is erased. If you blow the punch, you're going to get some dirty looks. Blow enough of them, and you're fired. It can be a nerve-wracking experience.

When I'm playing an instrument and engineering at the same time, I have to set up Pro Tools to punch in and out automatically, so I don't have to touch the keyboard. In the days before Pro Tools, I had to put the tape machine remote control on the floor, take my shoes off, and punch in with my toes, while playing my guitar. This method worked, but it was still distracting. Once I started using Pro Tools, I got so accustomed to punching in automatically that I use this technique even when I'm punching in other people. It enables me to close my eyes and listen to the performance without having to worry about pushing a button at the right time.

With this method, you also have the luxury of being able to adjust the punch-in and punch-out points after the fact. This is why I prefer to punch in about a second ahead of the area to be repaired and punch out a second or so after. This method gives me some leeway to use the Trimmer to move the punch points around once I have a good take.

In the following steps, you will play along with the previously recorded track. At the punch-in point, Pro Tools will go into Record, and the undesirable part of the RHYTHM track will be replaced. At the punch-out point, Pro Tools will go out of Record and stop automatically.

1. Listen through the song and pick out a three- or four-second section on the RHYTHM track to punch in on (pretend there's a mistake there).

2. Using the Selector, drag the cursor across the section to be repaired, just as you would highlight a sentence to be retyped. Leave a little overlap by selecting an area that will cause Pro Tools to punch in early and punch out late,

as shown next. This way, you'll have plenty of overlap to adjust the transitions or the points at which playback goes from the old sound to the new and back.

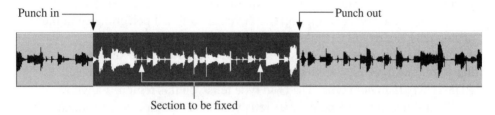

Punch in

Punch out

Section to be fixed

3. Open the Regions list by clicking the double arrow (>>) in the lower-right corner of the screen. (This window can be easily resized by dragging its border.) At this point, there should be at least two regions in the list: DRUMS_01 and RHYTHM_01. (If there are more, don't worry about it.)

4. Put the RHYTHM track into Record-Ready by clicking its Record button.

5. Make sure the monitor mode is set to Auto (OPTION+K / ALT+K, remember?), so that you will hear the previous RHYTHM track up to the punch-in point. The Input mode indicator(s) should *not* be glowing green.

6. Make sure the pre-roll is turned on (⌘+K / CTRL+K).

7. Drag the green pre-roll flag in the Timeline to the left to lengthen the pre-roll, so that you can get into the groove before punching in. Try about six seconds of pre-roll at first. Then lengthen or shorten it as desired. The pre-roll field in the Transport window shows the pre-roll value as you move the flag.

8. Set the post-roll to a short length, about two seconds.

9. When you're ready to record, press either ⌘+SPACEBAR (CTRL+SPACEBAR) or F12, and play along with the track. After the selected pre-roll, Pro Tools will punch in and out automatically across the range you have selected, and then stop at the end of the post-roll.

10. When Pro Tools punched out, you may have heard a dropout in the audio. This is normal. You can't tell how well the punch worked until you listen back. Press Play (SPACEBAR) to check out the punch. Don't worry if the transitions at the in and out points don't sound right. We'll fix that later.

When this punch is completed, you will see that Pro Tools has created and numbered a new region representing the new performance. The punch-in and punch-out points are now the borders of the new region. This is the virtual equivalent of the "piece of tape" pasted over the original performance in the analog tape analogy in Chapter 3.

Note that this new region has been added to the Regions list. In fact, there are now three new regions. The original RHYTHM track is labeled RHYTHM_01 in bold type. The bold type tells you this region is a whole, unedited sound file. The number 01 tells you this is the first region created on the RHYTHM track. When you punched in on the RHYTHM track, Pro Tools automatically created and numbered two new regions from RHYTHM_01: RHYTHM_01-01 (the region before the punch) and RHYTHM_01-02 (the region after the punch). Regions that are automatically created as a by-product of editing are referred to as *auto-created regions*. These regions are in plain type to show they are not whole sound files, but regions created from RHYTHM_01, the parent sound file.

The new region you created when you punched in on the RHYTHM track is also in bold type, because it's also a whole, unedited sound file.

11. Let's pretend that your first punch wasn't satisfactory, and you need to try it again. Simply press Record again to "go over" the first attempt.

12. Select the Grabber and double-click the new region and rename it **Best**.

13. Press the RETURN (ENTER) key to close the Name dialog.

14. Save the session, and then save it again as **Demo 4rhythm**.

Trimming the New Region

Let's get clear in our minds what's happening when you play back the new take. As I mentioned before, the original track has not been erased by the punch; it's just covered up by the new region named Best. What we're doing is giving the computer a set of instructions, as follows:

1. Play the original RHYTHM track up to the beginning of Best.

2. Jump to Best and play to the end of it.

3. Jump back to the original RHYTHM track and continue.

In the analog tape analogy in Chapter 3, we visualized "peeling back" the new take to reveal the original. I also talked about moving the punch points around to make the transitions sound better. The tool we use to accomplish this is the Trimmer.

1. Best should still be selected. If not, click it with the Grabber to select that region.

2. Go to Zoom preset 2 by typing the number **2** (use the alpha key above the QWERTY keys, not the numeric keys on the right side of the keyboard).

3. Select the Trimmer (F6) and move the Trimmer back and forth over the beginning of the region without clicking. Again, note how the tool changes direction. This provides a visual indication of which end of the region you'll be trimming.

4. Click just to the left of the punch-in point and drag the Trimmer an inch or so to the right as shown here:

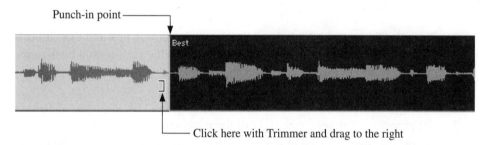

Punch-in point ⎯

⎯ Click here with Trimmer and drag to the right

As you drag the Trimmer, you are peeling back the new region to reveal the original RHYTHM track. Don't go too far or Best will disappear altogether. Note that the separation line between the regions changes appearance once it has been trimmed. The "dog-eared" angle at the top tells you in which direction the region was last trimmed.

> **NOTE**   *If you don't see the angle at the top of the region go to View > Region and enable Overlap.*

Look at the Regions list, and note that any selected region in the Edit window is also highlighted in the Regions list. If you find the Regions list bewildering now, wait until it fills up with hundreds of auto-created regions! Don't worry, most of the time you can pretty much ignore this list. The main concept you need to grasp at this point is this: the original RHYTHM track region (RHYTHM_01-01) is no longer visible in the Edit window, because it was divided into subregions when you punched in on it. If you ever need it again, you can drag it from the Regions list onto a new track without disturbing your edited RHYTHM track.

Because you clicked the region to the left of Best with the Trimmer, that region is now selected instead of Best. Pro Tools normally plays from the beginning of whichever region is selected. Therefore, to listen to the front of Best, you must reselect it by clicking it with the Grabber. Switching tools via the function keys will enable you to work much faster. If you use a different finger for each tool, you will eventually be able to select tools without looking at the keyboard.

5. Place the Trimmer to the right of the punch-in point. Click and drag it back to the left until it won't go any farther. This puts the Best region back to its original starting point.

6. Shorten the pre-roll to about one second.

7. Keeping the Trimmer to the right of the punch-in point, use it to trim the Best region to different lengths, listening to the results each time by pressing Play (SPACEBAR).

Experiment with different transition points until you find the one that sounds the best. As long as you keep the Trimmer to the *right* of the punch-in point, the Best region will stay selected and can be auditioned by merely pressing Play. Click the RHYTHM track's Solo button (marked with the letter *S*) to turn off the drums, so you can more easily hear any pops or thumps at the transition. Chances are, you will be able to minimize them by moving the punch-in point slightly one way or the other. Use the Zoom preset buttons to get a closer look at the edit. I've found that you can often mask a strange-sounding edit by placing it at the exact point at which a kick or snare drum hits, so you may want to take the RHYTHM track out of Solo and give that a try. If clicks persist, they can often be eliminated by crossfading the transition points—a topic we turn to next.

8. Using the scroll bar at the bottom of the screen, scroll to the right (if necessary) until you can see the punch-out point. Apply this same trimming technique to listen for the punch-out point as well. Just remember to keep the Trimmer to the right of the transition whenever possible to make auditioning easy.

9. Save the session, and then save it again as **Demo 5edit**.

Punch in on at least four other spots in the song (whether they need it or not) and go through the same trimming procedure each time. Don't label them Best. Pro Tools won't allow two regions with the same name. Give them different names or just let Pro Tools label them automatically. Keep at it until you get used to switching tools and feel confident about what you are doing. Don't get discouraged. Nearly everyone has trouble with this at first. Every time you finish a punch, save your session. Try to get into the habit of saving your session every time you complete a command. Train your left hand to reach over and do it automatically without looking.

Mangling the Session

As you've probably noticed, once you get into using the Trimmer and the Grabber, your chances of screwing up increase exponentially. Operator errors can cause regions to disappear from the screen, get accidentally shifted in time, or be dragged onto the wrong track. If none of these things has happened to you yet, they will sooner or later. When these little snafus occur, you need to know what to do to straighten them out. The purpose of this exercise is to simulate some of the more common mistakes, and then learn how to fix them.

At this point, you should have performed several punches on the RHYTHM track. This represents a fair amount of work on your part. Let's say you've gotten your session out of whack somehow. Obviously, the first thing you would do in that case is choose Edit > Undo (or press ⌘+Z / CTRL+Z).

If you have Auto Backup enabled, you can look through the backup sessions in the Session File Backups Folder and double-click recent backups of your session to look for one that predates the mistake. This may not help you if the mistake was made hours ago. Plus, you will lose all the work you did since the mistake was made. So, with that happy thought in mind...

Let's Mangle

Are you ready to do some damage?

1. Go back to Zoom preset 1. Using the Grabber, select the region we labeled Best and press DELETE. Whoops!

2. Using the Selector, select a small section in the middle of the audio region on the DRUMS track and press DELETE. Now there's a hole in the region, dividing it into two separate regions.

3. Using the Grabber, drag the second of the two newly made drum regions a little to the right. Now the drums are out of sync in the second half of the song.

4. Record-enable the DRUMS track. Make sure none of the other tracks is in Record. With the Selector tool, click somewhere in the middle of the first of the two newly separated audio regions on this track, and record a few seconds of silence.

5. Take the DRUMS track back out of Record. Step back and view the carnage.

Repairing the Session

We have several methods at our disposal to get the session back to normal. Let's replace our deleted take first.

Spotting a Region

You should currently be in the default *Slip mode,* indicated by the illuminated Slip button in the upper-left corner of the Edit window. This mode enables you to place regions anywhere you want. When you want a region placed precisely at its original location, you must switch to *Spot mode.* Spot mode enables you to place a region at its original location, or any location you specify. This is referred to as *spotting a region.* Here's how it works:

1. Switch to Spot mode by pressing F3 or clicking the Spot mode button near the upper-left corner of the Edit window.

2. In the Regions list, find the subregion labeled Best. As I mentioned earlier, the original sound file you recorded will be labeled in bold type. This means that it is a whole (untrimmed) file. You don't want the original file; you want the trimmed version in plain type below it. If you see more than one file, select the most recent (highest numbered) region. Drag this region onto the RHYTHM track and release the mouse.

3. The Spot dialog will appear. Click the upward-pointing arrow next to Original Time Stamp, and then press RETURN (ENTER). Note that the region has been spotted to its original location (it may be necessary to trim the end of the region again).

4. Close the Regions list, and go back to Slip mode (F2).

The Heal Separation Command

The Heal Separation command is used when you want to return separated regions to their original state. For this command to work, certain conditions have to be met, as this exercise will demonstrate.

1. On the DRUMS track, grab (with the Grabber, of course) the silent region you created by "accidentally" recording over the drums and delete it by pressing DELETE. Note that this leaves a gap in the region.

2. Using the Selector, make a selection across this gap, making sure the selection overlaps onto the regions on either side.

3. Choose Edit > Heal Separation or press ⌘+H (CTRL+H). The gap in the region is now healed.

4. Using this method, attempt to heal the separation we made earlier in the middle of the region on the DRUMS track. Nothing happens! This is because the Heal Separation command will only repair holes in regions that are *contiguous*. For this command to work, the regions you want to heal need to have been part of the same audio file at some point (which is the case here), and they have to be *in their original locations*. It worked in the previous step because the regions on either side of the gap had not been moved. It's not working here because the drum region on the right was moved from its original location.

5. Go back to Spot mode (F3) and use the Grabber to select the portion of the region on the DRUMS track you moved earlier.

6. When the Spot dialog appears, click the arrow next to Original Time Stamp to spot the region back to its original location, and then click OK to close the dialog.

7. Now you can go back to Slip mode and repair the hole in the middle of the region by using the Heal Separation command as in Steps 2 and 3.

8. Save the session, and then save it again as **Demo 6**.

Retrieving Deleted Tracks

Now we're really going to wreak havoc on the session. Wait at least five minutes after creating Demo 6, so that Auto Backup has time to make a backup.

1. Save the session again as **Demo 7td**. ("td" stands for "Total Disaster.")

2. For the next step, all three tracks need to be selected. If they are, the track names will be illuminated. If they are not, OPTION+click (ALT+click) DRUMS, the track name for the DRUMS track. This will cause all tracks in the Edit window to be selected.

3. Choose Track > Delete. A warning dialog will pop up. Foolishly ignore it and press DELETE.

4. Boom! Your tracks are gone, and Undo won't bring them back. In your panic, you save the session (go ahead and save the session).

5. Oops, that wasn't a good idea. You could have invoked the Revert to Saved command under the File menu and gotten things back to where they were when you last saved the session but, instead, you listened to me and saved the session *after* the screw-up.

6. Look under the File menu. You'll see that Revert to Saved is grayed out. Are you sweating yet? Just imagine this happening in a big session!

At this point, the producer has his hands around your neck, and you're starting to pass out. A guy from *Tape Op* magazine is in the corner scribbling furiously on his notepad and taking pictures. One of the band members is calling all the other bands in town to tell them what you just did. Not to worry. Luckily, you have been saving copies of your session all along, and you also have Auto Backup enabled.

7. Close the session (ignoring the gasps of everyone present) and go to the Demo Folder and open it.

8. While the producer goes out to his car to search for a firearm, open the Session File Backups Folder and look for the most recent backup of Demo 6.

9. Double-click this session to open it. Voila! You are back where you were, and everyone in the room applauds your genius. Note that the session is named **Demo 6recovered** to show that it came from a backup. You don't want to be reminded of your recent debacle, so you save the session as **Demo 8**.

Think about what would have happened if Auto Backup had not been enabled. Because you were saving versions of the session as you went, you could have opened Demo 6 and been in good shape because no work was done on the session after you saved it. That's not how it happens in real life, though. If you had worked on the Demo 7td session for an hour without Auto Backup enabled, and *then* deleted the tracks accidentally, you would have lost an hour's worth of work by going back to Demo 6. With Auto Backup enabled, you would have lost no more than five minutes' worth of work. Frustrating perhaps, but hardly grounds for murder. Now think about what would have happened if Auto Backup hadn't been enabled and you hadn't bothered to save any other versions of the session. It's not a pretty picture, is it?

Crossfading Basics

Upon listening to your punches on the RHYTHM track, you may have encountered pops or glitches where the transition from one region to another didn't sound quite right. In Nondestructive recording mode, these can be smoothed over by using crossfades.

The purpose of a *crossfade* is to smooth the transition between regions for a more natural sound. Placing a crossfade across the transition point between two regions tells the computer to fade out the old region, while simultaneously fading in the new one, thereby overlapping the two regions for the duration of the crossfade. If no crossfade is used at a transition, Pro Tools just bangs instantly from one region to another, like flipping a switch. If this occurs during a gap in the audio it may not be a problem, but if the transition occurs while audio is present, you'll probably hear pops or thumps. In the following exercise, we will use the Signal Generator plug-in to record a tone onto an audio track. Then, we'll do some crossfades on the resulting audio, so you can see how they work. We'll use Demo 8 for this exercise. Before you start this lesson, close the Regions list if it is open, press RETURN (ENTER) to go to the start of the song, and make sure you are in Slip mode. Select Zoom preset 2 and mute the DRUMS track by clicking its M button.

1.   Go to View > Edit Window > Inserts View. You will see a new column labeled "inserts" with five insert selectors for each track. They appear as small rectangles containing arrows. This is how you access your plug-ins (you'll be reading more about this in Chapter 5).

2.   Turn your speakers or headphones all the way down.

3. Click one of the RHYTHM track's insert selectors and select Plug-in > Other > Signal Generator (mono) from the list of plug-ins that pops up.

4. Bring up the volume of your speakers/headphones slightly and you'll hear a 1000-Hz tone. Bring the level in the Signal Generator Plug-in window up to about -8 and change the Frequency to 200 Hz. (Watch your speaker volume!) Close the plug-in window.

5. Click the RHYTHM track's Output label (OUT 1-2) and reassign its output to Bus > 1 (Mono).

6. Assign the input of the LEAD track to Bus > 1 (Mono).

7. Record-enable the LEAD track by clicking its R button. The tone is now internally routed to the LEAD track. You should now be able to see a meter reading on the LEAD track and hear the tone.

8. Press RETURN (ENTER) to rewind to the song start, and record three seconds of tone.

9. Select roughly a one-second section in the middle of the tone and record over it with the same tone.

10. Make sure you are in Auto Input mode (no green lights), press RETURN (ENTER), and play back the tone. If you don't hear an audible pop at both transitions, undo and try the punch again. Keep trying until you get an audible pop at each transition.

11. Take the LEAD track out of Record. Click the Signal Generator plug-in's insert selector (*not* the plug-in—the rectangle next to it) and select No Insert to get rid of the plug-in. Reassign the output of the RHYTHM track to interface > OUT 1-2.

12. Go to View > Edit Window > Inserts again to remove the inserts display from the Edit window.

13. The tone is now divided into three regions. Click the first region with the Grabber to select it. Hold SHIFT and click the other two regions to include them in the selection.

14. Press OPTION+F (ALT+F) to cause your selection to fill the window. Click in the empty space after the tone to deselect the regions. Your LEAD track should now resemble Figure 4-1.

FIGURE 4-1   Zoom in on the tone exercise

What Causes the Pops and Clicks?

To find out why the transitions are popping in the tone exercise, let's look closely at the punch-in point.

1. Use the Selector to make a short selection across the punch-in point (about half an inch), with the transition line in the center, as shown here:

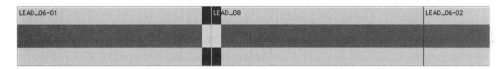

2. Press the E key to zoom in and expand the track height. This is the Zoom Toggle command. At this zoom level you can see that the waveform is chopped off at some point. This sudden truncation of the waveform causes the popping that you hear.

3. Press the E key again to return to the previous zoom setting.

What's the Difference Between an Audio File and a Region?

To understand crossfading, you have to understand the definition of these two terms. As you know, whenever you record anything in Pro Tools, you create an audio file—a whole, contiguous (uninterrupted) chunk of audio data that resides on your hard drive in the Audio Files Folder. The resulting waveform that appeared in the Edit window when you recorded the original three-second tone represents the *entire* audio file.

As we have learned, a region is a user-defined *area* derived from the parent audio file. Its boundaries are created by adjustable pointers that you can control by trimming, separating, and so forth. Therefore, you can use the Trimmer to make a region shorter, but you can't extend its length beyond the boundaries of its parent file.

The Link Edit and Timeline Selection Command

Before you place a crossfade at a transition point between two regions, you may need to move the transition points around first with the Trimmer until you find the spot that sounds the best musically. The idea is to make the transitions as seamless and transparent as possible. Obviously, every time you move the transition point, you have to audition, or listen back to, the changes.

You have probably noticed that clicking a region with the Trimmer highlights that region, and when you press Play, Pro Tools starts at the beginning of the highlighted region (with pre-roll, if activated). When using the Selector, playback starts wherever you click (along with any pre-roll you may have entered).

This is sometimes inconvenient, as you may want to start playback from the same place each time, regardless of which region is highlighted. While working on our tone exercise, we want playback to always start at the beginning of the tone, so we can hear the whole thing. As we click here and there with the Trimmer, the point at which playback starts will be constantly changing. We can get around this by disabling the Link Edit and Timeline Selection feature. This is accomplished by clicking the Link Edit and Timeline Selection button, shown next. Pro Tools defaults to the "on," or *linked*, position, which is denoted by a blue border around the button.

The Link Edit and Timeline Selection button

1. Click the Link Edit and Timeline Selection button to turn it off.

2. Press RETURN (ENTER) to go to the start of the tone. Make sure pre-roll is deactivated.

3. Press Play with the RHYTHM track muted and note that you can now click anywhere with the Selector, but the playback always starts at the beginning of the tone exercise. Pro Tools users who aren't familiar with this feature sometimes click this button accidentally, and then wonder why the playback isn't following the Selector. Playback will continue to start from the same place until you click the Link Edit and Timeline Selection button back on.

4. To illustrate a point, we'll attempt to place a crossfade at the first transition.

5. Once again, use the Selector to make a short selection across the first transition.

6. Press ⌘+F (CTRL+F) to bring up the Fades dialog, and click OK.

A dialog will appear, informing you that not enough audio data is available to make the fade. That's because crossfades cannot be placed at the *boundaries* (the very end or beginning) of an audio file. The regions' parent audio files must contain enough extra audio for the regions to *overlap*, so that Pro Tools can fade out the old region while fading in the new one. Therefore, when you attempted to place a crossfade at this transition, this dialog popped up asking for permission to move the transition over into an area where the audio files overlap to accomplish the fade. Letting Pro Tools choose where to put the crossfade isn't always a good idea. In general, you need to use your ears to determine where the transition sounds the best.

This is why I like to punch in a little early and punch out a little late when I'm overdubbing on a track. It provides the overlap necessary to be able to move the transitions around with the Trimmer. In the following steps, we will use the trimmer to manually adjust the transition points.

7. Choose Skip Invalid Fade(s) to close the dialog and use the Trimmer to move the first transition a half an inch or so to the right.

8. Move the second transition half an inch or so to the left. If you don't hear a pop or thump when you play through the transitions, keep moving them around, listening back each time until you hear one. In real life, you would be looking for the most musically transparent place for the transition by avoiding pops but, for the purpose of this exercise, you need to find pops so that you can try to get rid of them.

9. Now that the transition points have been moved so that the regions are overlapping, use the Selector again to make about a half-inch-wide selection across the first transition.

10. Once again, press ⌘+F (CTRL+F) to bring up the Fades dialog. Under "link," choose Equal Gain and press RETURN (ENTER).

11. If you followed the steps correctly, the pop will probably be gone, but you should be able to hear a dip in volume when you listen to the crossfade. That's because your fade is too long for an Equal Gain fade. (Check the Pro Tools *Reference Guide* for a more detailed explanation of the different types of fades.) Your crossfade probably looks something like the one shown here:

You should also be able to see a narrowing of the waveform across the fade. Pro Tools draws it this way to give you a visual indication that the amplitude or volume of the audio is dropping at the fade. Let's see if we can improve the situation by choosing a different type of fade.

12. Double-click the fade with the Grabber to bring up the Fades dialog again, and choose Equal Power instead. Note the difference in the way the fade curves are drawn in the Fades dialog. As you can see, the Equal Power fade keeps the volume up longer, and then drops more suddenly, making it a better choice in this particular case.

13. Click OK. Now, when you audition the fade, you should hear less of a dip in the volume (if any). If the volume is still dipping, that means the fade is too long. In some cases an equal gain fade will result in an undesirable *increase* in volume over the fade. The goal here is to make the transition as inaudible as possible.

14. Go to Zoom preset 4 or 5 for a much closer view of the fade. Experiment by using the Trimmer to shorten or lengthen the fade for the best sound.

15. When you are through experimenting, turn Link Edit and Timeline Selection back on.

16. Unmute the DRUMS and RHYTHM tracks. Go back to your RHYTHM track and place crossfades at all the transition points. Tweak them until you get the hang of it. Save often. When you're finished, do a Save As and name the session **Demo 9xfade**.

Recording the Lead Track

Now it's time to record a short solo section on the LEAD track. It can be a lead vocal, guitar solo, kazoo, keyboard, or the like, as long as it's a melodic figure. Whatever you use will be referred to as the lead.

1. Select the audio regions on the LEAD track from the tone exercise and delete them.

2. Pick a spot somewhere in the middle of the song to play the lead. Keep it down to four or eight bars.

3. The LEAD track input is probably still set to Bus 1. Reassign it to IN 1 and make sure the LEAD track is in Record-Ready.

4. Enter a suitable pre-roll (probably about five seconds) and place the Selector at the start of the lead.

5. Record a take.

Now let's imagine that we're at the point where we've gotten a pretty good take and we're not sure whether it's going to get any better. We could create another track for a new take, but it's easier to just open a new playlist.

Introducing the Playlist

One of the most important features in Pro Tools is the ability to create *playlists*. Playlists enable you to record and keep an almost unlimited number of takes for any instrument or group of instruments. You may run out of tracks, but it's doubtful you'll ever run out of playlists. The following exercise will give you a basic idea of what you can do with playlists, but I recommend reading the chapter on playlists in the *Pro Tools Reference Guide* for the full story.

1. Rename the LEAD track **LEAD 1** (the track—not the audio region).

2. Click the pop-up menu next to the track name, as shown next. This is the Playlist selector pop-up menu.

3. Select New, name the playlist **LEAD 2**, and then click OK. Now you have a new track you can record onto without affecting the original.

4. Record another lead in the same spot.

Playlist selector

Playlists vs. Additional Tracks

At this point, you may be wondering, "What's the difference between using playlists to record additional takes and creating new tracks to accomplish the same thing?" There are definite advantages to using playlists as opposed to creating a new track for each additional take:

- Every time you create a new track, Pro Tools assigns it a "voice." Your computer can only play a limited number of these voices at a time. However, a track can have an unlimited number of playlists associated with it, because they all *share* the voice assigned to that particular track, the way the limbs of a tree all share the same trunk.

- Additional playlists are no extra burden on your computer, because it only sees one playlist at a time.

- It takes longer to create more tracks because more steps are involved. (Inputs and outputs have to be assigned, and so forth.)

The only disadvantages of using playlists I can think of are as follows:

- Because they all share the same voice, you can only play one playlist at a time.

- You can only *see* one playlist at a time. This can be a disadvantage if you want to combine the best elements from multiple takes to create a single track. This process of creating a composite performance is known as *comping*.

Comping the LEAD Tracks

In my mind, one of the greatest advantages of using Pro Tools for recording is that comping tracks in Pro Tools is much faster and easier than on tape-based systems. In this exercise, we will do a simple comp of our two lead tracks to acquaint you with this technique. Imagine that you want to use the first half of LEAD 1 and the second half of LEAD 2.

1. Click the LEAD track's Playlist selector again and select LEAD 1.

2. Use the Selector to highlight the first half of the lead.

3. Press ⌘+C (CTRL+C) to copy the selection.

4. Return to the LEAD 2 playlist and press ⌘+V (CTRL+V) to paste the selection onto the second lead.

5. Listen to your new comp and use the Trimmer to adjust the point at which LEAD 1 switches over to LEAD 2 until you get something that works. If necessary, use a crossfade to smooth the transition.

6. Save your session, and then save it again as **Demo 10comp**.

This is a technique commonly used to comp vocals, solos, or any group of related takes to create a single track containing the best parts of each performance.

Consolidating Your Regions

Once you're finished editing a track, a good idea is to consolidate the audio regions in the track. This is accomplished using the Consolidate Selection command, which can be found under the Edit menu. The shortcut is OPTION+SHIFT+3 (ALT+SHIFT+3). This command turns a group of selected regions into a single uninterrupted new audio file in your session and on your hard drive. This can be advantageous for several reasons:

■ A single region is a lot easier to work with than a bunch of little ones.

■ This is a good way to protect your edited regions from being accidentally mangled or pulled apart. Consolidation incorporates all your edits and crossfades into the new audio file.

■ Consolidation relieves Pro Tools of the burden of performing all those crossfades in real time. Crossfades are calculated by Pro Tools and loaded into playback RAM. Having tons of crossfades in a session can slow your system to a crawl.

■ Consolidating your regions makes it much easier to clean up your session and get rid of unused audio.

■ If something goes wrong and your session becomes corrupted, you have a much better chance of salvaging a single uninterrupted audio file. Remember Humpty Dumpty?

> You should always listen carefully to make sure you are finished editing a track before you consolidate. In the real world, you may be hesitant to make the commitment this command entails. In such a case, the thing to do is to make a duplicate playlist of the track for a backup copy before consolidating. This is accomplished by clicking the track's Playlist selector and selecting Duplicate. Now you can consolidate the duplicate playlist while preserving the original for further editing at a later date. Be aware that if you go this route, you will be unable to free up hard drive space by dumping the audio files that make up your comp.

At this point, the audio on the RHYTHM track consists of several edited regions with crossfades. To consolidate the RHYTHM track, you must first select these regions.

1. Click the first region with the Grabber to select it.

2. SHIFT+click the last region in the RHYTHM track. The entire performance is now selected.

3. Choose Edit > Consolidate or press OPTION+SHIFT+3 (ALT+SHIFT+3) to consolidate the selection.

4. Do the same thing to the LEAD 2 track. Rename the track **Lead Comp**.

5. Save your session as **Demo 11cons**.

Cleaning Up the Session

During the editing portion of a project, you should occasionally clear the unused regions from your session. All the little bits and pieces of regions that are the by-product of editing can place an unnecessary burden on your computer. Our little session isn't going to put much of a strain on your computer, but imagine a full-blown 48-track session with tons of drum edits across 12 tracks, several tracks of vocal and background vocal comps, and lots of automation. If you don't streamline a session like that, your computer may start sending you nasty little messages like, "DAE was unable to complete this operation."

There are two different commands for clearing unused audio: Remove and Delete. It sounds like the same thing, but there's a huge difference between the two:

- *Remove* clears the audio from the current session only.

- *Delete* clears the audio files from the hard drive.

Let's start with the safest one first.

Removing Unused Regions from the Session

Any regions that are not visible in the Edit window (except for regions hidden by the Tracks list) are considered by Pro Tools to be unused. The Select Unused Regions command selects these regions and highlights them in the Regions list. The Clear Selected command removes these regions from the session. This command cannot be undone by choosing Edit > Undo. Therefore, it's a good idea to always do a Save As beforehand, in case you accidentally delete something you intended to keep.

When using the Clear Selected command to get rid of extra regions, it's important to make sure none of the regions in the Edit window are selected. Pro Tools will assume you want to delete them.

1. Deselect all audio by clicking any open space in the Edit window where there's no audio.

2. Open the Regions list. Click the word "Regions" at the top.

3. In the pop-up menu that appears, choose Select > Unused (or press ⌘+SHIFT+U / CTRL+SHIFT+U). Regions that don't appear in the Edit window or in a playlist are now highlighted in the Regions list.

4. Go back to the Regions pop-up menu and choose Clear (or press ⌘+SHIFT+B / CTRL+SHIFT+B).

5. In the Clear Regions dialog that appears, choose Remove. Note that all of the unused regions have disappeared from the Regions list. Save the session as **Demo 12rem aud** (for remove audio). Your computer has just breathed a sigh of relief.

The session has now been reduced to only the regions that appear in the Edit window and any playlists you have created. The regions and crossfades that originally made up the RHYTHM track have been removed, leaving only the consolidated version that incorporates all those elements. The LEAD 1 region hasn't been removed because it's on a playlist—therefore, Pro Tools assumes you want to keep it.

It's important to understand that the unused regions have only been removed from the session, *not from the hard drive.* Choose File > Open Recent > Demo 11cons. (If a dialog pops up asking you to locate a Fade or Audio File, click Skip All.) When the session is open, look in the Regions list. You will find that the unused regions are still present in this earlier session.

Deleting Unused Regions from the Hard Drive

One novice Pro Tools user called me and said, "I've only got three songs on my hard drive, but it's full! How can that be?" What he didn't realize was that all the nondestructive punching in and overdubbing he had been doing for the last two weeks had filled his hard drive with unused audio regions. When I told him he needed to delete these regions from his hard drive to make space for new audio, he was afraid to do so, and rightly so. This is not an operation that should be taken lightly. As I mentioned earlier, *removing* the unused regions only clears them from the current session—*deleting* them tells your hard drive that it's okay to overwrite them, similar to dragging the files into the Trash. As your computer will tell you, it's not undoable.

You should be wide awake when invoking this command. If possible, back up your session first. One quick and easy way to do this is the Save Session Copy In command. This command will let you save an exact copy of your current session to a different location. I normally back up sessions to a separate FireWire drive for archiving. If you don't have another hard drive, you can just save it to another location on the same hard drive. In a situation where your audio drive has become full, burning your sessions onto a CD-ROM or DVD-R may be an economical option for you. For our purposes, let's just copy it onto the same drive you've been using.

1. With Demo 11cons still open, choose File > Save Copy In. In the Save window that appears, be sure to check the All Audio Files box under Items To Copy. (In future sessions, you'll want to save your plug-in settings as well.) Pro Tools will name the new folder Copy of Demo 11cons. Choose your audio hard drive and click Save.

NOTE

Once you click Save, the copying process should take a few seconds at least. If it saves in the blink of an eye, it's probably because you've neglected to check the All Audio Files box, in which case you have only saved the session data and not the audio files. Obviously, the session data's pretty useless without the audio files.

2. Now we're going to permanently remove the unused audio from the session. Click any empty space in the Edit window to deselect any regions that might be selected.

3. Use the shortcut ⌘+SHIFT+U (CTRL+SHIFT+U) to select the unused regions. Note that they become highlighted in the Regions list.

4. Press ⌘+SHIFT+B (CTRL+SHIFT+B) to bring up the Clear Regions dialog and click Delete.

5. Pro Tools will put up a warning dialog informing you that the audio will be gone forever. It will put up a separate dialog for every single piece of audio you delete. OPTION+click (ALT+click) Yes to delete them all at once.

6. Save the current session as **Demo 13aud del**.

7. Go to File > Open Recent and open Demo 11cons. You will get a Pro Tools dialog informing you that files are missing. Select Skip All and click OK to get the session open. The files you deleted are still listed in the Regions list, but they are grayed out to signify that Pro Tools can't find them.

8. Go to File > Open Recent and open Demo 9xfade (there's no need to save the current session).

9. Select Skip All again and note that the missing audio files are displayed as *ghost regions* because they have been sent to Audio File Heaven. This is a sight that truly strikes fear into the heart of the Pro Tools user.

The next exercise will start with Demo 13aud del.

Chapter 5

The Pro Tools Virtual Mixer

At this point, our demo is ready for *mixdown,* which is the process of balancing the tracks to create a stereo mix that can be burned onto a CD-R. Owners of Pro Tools systems using multichannel interfaces would normally have two choices at this point. You could use the virtual mixer inside Pro Tools to mix the song or you could route the instruments to separate outputs on your interface and use an external mixer. Users of two-channel Pro Tools systems like the Mbox 2 have to mix internally because they only have one stereo output. In audio engineering lingo, this is referred to as mixing "inside the box." Like everything else, there are advantages and disadvantages to using the virtual mixer in Pro Tools.

Advantages:

- You don't have to go out and buy a mixer.

- Every fader, send, and plug-in can be automated.

- Every single aspect of your mix can be saved and easily recalled if you want to make a change at a later date.

- All the music stays in the digital domain. When using an external analog mixer, all signals must be converted back to analog for mixing, and then most likely converted back to digital again. This can cause degradation of the audio quality, especially when using a cheap, noisy mixer.

Disadvantages:

- Unless you have some type of external controller, you have to use your mouse to make all the fader moves, EQ adjustments, and so forth. This is much more cumbersome than using an external mixer, especially when you have a lot of tracks going.

- Mixing within Pro Tools usually involves using plug-ins for effects. Using a lot of plug-ins and automation can max out your computer pretty quickly, especially with host-based systems running LE software.

- Your ability to use outboard gear, such as compressors, equalizers, and reverbs, is severely limited with an eight- or two-channel interface.

Having Fun with Plug-ins and Aux Sends

In this chapter, you will learn how to use aux sends, aux returns, busses, and plug-ins for reverb and delay effects. Then you'll learn how to use automation to create effects, control plug-in parameters, and program fades. When you're through playing with the toys, you'll learn different methods of creating a final stereo mix.

What Are Plug-ins?

One of the most enjoyable aspects of working with Pro Tools is the ability to use a wide variety of plug-ins. *Plug-ins* are useful little pieces of software that usually perform signal processing, such as equalization, compression, and reverb and delay effects. Pro Tools systems always come with an assortment of free plug-ins. A staggering variety of third-party plug-ins is available for Pro Tools systems nowadays, and most are available in versions that will work on both HD and LE systems. Plug-ins can be quite expensive—but not as expensive as the outboard devices they simulate. Most plug-ins can be downloaded free of charge as fully functional demos that will work for several days before you have to pay to keep them.

One of the reasons Pro Tools HD (High Definition) systems cost so much more than their LE counterparts is that they provide DSP (Digital Signal Processing) cards to handle the load, so the computer won't have to do all the work. Pro Tools systems running LE software use *host-based* processing, which means the computer's CPU is providing the processing power in addition to performing all of its other tasks. With a host-based system, the more powerful your computer is, the more tracks, plug-ins, and automation you can pile on.

After you complete this lesson, it is strongly suggested that you read Digidesign's *Plug-In User's Guide*. It's loaded with useful information about getting the most out of your computer and is accessible under the Help menu.

Plug-In Formats

Pro Tools plug-ins come in three different formats:

- TDM (Time-division multiplexing) (or HD) plug-ins
- RTAS (Real Time AudioSuite) plug-ins
- AudioSuite plug-ins

TDM (or HD) plug-ins are designed to be used only on HD systems. They are used in track inserts and work in real time. They are nondestructive, which means they don't permanently alter the audio files. They are powered by DSP chips on the Digidesign PCI cards that come with these systems.

RTAS plug-ins basically work the same way, but they are powered by the host processor and can be used in non-HD systems as well.

AudioSuite plug-ins are available in all Pro Tools systems. They are accessed via the AudioSuite menu and use *file-based processing,* which means they create a new audio file with the effect permanently applied. They require no DSP and place no burden on the computer.

What Are Busses and Aux Sends?

In the Pro Tools environment, *busses* are virtual pathways that you can use to route signals from one place to another. In the tone exercise in Chapter 4, for instance, we used a bus to bounce a 200 Hz tone from one track to another. If you recall, we accessed the bus by routing the output of the track directly to the bus. Another way to route a signal to a bus is to insert an aux send (short for auxiliary send) on a track. A common use of an aux send is to split off a portion of a track's signal to send it to a reverb plug-in for processing.

What Are Aux Returns?

Once you process a signal using an aux send, you need a way to return the processed signal to the stereo mix. Pro Tools provides aux return channels for this purpose. The ability to build your own network of sends and returns gives you a great deal of flexibility, but it has the potential to cause a great deal of confusion for someone who has never used a mixing console. The flow chart in Figure 5-1 shows a simple setup for putting mono reverb on the DRUMS track. The arrows show the direction of signal flow.

In this example, you can see how a mono aux send routes a portion of the DRUMS track's signal to a bus. Think of the bus as a patch cord used to connect the aux send to the reverb. The *fader* on the aux send controls how much of the signal is sent out. An aux return channel has been created with its input set to receive Bus 1, and its outputs are set to feed the processed, or "wet," signal back into our stereo mix. A reverb plug-in has been placed on one of the aux channel's inserts. This setup bears certain similarities to your shower at home, as shown in Figure 5-2. The cold water is diverted (sent) into a water heater, where it is heated (processed).

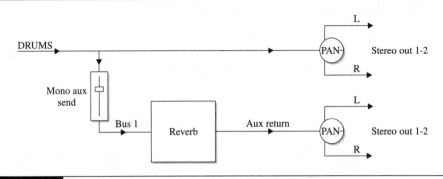

FIGURE 5-1   Mono drum reverb flow chart

Then it returns to the hot water faucet, where it is mixed with the cold water before it reaches the shower head (which may or may not be stereo).

Of course, the easiest and most obvious way to put reverb on the drums would be to simply insert a reverb plug-in on the DRUMS track. That's not going to work very well if you have eight tracks of drums, however. Many novice users unknowingly squander their DSP resources by trying to put a separate D-Verb plug-in on every track. This eats up their CPU power like there's no tomorrow, and it's completely unnecessary. If you were mixing a 24-track song on a traditional tape machine/mixer setup, it's highly unlikely that you would use a separate reverb device for each track, even if you wanted them all to have reverb. It makes a lot more sense to use auxiliary effects sends to put *groups* of tracks through a smaller number of reverb devices. Pro Tools provides plenty of aux sends and returns for effects, but many beginners shy away from using them because they haven't had enough experience with analog mixers to understand how they work.

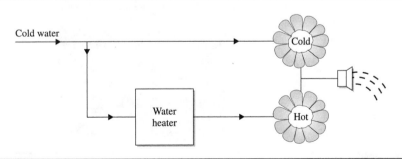

FIGURE 5-2   Plumbing analogy

Setting Up Aux Returns with D-Verb

In the first exercise, we will create a slightly more complex version of the setup in Figure 5-1 using a stereo reverb setup with D-Verb. *D-Verb* is a Digidesign reverb plug-in that is included with the Pro Tools software.

1. Open Demo 13aud del and save it as **Demo 14mix**. Close the Regions list if it is open. Pro Tools provides a window that tells you how much strain you're putting on the computer. Choose Window > System Usage to display this window in the Edit window. Put it in the upper-right corner, so you can keep an eye on it.

2. Press ⌘+SHIFT+N (CTRL+SHIFT+N) to bring up the New Track dialog. Click the Track format pop-up menu (currently set to Mono) and select Stereo. Click the Track Type pop-up menu (currently set to Audio Track), select Aux Input, and then click Create.

3. Rename the new track **D-Verb**. From now on, this book will refer to these aux returns as *channels* instead of tracks because they don't contain audio files.

4. Set the D-Verb channel input to Bus 1-2 (Stereo).

5. Here's another way to show the Inserts view. In the upper-left corner of the Edit window, find the small View Selector icon shown in Figure 5-3 and click it. Select Inserts View from the pop-up menu.

6. Click one of the D-Verb channel's five Insert selectors and select Multichannel Plug-in > Reverb > D-Verb (Stereo). The D-Verb plug-in window appears.

View Selector icon ——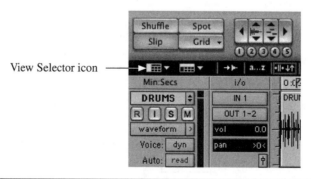

FIGURE 5-3   Click the View Selector icon to enable the Inserts view.

7. In the D-Verb plug-in window, turn the Input level up to zero. (For some reason, it defaults to –4.)

8. In the Edit window, click the View Selector icon again and choose Sends A-E. The Sends view appears. Note that there are five Send selector buttons for each track. (The Sends F-J view provides an additional five Send selector buttons for a total of ten possible send assignments.)

9. On the DRUMS track, click the first Send selector button and choose Bus > Bus 1-2 (Stereo). A Send window for the DRUMS track appears with a virtual sliding volume control, resembling a fader on a mixing console. This *fader* will be used to control the level of the signal from the DRUMS track to the D-Verb plug-in. Drag the Send window to the right side of the display to get it out of the way.

10. Mute the RHYTHM and Lead Comp tracks (by clicking the M button) and play the DRUMS track. Click the fader in the Send window and move it upward until you can plainly hear reverb on the drums. The reverb effect you hear is coming from the D-Verb plug-in which you have inserted on the D-Verb channel. You should be able to see its meters moving.

CAUTION   *It's not a good idea to run the Send faders much higher than zero, because this can overdrive the plug-in. If you've got the fader up to zero and you still want more reverb, you can raise the output level of the D-Verb channel by clicking its Volume button and adjusting the slider control. Make sure the red clip indicator in the D-Verb plug-in window doesn't light.*

11. If you are using a Mac, click the small round button on the right at the top of the Send window (it turns green when you place the cursor over it) and it will expand to show a stereo send meter. On a Windows machine, this button appears as a small rounded rectangle, located to the left of the X (or Close) button in the Send window. It does not change color, but it will expand the meter window when clicked.

12. Click the Pan knob in the Send window and pan the send all the way to the right. Note that the dry drums are still in the middle, but the reverb mostly comes out of the right channel.

13. OPTION+click (ALT+click) on the Pan knob to return it to the center position.

14. Close the Send window. The flow chart in Figure 5-4 illustrates your current setup.

15. Unmute the RHYTHM and Lead Comp tracks.

16. Click the first Send selector button on the RHYTHM track, but this time hold down the OPTION (ALT) key while doing so, and choose Bus > Bus 1-2 (Stereo).

NOTE   *Send assignments appear on all the remaining tracks. This feature saves you the trouble of manually putting a send assignment on each track but, in this case, it presents a problem. It has also put a send assignment on the D-Verb channel, which is a definite no-no. Raising the send fader on the D-Verb channel will cause this channel to feed a signal to itself, resulting in a feedback loop that will make your speakers howl. For the remainder of this book, these send assignments will be referred to simply as "sends."*

17. To remove the unwanted send, click the Send selector button for the D-Verb channel and select No Send.

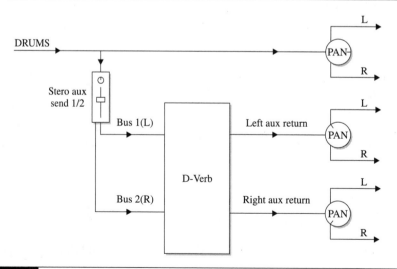

FIGURE 5-4   Stereo drum reverb flow chart

18. Unmute the Lead Comp track, click its send to open the Send window, and put some reverb on the Lead Comp track. Take some time to experiment with the different reverb algorithms in the D-Verb plug-in window. Check the System Usage meter. LE system users should see a slight increase in CPU usage as a result of adding these sends.

19. Save your session, and then save it again as **Demo 15verb**.

Using Multimono D-Verb

In the previous scenario, D-Verb is configured as a stereo (multichannel) reverb. The reverb controls are ganged together, so changes you make will apply to both the left and right channels. The reverb outputs are panned left and right. Let's say you want to put a short reverb on the DRUMS track and a long reverb on the Lead Comp track. You can accomplish this by using the multimono version of D-Verb instead, in which the plug-in is configured as two separate mono reverbs.

1. Click the D-Verb plug-in insert and select Multimono Plug-in > Reverb > D-Verb (Mono).

2. In the Edit window, OPTION+click (ALT+click) the D-Verb channel Pan settings (under the Volume control in the channel's I/O column) to set them to the center position (>0<) as shown here:

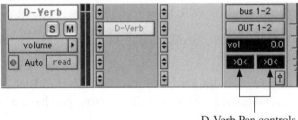

D-Verb Pan controls

3. Figure 5-5 shows the upper half of the D-Verb plug-in window. An illuminated Master Link button with a chain-link icon indicates that the controls for the left and right channels are linked. Click this button to unlink them, so we can set different parameters for left and right.

4. Make sure the Channel selector is set to L for left channel. Set the algorithm to Room 2. This will be the short reverb.

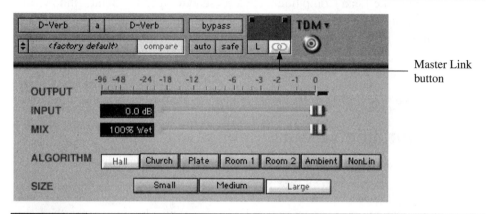

Master Link button

FIGURE 5-5   D-Verb plug-in window

5. Click the L and choose Right in the Channel selector pop-up menu. This will be the long reverb.

6. Click the DRUMS track's send to bring up its Send window, and play the song.

When you play the DRUMS track, you'll notice that panning its aux send to the left sends the drums to the short reverb, and panning to the right sends the drums to the long reverb. It would be much more convenient to have a separate send for each reverb. Here's how:

7. Use the DRUMS track's Send selector button to reassign the send to Bus 1 > (Mono).

8. Create a new send on the DRUMS track and set it to Bus 2 > (Mono). Leave this send turned all the way down. Now you have a separate send for each reverb.

It would be best to have the sends on the other tracks set up this way as well. You should use the OPTION (ALT) key to do them all at once but, first, you need to hide the D-Verb channel, so that you don't have to go to the trouble of deleting the sends from it again.

9. To accomplish this, open the Tracks list by clicking the double-arrow button in the lower-left corner of the screen. At the top, you will see a highlighted list of your tracks.

10. Click D-Verb in this list to hide it from view. Note that the D-Verb disappears from the screen and is no longer highlighted, but you can still hear it working.

11. Holding down the OPTION (ALT) key, create two Mono sends on the RHYTHM track, one for Bus 1 > (Mono) and one for Bus 2 > (Mono) the same way you did on the DRUMS track. Identical sends will appear in all the remaining tracks, but the D-Verb track will not be affected because it is hidden.

12. On the Lead Comp track, click the Bus 2 send (long reverb) and bring up the fader to send the Lead Comp track to the long reverb.

Look carefully at the flow chart in Figure 5-6. This diagram shows the signal flow for your current setup.

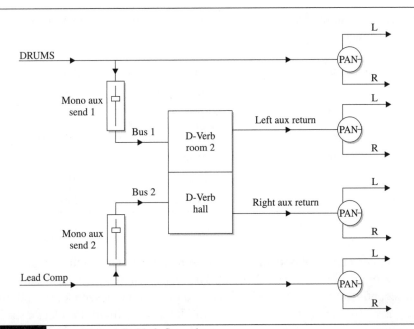

FIGURE 5-6   Dual Mono D-Verb flow chart

Setting Up an Aux Return for Digital Delay

Now let's create another aux track for some digital delay using the techniques we've learned. Close any open send or plug-in windows.

1. Create a new track, and this time make it a Mono Aux Input channel.

2. Label it **Delay** and set the input to Bus 3 > (Mono).

3. In the Inserts view, choose Plug-in > Delay > Long Delay II (Mono/Stereo) on the Delay channel. Note that this mono channel has been transformed by the plug-in into a mono-in, stereo-out channel.

4. Hide the Delay channel as before, by clicking its name in the Tracks list.

5. Using the OPTION (ALT) key as before, add a new Bus 3 > (Mono) send to all channels.

6. Use the Tracks list to unhide the D-Verb and Delay channels, and then ⌘+click (CTRL+click) their Solo buttons to put them in Solo Safe mode. Note that the Solo buttons are now grayed out.

7. Let's set up the Delay plug-in for a simple stereo setting for the lead instrument using the following table:

Gain	0.0	Gain	0.0
Mix	100% Wet	Mix	100% Wet
LPF	Off	LPF	Off
Delay	400 msec	Delay	200 msec
Depth	0%	Depth	0%
Rate	0.0 Hz	Rate	0.0 Hz
Feedback	25%	Feedback	25%

The Mix percentage of both channels is set to 100 percent, so that no dry signal comes from the Delay return channel. The Delay lengths are measured in milliseconds (msec). A *millisecond* is one-thousandth of a second, so 400 msec is slightly less than half a second in length. It can be difficult to select a specific Delay value using the sliders. Instead, click the current Delay value, type in the new Delay value, and press RETURN (ENTER). The Feedback setting determines the number of times the echo repeats.

Solo Safe Mode

Before we start playing with the digital delay, I want to introduce you to Solo Safe mode. You may have noticed that clicking the Solo button on a track mutes all the other tracks. This is a useful tool for mixing. However, when you solo a track, you still want to be able to hear the reverb and other effects associated with that track. Putting the aux channels in *Solo Safe* mode will prevent them from being muted when a track is soloed.

8. Solo the Lead Comp track.

9. Click its Bus 3 send and bring up the fader during playback. You should be able to hear the delay and see some meter action on the Delay channel.

10. Put a send on the Delay channel and select Bus 2 > (Mono). Raising the fader on this send will route the delay back into the long reverb for a more ethereal sound.

11. Take the Lead Comp track out of Solo and listen to the whole mix. It should be pretty well drenched in effects by now. Are we having fun yet?

12. To reduce screen clutter, close any send and plug-in windows that are open and close the Tracks list. Save the session, and then save it again as **Demo 16fx**.

The Leslie Effect

This delay setting mimics the effect achieved by a rotating speaker device, such as the Leslie cabinet commonly used with Hammond organs.

1. Insert Plug-in > Delay > Short Delay II (Mono) on the RHYTHM track.

2. Solo the RHYTHM track and set the Delay plug-in's parameters as the following table shows. This time, click the first parameter you need to

change, type in the new setting, and then use the TAB key to scroll through the other parameters, typing in the new values as you go.

Gain	0
Mix	30%
LPF	Off
Delay	0.16 msec
Depth	22%
Rate	3.00
FB	0

3. As you listen to playback, try changing the Rate to vary the speed of the effect.

4. When you're done, close the plug-in window and take the RHYTHM track out of Solo.

Creating Effects with Automation

Pro Tools *automation* can manipulate the various controls, so you don't have to do it manually. Many new users don't take advantage of automation out of fear that it will be too complicated, but Pro Tools automation can be edited graphically, which makes it easy to use. Almost anything you can do in Pro Tools can be automated. It's a powerful tool for creating effects. Here are a few examples that give a brief demonstration of its capabilities.

The Auto Panner

We can use the automation to automatically pan things left and right. Let's try it on the Lead Comp track.

1. Use the Grabber to select the audio region on the Lead Comp track and press OPTION+F (ALT+F5) to make the selection fill the Edit window. Close any send or plug-in windows that are in the way.

2. With the Selector, click somewhere in the Edit window to deselect the region.

3. Click the Lead Comp track's Pan control and drag to the right to pan the Lead Comp track all the way to the right.

4. On the Lead Comp track, click the Track View selector (currently set to Waveform) and select Pan.

5. While in this view, you will not be able to edit anything except pan data. You will see a line across the bottom of the Lead Comp track that represents the pan setting. Move the Pan control to different settings and note how the line changes accordingly. (You have to let go of the mouse button before it will change.) Panning to the left moves the line up; panning to the right moves the line down.

6. Once again, pan the Lead Comp track all the way to the right.

7. Click the Main counter pop-up, as shown here, and select Bars: Beats.

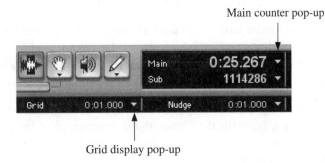

Main counter pop-up

Grid display pop-up

8. Click the Grid display pop-up, shown in the previous illustration, and select 1/16 Note.

9. Choose View > Transport > MIDI Controls. Note that your Transport window is now expanded.

10. Locate the Conductor button (there's a picture of a conductor on it) and turn it off if it's illuminated. This will enable you to manually select a tempo.

11. Locate the Tempo slider below the Conductor button and slide it to the left for a tempo of 30 bpm (beats per minute) or enter **30** into the Tempo field.

12. Click and hold on the Pencil tool icon (the last tool on the right in the Edit window toolbar) and select Triangle from the pop-up menu.

13. Click the pan line at the bottom of the Lead Comp track at the point where the lead starts, as shown here:

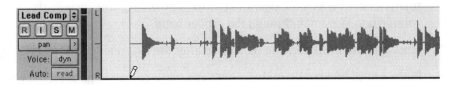

14. Drag upward to the top of the Lead Comp track, and then continue dragging to the right until you reach the end of the lead. The resulting automation data should appear as shown here:

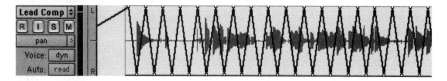

If it doesn't, start in the same place and try again.

15. Click the small fader icon under the Pan control on the Lead Comp track. The Output window appears, which shows the volume and pan settings for that track. Now when you play the lead, the Pan knob should swing rapidly from side to side, and you can hear the lead panning from left to right.

16. Change the pan speed by changing the Tempo slider and drawing the waveform again. Note the difference in the appearance of the automation data. You can also select a different shape for the Pencil tool or draw a freehand panning pattern.

17. Remove the effect by dragging the Selector across all of the automation data and pressing DELETE. Because you are still in the Pan Track view, only the automation is deleted, not the audio. OPTION+click (ALT+click) the Pan control to pan the lead back to the center.

The Tremolo Effect

We can use volume automation to create a tremolo effect.

1. On the Lead Comp track, click the Track View Selector and choose Volume. The black line now represents the volume level of the track. Think of the volume line as though it were a rubber band stretched across the width of the track.

2. Using the Grabber, click the volume line somewhere during the lead. A small dot known as a breakpoint appears. The *breakpoint* anchors the volume line like a nail through the rubber band.

3. Place another breakpoint an inch or so after the first one.

4. Place a third breakpoint midway between these two and pull it all the way down to the bottom of the track to make a V-shaped notch in the volume line. You have just programmed the automation to fade the lead down and back up.

5. Play the Lead Comp track across the fade and note that the fader moves as the volume goes down and back up.

6. This time, we'll use the Grabber to remove the automation data. Delete all three breakpoints by OPTION+clicking (ALT+clicking) on them with the Grabber.

7. Set the tempo to around 160 bpm.

8. Use the Pencil tool (still set to Triangle) to click the volume line and drag it downward to the middle of the track (not all the way to the bottom), and all the way across the lead region.

9. Play back the lead. This creates an effect similar to the tremolo effect on a guitar amp. One cool thing about it is that you can match it exactly to the tempo of the song.

10. To return to normal, use the Selector to select across the automation breakpoints and press DELETE.

11. Change the Lead Comp Track view back to Waveform.

12. Close the Output window and save the session, and then save it again as **Demo 17auto**.

The Wah-Wah Effect

We can automate the EQ plug-in to emulate the effect of a wah-wah pedal.

1. On the RHYTHM track, ⌘+CTRL+click (CTRL+START+click) on the Short Delay plug-in to deactivate it. This is a good way to turn plug-ins off without losing your plug-in settings. It's better than clicking the Bypass button because it frees up the DSP that was allocated to that plug-in. If you're not into the Leslie effect, just delete the plug-in altogether by clicking on the insert and selecting No Insert.

2. Insert the 1-Band EQ 3 (Mono) plug-in on the RHYTHM track and set the parameters as follows:

Input	−8.0 dB
Type	Peak
Gain	12.0 dB
Freq.	doesn't matter
Q	2.50

3. Play the RHYTHM track and move the Frequency slider back and forth for a wah-wah pedal effect. It's more realistic if you stay in the middle area. Find the range that sounds best to you.

To automate this effect, do the following:

4. In the EQ plug-in window, click Auto. A dialog that appears enables us to choose which plug-in controls we want to automate. Select Frequency in the column on the left and click Add. Click OK to close the window. A green light below the Frequency knob lights to show that it has been selected for automation.

5. Locate the Automation Mode selector on the RHYTHM track. (It's the button next to the word "Auto" that says "read.") Click it and select Touch. The light below the Frequency knob should now glow red to indicate it is ready to record automation data as soon as you touch it.

6. Play the first eight bars or so, while moving the Frequency knob.

7. Play back the same section of the song and note that the automation re-creates your performance. Clicking the Frequency knob during playback will overwrite the previous automation data.

8. Click the Automation Mode selector again and choose Read to prevent further automation from being written.

Pasting Automation

Automation data can be copied and pasted like text. Here's how this works:

1. On the RHYTHM track, click the Track View selector and notice that new options have appeared. Set the Track View selector to 1-Band EQ 3 > Frequency. In this view, the Frequency knob automation data appears as a series of breakpoints, which can now be edited. The RHYTHM track view should look something like this:

2. Go to Zoom preset 1 and drag the Selector across the breakpoints to highlight them. Select only the area that contains breakpoints.

3. Press ⌘+D (CTRL+D) to duplicate the automation data and place it adjacent to the original data.

4. Continue to press ⌘+D (CTRL+D) until you've pasted automation breakpoints all the way to the end of the song. Now the entire RHYTHM track has the wah-wah effect applied.

5. Close the EQ plug-in window and save your session.

The Backwards Lead

This effect is accomplished using the Reverse AudioSuite plug-in. As I mentioned before, AudioSuite plug-ins create a new audio file with the effect permanently applied and place no DSP burden on the computer. Therefore, you should duplicate the playlist and process only the copy, so that you can easily return to the original playlist, if you so desire.

1. On the Lead Comp track, click the Playlist button (next to the track's name) and select Duplicate. Name the new playlist **BW Lead**.

2. Use the Grabber to select the Lead region in the Edit window.

3. Choose AudioSuite > Other > Reverse.

4. In the window that appears, select Process, and close the window.

5. Make sure the Lead Comp track is unmated and play back your creation. By now, it should be sounding downright psychedelic. Save your session as **Demo 18fx**.

Finishing Your Mix

Now it's time to take all the elements of your song and balance them in a way that sounds good to you. Play with the levels and effects sends, and explore the parameters of the different plug-ins at your disposal. Read the automation chapter in the *Reference Guide* and experiment with the automation. The best thing about recording at home is that you can take all the time you need to experiment with your recordings.

There are basically two options for recording a stereo mix of your song to disk. You can create a new stereo track (or a pair of mono tracks) and record your stereo mix onto those. If you need to convert your mix to a different format (to make it compatible for CD burning, for instance), you can use the Bounce to Disk command. In the following steps, we will do both. If you have time, read the mixdown chapter in the *Reference Guide*.

Submixing

In engineering lingo, the routing of signals from one place to another in a mixing console is known as *bussing*. The virtual mixer in Pro Tools provides a number of busses. In earlier parts of the tutorial, you assigned aux sends to busses to send signals to effects. In the tone exercise in Chapter 4, you used a bus to route or "bounce" a tone from one track to another. To create a stereo mix of your session, you'll change your outputs from OUT 1-2 to a stereo bus, place a Master Fader track across that bus so you can control the volume of the entire mix, and then create a new Mix track that will be fed from that bus. This process is known as *submixing*.

1. Look in the Tracks list to make sure all tracks and return channels are visible in the Edit window.

2. Bring up the New Track dialog and create a Stereo Master Fader. This fader is analogous to the stereo master fader on a recording console. It will default to the name Master 1. Set its output to Bus 15-16 (Stereo).

NOTE   *Master faders use no additional DSP.*

3. Hold down the OPTION (ALT) key and click any track's output (in the I/O column) and reassign all the outputs to Bus 15-16 (Stereo).

4. Hide the D-Verb and Delay channels.

5. Create a new Stereo Audio track and name it **MIX**.

6. Set the input of the Mix track to Bus 15-16 (Stereo).

7. ⌘+click (CTRL+click) the Mix track's Solo button to place it in Solo Safe mode.

8. All the audio tracks are now routed through the Master 1 channel. This channel also provides plug-in inserts which we can use to process the entire mix. On the Master 1 fader channel, insert Multichannel Plug-in > Dither > POW-r Dither (Stereo). Bypass the plug-in for now, and close the plug-in window. (We'll discuss dither in the upcoming section "Bouncing to Disk.")

9. Record-enable the Mix track and set the Monitor mode to Input (OPTION+K / ALT+K). Now that your entire mix is routed through the Master 1 channel, you can use volume automation to fade out the end of the song.

10. Pick a spot about 20 seconds before the end of the song and put a breakpoint on the Master 1 channel's volume line.

11. Put another breakpoint at the end of the song and pull the volume line all the way down to the bottom of the track, as shown here:

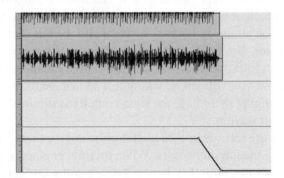

12. If you followed all these steps correctly, you should be able to hear your mix playing from the output of the Mix track. At the end of the song, you should hear your 20-second fade-out.

At this point, you may be saying to yourself, "I followed all the steps and it works like it's supposed to, but I still don't understand what the heck I just did." It may help to refer to the flow chart in Figure 5-7 to see how the signals in our session are routed. All the audio tracks are now bussed through the Master 1 channel, where processing can be applied to the entire mix, which is then bussed to a stereo audio track for recording. We are monitoring the output of the stereo Mix track (OUT 1-2).

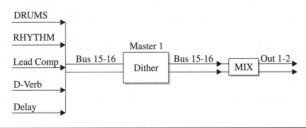

FIGURE 5-7   Mix flow chart

Gain Structure

To put it in the simplest terms possible, *gain structure* is a term used to describe the way you have your volume controls set. It's important to pay attention to gain structure when mixing. Guitar players know that the higher they set the Gain knob on their amp, the more distortion they'll hear (if they have any hearing left). When they do this, they're changing the gain structure of the amp.

Pro Tools provides clipping indicators on every meter to let you know when you're overdriving the different gain stages. If you insert a plug-in on a track and boost its gain too much, it will cause clipping (distortion) on that track. If you have the faders too high on all the audio tracks, you'll clip the bus that feeds the Master fader channel, causing distortion. In this case, you would have to back off the level of all the audio track faders until the Master fader meter stops clipping. If the faders are set too low, you will not be taking full advantage of the dynamic range of your system. In digital recording, the sound quality is diminished at low levels, especially in a 16-bit session.

Once the tracks are recorded, it's a matter of balancing them in such a way as to avoid overdriving the internal busses. When mixing, engineers tend to bring the faders up a little at a time, until they have a good, healthy level at the Master fader channel without clipping.

Recording a 24-Bit Mix

Once you're satisfied with the mix and are sure that nothing is clipping, you're ready to record a stereo mix of your session.

1. Using the Selector, select the entire song from the first audio in the song to the end of the fade. It doesn't matter which track you select it on.

2. With no pre- or post-roll, begin recording and let it run. Pro Tools will stop at the end of the selection.

3. Your mix now appears on the stereo Mix track as a stereo file. Double-click this file with the Grabber and rename it **24-Bit Mix**.

4. Look in the Audio Files folder for the session and note that your "stereo" mix appears as two separate mono files; 24-Bit Mix.L and 24-Bit Mix.R. That's because Pro Tools does not support stereo interleaved files within a session. Stereo tracks in Pro Tools are merely two mono tracks grouped together.

Bouncing to Disk

In engineering lingo, *bouncing* is simply the process of recording the output of a track (or combination of tracks) to another empty track. It comes from the world of tape machines.

When a 24-track session is running out of tracks, an engineer might bounce the backing vocals on tracks 17, 18, and 19 together onto track 21 to free up tracks 17 through 19 for additional overdubs. Tracks can easily be bounced in Pro Tools as well, but the Bounce to Disk command is used for something else entirely.

The Bounce to Disk command is the Swiss army knife of Pro Tools. It can create a stereo or mono file of your mix in a multitude of formats, including MP3 (the MP3 feature costs extra). The resulting file will not appear in your session. If you want to burn an audio CD of your mix, you need to create a file that your CD burning software can import. The safest bet would be to create a 16-Bit stereo interleaved .wav or AIFF file. These formats can be imported by most CD burning applications. When we bounce this mix to disk, we'll specify the bit depth, sample rate, and file format in the Bounce window.

Earlier, we inserted the Dither plug-in on the Master 1 channel. It was bypassed because dither is not needed when making a 24-bit mix. *Dithering* is a process (optional, but recommended) that improves the sound quality of low-level signals when bouncing to a lower bit depth, such as 16 bits. (Check the *Plug-In User's Guide* for more info about dithering.) The main thing to remember about dithering is that it must be the last process the mix goes through before converting to 16-bit.

1. Take the Dither plug-in out of Bypass.

2. Make sure the entire song is still selected.

3. Mute the Mix track and take it out of Record.

4. Unhide the aux channels and set the outputs of all tracks and channels to OUT 1-2.

5. Choose File > Bounce To > Disk.

6. In the Bounce window, set the Bounce options, as shown in Figure 5-8.

7. Click Bounce or press RETURN (ENTER).

8. When the Save window appears, name the file **16-bit Mix** and save it to the Demo Audio Files Folder (the default location).

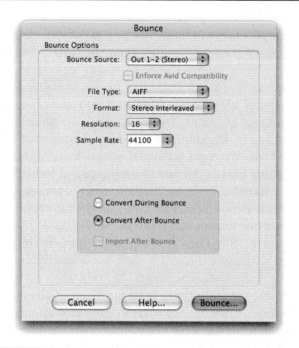

FIGURE 5-8 The Bounce window

TIP

For future reference, bouncing a large session to disk can put quite a load on your CPU. Don't try to do anything with the computer while it's bouncing; just leave it alone until the bounce is completed.

9. Click Bounce to start the process. The mix will play from beginning to end, and then Pro Tools will perform the conversion process.

10. Check in the Demo Audio Files Folder to make sure 16-bit Mix is there among the other audio files.

11. Save your session, and then save it again as **Demo 19mix**.

If you have a CD-burning program, such as Roxio's Toast, you would simply drag the 16-Bit Mix audio file into the Toast window, pop in a blank CD-R, and click Record.

Good Work...Now Do It Again!

The key to retaining what you have learned so far is repetition. The best way to drill these concepts into your head is to go through Chapters 3–5 at least one more time (with a different song) until you can record, edit, and mix a simple session without consulting the book. This will give you a good foundation before moving into the more advanced operations in Chapter 6.

Before we move on, I feel that a few important words about file organization and archival are in order.

Place Each Song in a Separate Session

It's not a good idea to have multiple songs in one session, because each song will have its own requirements in terms of plug-ins, routing, and so on. Having multiple songs in one session also makes them hard to separate later on. Get into the habit of creating a separate session for each song. If you want to borrow the track layout of one session to use for another, you can make a session template (the *Reference Guide* details this procedure).

The decision about where the song will go is made in the Session Setup dialog when the session is first created. All audio files for a session should be kept in one folder whenever possible. Bounced files like the 16-bit mix of the demo can be placed anywhere you like, because they don't appear in the session. Sessions with lots of tracks at high sample rates may need to have the tracks allocated to two or more hard drives. This is accomplished by changing the tracks' Disk Allocation (Setups > Disk Allocation). The bigger the session, the more critical it is to avoid the archiving nightmare of having elements of a session spread out over too many hard drives.

Backing Up Your Work

It's no fun losing hours of work because of a crash or hardware failure. This is the main reason many people are leery of recording with computers. Your music is out there in cyberspace somewhere, and you can't physically touch it like you can a tape. That's why it's important to implement a procedure for backing up your work. Any work that is not backed up should be thought of as being at considerable risk. A crash or hardware problem can cause your work to disappear forever in the blink of an eye and, sooner or later, it will happen to you.

CAUTION *Your music should always exist in at least two places, if not three. Personally, I prefer to back up to a pair of identical FireWire drives for redundancy at the end of a project. FireWire drives are so cheap nowadays, there's no good reason not to. Is it worth the extra hundred bucks or so for a spare backup drive to guarantee the safety of weeks or months of hard work?*

With smaller sessions, an economical option is to burn your session *as data* onto a CD-R or DVD-R with a program such as Adaptec's Toast or the software that came free with your computer. It's not the most convenient method, however, because you can't back up sessions incrementally as you go. You have to back up the *entire* project every time. Backing up dozens of versions of a song to CD-R is neither practical nor convenient. In addition, CD-Rs only hold 700MB, so you may have to spread a session out over a number of disks. DVD-Rs hold much more data and are good for archival purposes, but not for incremental backup. Therefore, this method fosters an understandable tendency to wait until the project is completely finished before backing it up, and that's not good. When problems occur, it's usually in the *middle* of a project. Therefore, important sessions need to be backed up every few hours. This is not as hard as it sounds.

Ideally, you should back up a project every time you get to a good stopping place. The most convenient method I've found to back up projects is to purchase a FireWire drive and back up to it regularly over the course of a project with an archiving program called Synchronize Pro X (Macintosh only). This program is extremely easy to use, and can be configured to back up automatically in the middle of the night. Synchronize is available at www.qdea.com and, at press time, costs about $100. Similar programs are available for Windows systems such as FolderMatch by Salty Brine Software at www.foldermatch.com. Every time I take a break, I quit Pro Tools and fire up Synchronize to back up the last few hours of work. It only takes a few seconds, and it does a lot for my peace of mind.

At the end of a project, I need to clear my main audio drives for the next project. Before I clear the drives, I back up again to a second FireWire drive or DVD-R, so that there are at least two copies for archival.

I don't do this because I'm anal retentive. I do it because I've had days of work go down the drain in the past. Hard drives are getting cheaper, flimsier, and less reliable every day. It will happen to you—count on it.

Part II

The Doormats Session

Chapter 6

Fixing the Drums

In this chapter, you'll be working on a multitrack session that needs a lot of "Pro Tooling." You'll be learning some of the editing techniques commonly employed for fixing drum tracks. Along the way, you'll be learning a lot of new commands and shortcuts. By now, you should have committed most of the items on the previous Cheat Sheet (for Chapters 1–5) to memory. Table 6-1 shows the new Mac Cheat Sheet for this chapter. As before, the Mac and Windows

Toggle Mix/Edit window	⌘+=
Zoom Toggle	E
Select the Smart Tool	F6+F7
Nudge Back by next Nudge Value	M
Nudge Back by Nudge Value	<
Nudge Forward by Nudge Value	>
Nudge Forward by next Nudge Value	/
Create Group	⌘+G
Suspend Groups	⌘+SHIFT+G
Lock/Unlock Region	⌘+L
Zoom Vertically	⌘+OPTION+[or]
Locate Selected Region Start	LEFT ARROW
Locate Selected Region End	RIGHT ARROW
Toggle Waveform & Volume view	DASH
Half speed playback	SHIFT+SPACEBAR
Fades window	⌘+F
Fade (without Fades dialog)	F
Go to next edit point	TAB
Extend selection to end of session	OPTION+SHIFT+RETURN
Undo	Z
Cut	X
Copy	C
Paste	V
Select Unused Audio	⌘+SHIFT+U
Clear Audio window	⌘+SHIFT+B
Delete Breakpoints	OPTION+click (Grabber)

TABLE 6-1   Macintosh Cheat Sheet for Chapter 6

cutout versions can be found in Appendix B, and on the Cheat Sheets PDF file on the Session Disc CD-ROM. To save space on the Cheat Sheets, CONTROL is abbreviated as CTRL.

Copy the Session Disc to Your Hard Drive

Macintosh   Remove the Session Disc CD-ROM from the back of the book and insert it into your computer's CD-ROM drive. When the Session Disc icon appears on the desktop, OPTION-drag the icon to your audio drive or main startup drive to copy the files and create a Session Disc folder at that location. This folder will contain the files you'll need for the remainder of the book.

Windows   Remove the Session Disc CD-ROM from the back of the book and insert it into your computer's CD-ROM drive. Then go to Start > My Computer and locate the Session Disc on your CD-ROM drive (usually the D drive). Right-click the Session Disc icon and choose Copy from the pop-up menu that appears. Right-click your audio drive or Desktop and select Paste to copy the files and create a Session Disc folder at that location.

Open the Love Bites Session

With Pro Tools running, open the Doormats folder and double-click the Love Bites session to open it.

Because this session was not created on your computer, various dialogs will appear with warning messages about the Playback Engine, the Disk Allocation, the I/O Setup, and so forth. Ignore them and keep pressing RETURN (ENTER) until the session opens.

Setting Preferences

Before you start working on any session that has been imported from another source, you should check these Preferences and reset them if necessary:

■ **Auto Backup**   Whenever you open a session that you didn't create on your system, some Preferences will be imported along with the session. Auto Backup may not be enabled in the Preferences menu. Go to Setup > Preferences > Operation and make sure that Enable Session File Auto Backup is enabled. Leave the default backup time set to five minutes.

- **Marker Colors**   Go to Display and make sure Always Display Marker Colors is checked.

- **Commands Focus**   Close the Preferences window, and in the Edit window, make sure Commands Focus mode is enabled (the a...z button's blue border is illuminated).

Preparing the Basic Tracks

Here's the scenario for the session: Last night you did a late-night session with The Doormats, a local bar band. They were in a hurry to make last call, so they deserted you shortly after recording a take of their new song "Love Bites." Today, you've opened the session and discovered that the tracks don't sound quite as good as they did the night before. It's basically a solid take, but there are a few unacceptable flaws. The band is now in a van headed for Lawrence, Kansas. They'll be back in a couple of weeks to do some overdubs. Now it's up to you to make them sound like they knew what they were doing.

The band played the take while listening to a *click track* (a drum machine used as a metronome), which they managed to stick to for the most part. There are a few bad bass notes, some muffled guitar chords, and a few places where the drummer rushed or dragged. Because the drums are the foundation of the song, we'll fix them first. Before we dig into the drums, however, we need to make our session a little easier to navigate.

Throughout the exercise, you'll be asked to find locations within the song. These locations will be given in minutes and seconds. Locate the Cursor display, as shown here:

Event Edit Area

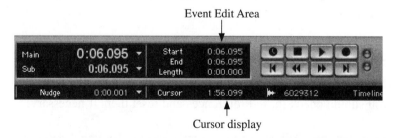

Cursor display

The *Cursor display* gives you the exact location of the cursor at any given moment. You can see it changing when you move the cursor. Also, when you make a selection, the length of the selection, as well as its start and end points, is shown in the Event Edit Area (how's that for a tongue twister?), as shown in the previous illustration. These Start, End, and Length values are also displayed in the Transport window.

In the Transport window, set the pre-roll to two seconds and the post-roll to one minute, as shown here:

The reason for setting the post-roll to such a long value is this—you usually don't need Pro Tools to stop the transport for you. When you're ready to stop listening, just press the SPACEBAR. It can be annoying when the transport stops before you want it to.

Using Markers

A handy feature of Pro Tools is the capability to create markers and display them across the top of the Edit window in the Markers ruler.

1. The Markers ruler should already be showing as a dark-gray strip above the top audio track. If not, choose View > Rulers > Markers.

2. Press RETURN (ENTER) to rewind to the beginning of the song.

3. Press the numeric ENTER key (on the right side of the keyboard) and type **START** into the Name field of the New Memory Location window (I like to use uppercase letters because they're easier to see). Mac laptop users will find the numeric ENTER key in the bottom row next to the right COMMAND key. Windows laptop users may press and hold the FN key and press ENTER.

4. Press RETURN (ENTER) to close the window.

Note that the Markers ruler has changed color, and a yellow marker labeled START has appeared. These markers can be entered anywhere in the session by clicking a spot with the Selector and pressing the numeric ENTER key. If you're familiar enough with a song, you can drop in markers "on-the-fly" during playback. Pro Tools will place a new marker in the session whenever you press the numeric ENTER key. If you press the key late or early, you can always move markers later by dragging them left or right. Dragging the markers downward will delete them.

For this exercise, you'll be given specific locations and names for marker placement. Make sure the Edit window fills your entire display. Zoom in until the Timeline displays about 35–40 seconds of audio across the length of the Edit window. Use the horizontal scroll bar to scroll through the song. Use the Selector and watch the Cursor display to place the markers.

5. We need to place a marker four bars after the guitar starts playing. With the Selector, click (in the Timeline or on any audio region) at about 12.2 (seconds).

6. Press the numeric ENTER key and name the marker **DRUMS IN**. Press RETURN (ENTER) to close the New Memory Location window.

7. Place another marker at the point where the bass comes in (about :20) and name it **V1** (for verse 1).

8. Place a marker titled **CH 1** at the first chorus (about :37).

9. Right after the stop, place a marker titled **V2** (about :54).

10. Place a marker titled **CH 2** at the start of the second chorus (about 1:10).

11. Right after the next stop, place a marker labeled **SOLO** (about 1:29).

12. Place a marker titled **V3** eight bars later (after the drum fill at about 1:46).

13. Eight bars later, place a marker titled **CH 3** (about 2:03).

14. Eight bars later, place a marker titled **OUTRO** (about 2:21). Save your session.

15. Press RETURN (ENTER) to return to the song start.

Using Memory Locations

Press ⌘+5 (CTRL+5) on the numeric keypad or choose Window > Memory Locations to open the Memory Locations window.

NOTE

On Windows machines the NUM LOCK key on the numeric keyboard must be engaged for this command to work. Mac laptops don't have separate numeric keypads. Instead, certain letter keys on the right side of the keyboard are designated for numeric entry by a small number in the lower-right corner of the key. These keys can be used for numeric entry when either the FN key in the lower-left corner is pressed or NUM LOCK is on. Unfortunately, there are other commands that won't work when NUM LOCK is on, so I recommend pressing the FN key. Better yet, get a full-sized USB keyboard and plug it into your laptop.

Note that all your markers are listed in the Memory Locations window. Click the button shown in the following illustration and make sure View Filter > Show

Icons is unchecked. This turns off a lot of bells and whistles for the sake of simplicity and makes the window smaller.

Click here to
turn off icons

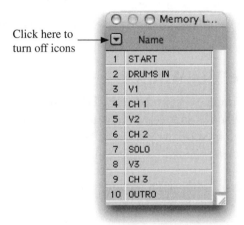

Click the resizing button in the lower-right corner of the Memory Locations window if necessary and adjust the window to make it as small as possible without obscuring the names of your memory locations. Drag it to the lower-right corner of the screen (but don't cover the Edit window's scroll bars).

The Memory Locations window is useful for getting quickly from one part of a song to another. You can instantly go to any of the marker locations by simply clicking them. Also, I find it helpful to have the yellow markers across the top as a color-coded map of the song structure. If I hear something that I want to be able to find later, I'll just tap the numeric ENTER key as it goes by and type in **Bass Muff** or whatever.

NOTE

The Memory Locations window is capable of performing a mind-boggling array of functions, many of which I haven't found a use for yet. If you feel like having your mind boggled, feel free to plow through "Memory Locations and Markers" in the Reference Guide. *Better drink some coffee first.*

Setting Up for Drum Editing

Drum editing is an area where Pro Tools really shines. Contrary to what people might tell you, you can't turn a bad drum performance into a great one with Pro Tools, but you can certainly make it more tolerable. When it comes to editing tracks of any kind, Pro Tools is a control freak's dream. You can spend weeks moving hi-hat beats around if you want. If you go too far, you can completely suck all the life out of a perfectly good drum performance. It's an easy trap to fall into because Pro Tools is essentially an audio microscope. You can zoom in and see timing discrepancies that no one will ever hear. Ultimately, you have to make up your own mind about what needs to be fixed and what doesn't, but it's good to know that the capability is there if you need it.

Introducing the Mix Window

So far, we've been working exclusively in the Edit window. Press ⌘+= (CTRL+=) to toggle to the Mix window, and resize the window to fill your screen. This is a command you need to memorize right away. You'll want to be able to quickly toggle to the Mix window to make volume adjustments.

> **NOTE** *Mac laptop users will need to disable the NUM LOCK key for this command to work.*

The Mix window has the same controls found in the Edit window, but they are graphically arranged to resemble an analog recording console. The large fader size makes volume adjustments easier.

Let's make a few changes to the mix:

1. Play the song and use the faders to turn the guitar and bass way down, but make sure you can still hear them in the background. This will help you keep track of where you are in the song.

2. Make sure the Kick and Snare tracks are louder than the other drum tracks.

3. Unmute the Click track and turn it up, so you can hear it clearly.

4. Press ⌘+= (CTRL+=) to toggle back to the Edit window.

Preparing the Edit Window

In this session, our goal is to make the drum tracks sound as if the drummer hadn't just polished off Budweiser number five. To accomplish this feat, we must first set up the Edit window, so that we can see what we're doing.

1. Set the Track Height to Small for all tracks.

2. Open the Tracks list (click the double-arrow button, in the lower-left corner of the Edit window) and hide the Guitar and Bass tracks. When editing groups of tracks, a good idea is to hide any tracks you won't be editing and

don't need to see. It keeps you from accidentally mangling them, and it will reduce the amount of time the computer spends drawing waveforms. This can make a big difference in scrolling speed when editing drums.

3. Close the Tracks list. Keep it closed whenever you're not using it. The Edit window should be kept as wide and uncluttered as possible.

4. Tracks can be rearranged in the Edit window by clicking the track name and dragging the track up or down to a new location. Rearrange the tracks from top to bottom, as follows: KICK, CLICK, SNARE, HI HAT, TOM, and OVERHEAD, as shown here:

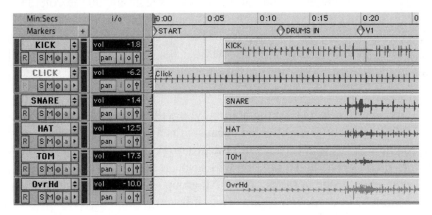

5. Save the session, and then save it again as **Love 2drums**.

Grouping Tracks

Because the drum tracks were all recorded live together, it's imperative that they be edited together as a *group* to preserve their relationship to one another. Pro Tools enables you to accomplish this by creating edit groups. In the following steps, you'll learn how to group the drum tracks, so any edits you make will be made across *all* the drum tracks simultaneously.

1. OPTION+click (ALT+click) one of the track names so that all tracks are selected. Be sure to click a track name on the left, *not* an audio region. Then ⌘+click (CTRL+click) the Click track to deselect it. The Click track is not considered a drum track; it's our timing reference and should not be edited. At this point all the track names in the Edit window should be illuminated except for the Click track.

2. Press ⌘+G (CTRL+G) or choose Track > Group to bring up the Create Group dialog. The tracks you selected in the previous step will be added to the group. Name the group **DRUMS** and press RETURN (ENTER).

3. Click one of the drum audio regions with the Grabber. Notice that *all* the drum regions in the group are selected.

4. Make a selection within any of the drum tracks with the Selector. Notice that the other drum tracks follow suit.

If you change the volume of one of the tracks in the group, all the volumes in the group will change accordingly. Any changes you make on a track will affect the other tracks in the group (with a few exceptions, such as panning). If you press the CONTROL (START) key while making a change, the group will temporarily be suspended, and only the track you're adjusting will change.

5. Open the Tracks list. At the bottom, you will see a list of groups. The DRUMS group is highlighted because it is active. Clicking the group name will suspend (deactivate) the group. (Leave it active.) Pressing ⌘+SHIFT+G (CTRL+SHIFT+G) will suspend *all* the groups. At present, the only other group in the list is the All group. This is a permanent group and cannot be deleted. You would select it if you wanted to group all the tracks in the Edit window.

6. Close the Tracks list.

Locking a Region

Because the Click track is our timing reference, we want to make sure it doesn't get moved accidentally, so we are going to lock it with the Lock/Unlock Region command.

1. Use the Grabber to select the Click track's audio region.

2. Press ⌘+L (CTRL+L) or choose Region > Lock/Unlock. Note that a small padlock icon appears in the lower-left corner of the region. Invoking this command will prevent you from accidentally performing any edits on the Click track.

NOTE   *Windows users should be aware that NUM LOCK must be turned off for this command to work.*

Setting Zoom Presets

In Chapter 3, we set the Zoom preset buttons for overdubbing. For editing drums, we need to set them a little differently.

1. Use the Grabber to select one of the drum regions and press OPTION+F (ALT+F) to fill the screen with your selection. ⌘+click (CTRL+click) on Zoom preset button 1 to make this your Zoom preset 1.

2. Zoom in four clicks of the T key (or the Horizontal Zoom button) and enter that setting for Zoom preset 2.

3. Zoom in one more click and enter that setting for Zoom preset 3.

4. Zoom in two more clicks for Zoom preset 4, and then two *more* clicks for Zoom preset 5. Return to Zoom preset 1. Save your session.

> **TIP**
>
> *Editing drums requires a lot of zooming. Try to get used to zooming by pressing numbers 1 through 5 with your left hand.*

5. With the Selector, click somewhere in the middle of the song and go to Zoom preset 4.

6. On the Kick drum track, place the Selector at the front edge of the nearest kick drum waveform and go to Zoom preset 5.

7. To get a better look at the kick drum, set its Track Height to Large.

8. Press ⌘+OPTION+] (ALT+CTRL+]) to make the waveform taller. This is the Vertical Zoom command.

> **TIP**
>
> *Vertical Zoom can also be changed by clicking the Vertical Zoom button in the upper-left corner of the Edit window, but we want to stay away from using the mouse for zooming purposes—it's much too time consuming. On a full-sized Mac keyboard, you can hold down the OPTION and COMMAND keys with the thumb of your left hand and tap the bracket keys with the two middle fingers of the same hand. Practice this without looking at the keyboard.*

9. Set the Track Height on the Click track to Medium.

Trimming the Drum Entrance

We need to get rid of any extraneous drum noises at the front of the song. In this instance, the drummer got excited and came in early. He was supposed to wait until the guitar played for four bars before coming in with the kick drum. That's why there is a marker at 12.2 seconds labeled DRUMS IN.

1. Go to Zoom preset 2 and click DRUMS IN in the Memory Locations window.

2. The kick drum beat closest to the DRUMS IN marker is the first drum sound we want to hear, so place the Trimmer to the left of this beat and click. Now all the drum tracks have been trimmed up to the point where the drummer was supposed to come in.

3. Go to Zoom preset 5 to get a closer look. Use the Trimmer to trim the drums up to about an inch from the front edge of the kick, as shown in Figure 6-1. This will leave enough room for a fade-in. If you get too close to the kick waveform, you could cut off the attack of the drum, and it will sound mushy. Save your session.

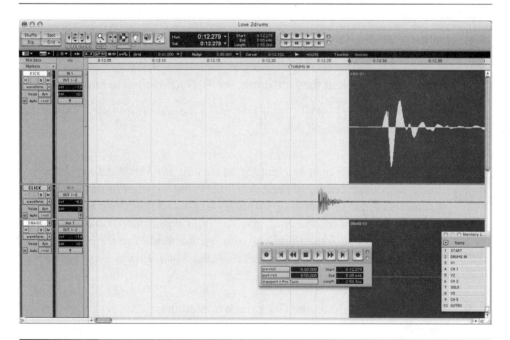

FIGURE 6-1   Trimming the drums

Introducing the Smart Tool

We need to fade in the drum tracks to keep the entrance from sounding too abrupt. The easiest way to do this is by using the Smart tool. The Smart tool switches automatically among the Trimmer, Selector, and Grabber, plus an additional Fade tool, depending on where the cursor is positioned within a region.

1. Select the Smart tool in one of three ways: by clicking the Smart Tool button as shown in Figure 6-2, by pressing F6+F7, or by pressing ⌘+7 (CTRL+7). Note that the Trimmer, Selector, and Grabber buttons all light up. Move the cursor in a circle around the kick drum waveform and take note of how the cursor changes. Use the Smart tool for the remainder of this chapter unless otherwise instructed. To deselect the Smart tool, simply click another tool.

2. Move the cursor to the upper-left corner of the kick region, so the cursor turns into the Fade tool (a square box with a diagonal line through it).

3. Click and drag the Fade tool to the right, but stop short of the front of the kick waveform. A fade-in will appear across the drum tracks, as shown in Figure 6-3.

4. Click an empty space to deselect the drums.

Aligning the Drums to the Click

Comparing drums to a Click track by ear to check for tempo discrepancies takes a little getting used to. To the inexperienced listener, it's hard to tell whether the drums are ahead of or behind the click. When the drums are spot on, they tend to mask the click. For those of you who aren't familiar with the terminology, playing faster than the click tempo is referred to as *rushing*. Playing slower than the click is known as *dragging*. In Pro Tools, it's easy to see when things are out of sync.

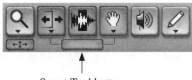

Smart Tool button

FIGURE 6-2   The Smart Tool button

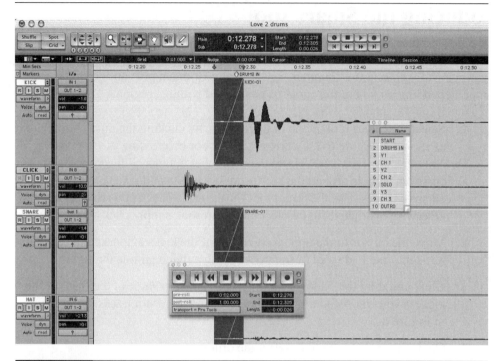

FIGURE 6-3   Fading in the drum tracks

In this part of the tutorial, you will learn to visually align drums and other instruments to a recorded Click track.

Solo the drums and the Click track, and listen to the first few bars. You can probably tell by listening that the drums aren't exactly tight with the click at the front of the song. It took the drummer a bar or so to get into the groove. The first five kick drum beats are dragged. By the sixth beat, the drummer had caught up with the click. This is a common problem. Here's how we're going to fix it:

■ We'll separate the first five kick drum beats from the rest of the song.

■ We'll separate and move the individual kick drum beats to line them up with the Click track.

■ We'll use the Trimmer to "clean up" the edit points.

When I speak of moving individual kick drum beats, it's important to understand that I'm not talking about *only* moving the kick drum region. You have to move *all* the drum regions together, because every microphone on the drum kit is picking up the kick drum. Therefore, the drum tracks must be grouped together, so that they can be edited as if they were one track. When I edit drums to a Click track, I usually zero in on the kick and snare waveforms. If some of your drum tracks are below the bottom of the Edit window where you can't see them, don't worry. It's not imperative to be able to see all the drum tracks in the Edit window. As long as they are not hidden in the Tracks list, they will be edited along with the rest of the group.

Separating the Intro Drums

Our first task is to identify the section we want to work on and separate it from the rest of the song. Before you start, save the session as **Love 3pre edit**, in case you make a mistake and need to return to this point in the exercise. Then immediately save the session again as **Love 4edit**.

1. The Kick and Click tracks should still be in Solo. The drum tracks should still be at the Large Track Height setting.

2. Go to Zoom preset 3. With the Smart tool still selected, notice that the cursor turns into the Selector (I-beam) when positioned over the upper half of the waveform.

3. Find the sixth kick drum beat and click a little to the left of it with the Selector.

4. Press the B key. This is the Separate Region command. Note that a separation has been placed at the spot you selected, creating a new set of regions containing the first five kick drum beats. You're now free to move these new regions around without affecting the drums in the rest of the song.

CAUTION *Before we start moving the drum intro around, it behooves us to lock the rest of the song down, so that we don't move it by accident. This is the number one source of frustration when editing drums, and it can easily happen before you realize it.*

5. Position the Smart tool cursor over the lower portion of the kick region to the right of the separation so that the Grabber appears and click to select the region. Lock the region using the Lock/Unlock Region command (⌘+L / CTRL+L).

6. On the *left* side of the separation, position the Smart tool cursor over the lower portion of the recently separated kick region, so the Grabber appears. Click the region to select it.

7. Go to Zoom preset 5.

Nudging and Trimming the Regions

Earlier you learned to use the Grabber to slide regions to the left or right, but you can also use the Nudge function to move a region in small, predetermined increments. *Nudging* is accomplished by selecting a region with the Grabber and pressing one of the nudge keys. Because we have Commands Focus activated, we have the four nudge keys: M, <, >, and /, as shown on your Cheat Sheet.

NOTE *The plus (+) and minus (−) keys on the numeric keypad (on the far right side of the keyboard) can also be used for nudging. The minus key nudges regions to the left, or back; the plus key nudges regions to the right, or forward.*

The nudge value is shown in the Nudge display, which is underneath the Main counter. Click the Nudge value pop-up menu to the right of the Nudge field and select 10 msec (milliseconds). Now, every time you press the < or > key (or a minus or plus key), the selected region will move forward or back ten milliseconds, which is one hundredth of a second. This is a good increment for editing drums. When you press the M or / key, the selected region will be nudged at the next higher nudge value, which, in this case, is 100 milliseconds, or one tenth of a second.

NOTE *You can also enter any nudge value you want by typing the desired number of milliseconds directly into the Nudge field. If you type in your own nudge value instead of using one of the presets, the M and / keys will not nudge to a higher value.*

In the following exercise we will separate the individual kick drum beats and use the nudge keys to align them with the Click track. Then we'll trim the regions to remove gaps in the audio.

1. The region containing the first five kick drum beats should still be selected. Use the < key to nudge the region to the left until the front of the kick waveform lines up visually with the front of the click waveform, as shown in Figure 6-4. Don't worry about lining it up perfectly; just get it as close as you can with the current nudge value.

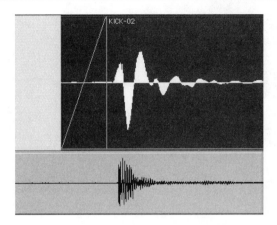

KICK-02

FIGURE 6-4   Aligning the Kick track with the Click track

2. Scroll to the right until you arrive at the next kick drum waveform. Notice that it's ahead of the click.

3. Position the Smart tool cursor over the front of the kick waveform and move it around until the Selector (the I-beam cursor) appears. Click with the Selector at the front of the kick waveform.

4. Place a separation at that point by pressing the B key.

5. Position the cursor to the right of the separation in the lower half of the kick region so that the Grabber appears, and click to select the region.

6. Nudge the region to the right to line it up with the click.

7. Position the cursor over the end of the waveform on the left to cause the Trimmer to appear.

8. Click and trim the region back to the right, stopping at the front of the kick. Release the mouse button.

Notice that you can see part of a kick waveform in the region on the left, as shown in Figure 6-5. What you are seeing is the same kick drum beat displayed twice. If you play across an edit like the one in this figure, you'll hear a double attack on the kick drum.

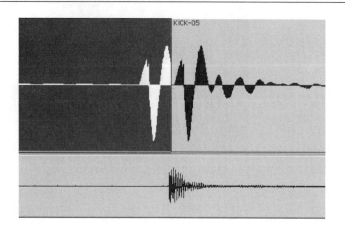

FIGURE 6-5   Partial kick region

9. Position the Trimmer over the unselected region on the right. Click and trim it back to the left until you have covered up the unwanted kick drum attack and gone a little way past it to leave room for a crossfade. The edit should now look like Figure 6-6.

10. Scroll to the right until you can see the next kick.

11. Repeat Steps 3 through 10, and then go to Step 12.

12. At this point, we are at the fourth kick (about 0.13.80 in the timeline). As you can see, it's already pretty well lined up with the click, so we'll leave it alone. Scroll on to the fifth kick.

13. Perform Steps 3 through 9 on this kick.

14. Scroll to the right until you come to the next region boundary. At this point, we're at the separation between the fifth kick and the rest of the song. Because you've locked the rest of the song, you can see the padlock on the kick region to the right.

15. Position the Smart tool cursor over the lower half of the locked kick region so that the Grabber appears. Select the region and unlock it with the Lock/Unlock Region command (⌘+L / CTRL+L).

16. Position the Smart tool Trimmer over the kick region on the left and trim back to the right, stopping at the front of the next kick.

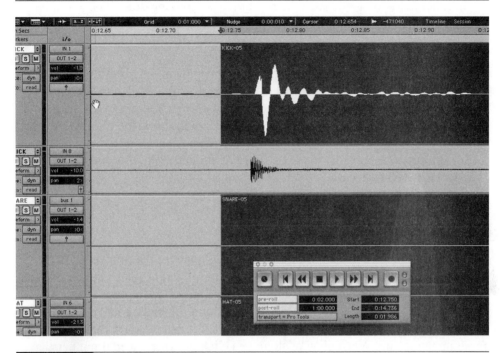

FIGURE 6-6   Finished edit

17. Position the Trimmer over the region on the right. Click and trim it back to the left until you have covered up the unwanted kick drum attack and gone a little way past it to leave room for a crossfade.

18. Go to Zoom preset 3. Save your session.

Our edit of the intro is now complete. Click DRUMS IN in the Memory Locations window and play back your handiwork. Listen to it again with the Click track muted. The edited area should sound fairly natural, with no pops or glitches. We'll crossfade the edits later for a more seamless sound.

At this point, you should be able to see a pattern emerging here. Going through a song like this and fixing trouble spots can be broken down into three main steps:

1. **Separate** the region to be fixed.

2. **Nudge** the region into place.

3. **Trim** the edit points.

In general, as you go through the rest of the song fixing drum hits, you'll be working chronologically from left to right.

In some cases, it is inadvisable to move drum parts without also moving the other instruments in the session. We can get away with it this time because the other band members' instruments were acoustically isolated from the drums. Because the click was the timing reference and all the band members were listening to it during tracking, there will be places where the drummer was a little off but the other band members stayed with the click. This was the case in the intro we just edited.

Fixing a Rushed Fill

The next drum fix is a rushed drum fill at the beginning of the first verse. Let's take a look at it. Click V1 in the Memory Locations window. Place the Selector a few seconds before the drum fill leading up to V1 and click to place an insertion point. Unmute the Click track and listen to the drum fill leading into the first verse. The drummer got ahead of the Click track during the fill, which is a common thing for drummers to do. When playing along to a click, inexperienced drummers have a tendency to rush the fills, and then slow down to wait for the Click track to catch up. This results in an unnatural-sounding tempo shift.

1. Go to Zoom preset 4 and scroll to start of the first verse (at 20.5 seconds, right at the end of the drum fill). Visually compare the kick and snare drum waveforms with the click. You can see that the kick drum at this location and the snare right after it are both ahead of the click. Sometimes it's easier to hear tempo discrepancies when listening at half speed. To play back at half speed, hold the SHIFT key and press the SPACEBAR. Make sure the Click track is loud enough.

NOTE   *Pro Tools records at half speed if you hold the SHIFT key when you click Record. Try it some time; it's a hoot.*

2. Using the Smart tool (you may need to turn it back on if it has become deselected), place the Selector at the front of the rushed kick near the

V1 marker (about 20.5 seconds). Click and drag to the right all the way
to the front of the following snare beat, as shown here. Release the
mouse button.

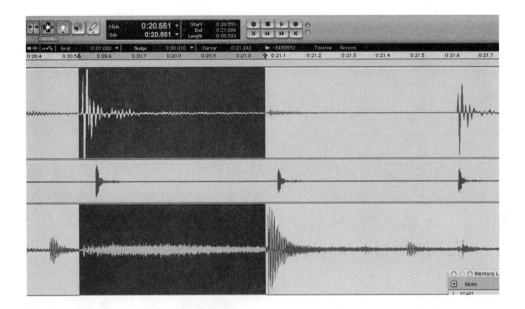

When you're editing in the middle of a song and you're zoomed in close, it's
easy to lose track of which regions are new and which are old. Therefore,
we'll be giving the new regions specific names to make them more easily
identifiable.

3. Separate the new region (B key).

4. Double-click the new kick region with the Grabber and name it **R KICK 1**
(*R* stands for rushed).

5. Position the Selector in front of the next kick drum beat (at 21.6 sec.) and
place a separation there. You should now have two new, separated regions,
one for the kick (R KICK 1) and one for the snare.

6. Double-click the second region (on the Kick track) and name it **R SNARE 1,** and then deselect it. The results should appear as shown here:

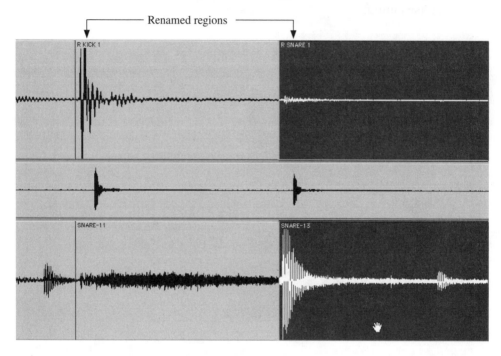

7. Save the session.

Although it may seem odd to type in the word "snare" on a kick drum region, it's best in the long run to always use the topmost track in the drum group for labeling purposes. You will quickly learn to tell which type of drum you're looking at solely by the appearance of its waveform.

Remember that the old regions before and after R KICK 1 and R SNARE 1 must not be moved! If you accidentally grab these regions and move them, they'll have to be spotted back to their original location.

8. Select R KICK 1 with the Grabber. Go to Zoom preset 5 and nudge R KICK 1 to the right until the kick drum lines up with the click.

9. Place the Trimmer on the old region to the left of R KICK 1 and trim to the right, stopping at the front of the newly separated kick drum. As before, part of the old rushed kick will be exposed.

Editing at the Zero Crossing Point

These peaks and valleys represent the *amplitude,* or volume level, of the waveform. The horizontal line running through the center of the waveform represents zero amplitude; therefore the waveform is quietest where it crosses the centerline. That's why the *zero crossing point* is the most sonically transparent place to make an edit. Shown here is a worst-case scenario, in which the edit takes place at the waveform's highest amplitude, which will result in a loud pop at the transition point:

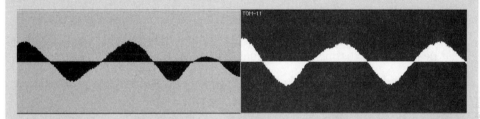

The edit shown next is also undesirable, because the edit is made at the peak of two waveforms of different amplitude:

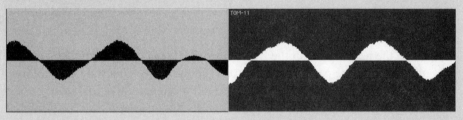

The idea is to observe the pattern in the waveform on the left, and then try to nudge the regions and adjust the edit points in an effort to continue the pattern in the waveform on the right, as shown here:

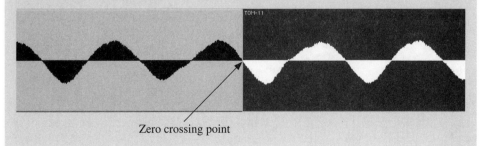

Zero crossing point

10. Position the Trimmer over the beginning of R KICK 1 and trim back to the left, covering up the rushed kick drum and leaving some space for a crossfade.

11. Mute the Click track and listen back to the edit. You should be able to discern a pop at the transition point. When an edit like this one doesn't sound right, the Tom track is a likely culprit. If you can't see the Tom track, scroll down to bring it into view (using the scroll bar on the right side of the screen).

12. Zoom in on the transition point horizontally and vertically until the rise and fall of the tom waveform is in plain view, as shown in the sidebar "Editing at the Zero Crossing Point."

13. With the Trimmer, trim the new region on the right in either direction to the nearest zero crossing point for that region, as shown here:

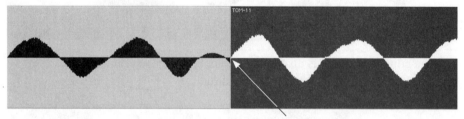

Trim to zero crossing point

14. Grab the new region on the right and slide it (don't use the nudge keys) to the left until the patterns match up, as shown here. This should go a long way toward making the Tom track sound more natural across the edit. We have shifted the R KICK 1 region in time, but only by a tiny fraction of a second. Don't worry if it still doesn't sound quite right. We'll come back to it later and try something else.

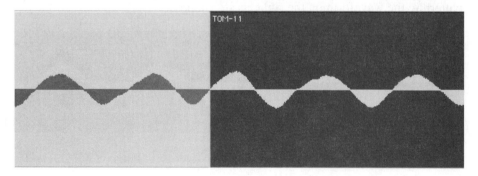

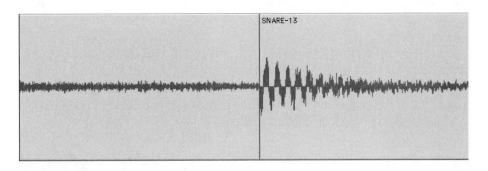

FIGURE 6-7   Covered snare hit

15. Go back to Zoom preset 5.

16. Scroll back up to the top of the Edit window to view the Kick and Snare tracks again.

17. Scroll to the right to locate the next edit, which will be at the front of R SNARE 1. When you look at the Snare track, you will notice that when you nudged R KICK 1 to the right, you partially covered up the snare hit in R SNARE 1, as shown in Figure 6-7.

18. On the Snare track, click with the Trimmer and trim it back to the left until the entire snare hit is in view.

19. Nudge R SNARE 1 to the right to line it up with the Click track.

20. Trim the end of R KICK 1 to the right, stopping at the front of the snare hit.

21. Trim the front of R SNARE 1 back to the left to leave enough space for a crossfade, as shown in Figure 6-8.

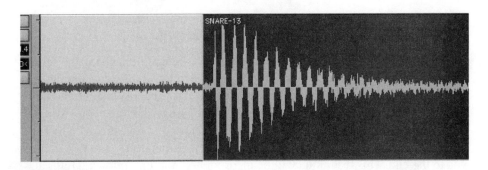

FIGURE 6-8   Finished edit

22. Scroll right to view the next edit point, which is the next kick drum hit.

You are now at the boundary between the tail end of R SNARE 1 and the kick drum hit at the front of the rest of the song. We do not want to slide or nudge either of these regions; we just want to use the Trimmer to adjust the edit point. You'll notice that most of the kick drum has gotten covered up in the process of moving the R SNARE 1 to the right.

23. Position the Trimmer over the kick waveform on the right. Click and trim back to the left to uncover the kick drum, leaving a space in front of it for a crossfade.

24. Go to Zoom preset 3 and play back the edits at the beginning of the first verse. The drums should now sound smoother through the transition into the first verse. Save your session.

Fixing a Dragged Snare Hit

Scroll forward to the snare hit at 27.4 seconds. The drummer hesitated slightly, resulting in a dragged snare hit. A soft snare hit right after it is also dragged. In this section, we are going to fix these dragged snare hits. While doing so, we are also going to use another technique to make a selection, SHIFT+clicking.

1. On the Snare track, use the Selector to click at the front of the snare hit at 27.4 seconds, and go to Zoom preset 4.

2. SHIFT+click the front of the following kick drum beat on the Kick track. Note that the area between the two selections is now selected.

3. Separate the region.

Using the Left and Right Arrow Keys

At Zoom preset 5, you usually can't see both ends of a region. Using the scroll bar to get to the next edit point at this zoom setting can be time consuming. You can use the TAB key to skip to the next edit point, but I feel the fastest and most intuitive way to zip from one end of a *selected* region to the other is by using the LEFT ARROW and RIGHT ARROW keys at the bottom of the keyboard. The LEFT ARROW key takes you to the beginning of the region; the RIGHT ARROW key takes you to the end. This technique will be incorporated into the following tutorial.

4. On the Kick track, double-click the newly separated region and name the new region **D SNARE 1**.

5. Go to Zoom preset 5 and nudge the snare drum to line it up with the click.

6. Use the RIGHT ARROW key to go to the tail end of D SNARE 1. Note that nudging D SNARE 1 to the left has created a gap in the audio.

7. Trim the end of D SNARE 1 to the right to close the gap. This exposes a piece of an early kick drum beat.

8. Position the Trimmer over the region to the right and trim back to the left to cover up the early kick drum beat, leaving the usual space for a crossfade.

9. Go to Zoom preset 3 and listen to the edit (with the Click track unmuted).

10. At 52.4 seconds, there is another dragged snare hit. Repeat Steps 3 through 9 to fix this one, naming the separated region **D SNARE 2** (there won't be an early kick beat after this one).

11. At 1:05.9, the snare and the kick after it are both rushed. Because they're both rushed by the same amount, create one separated region containing both drum hits. Name it **R KICK & SNARE**. Use the techniques you learned in Steps 3 through 9 to align this region with the click.

12. At 2:35, the drummer's headphones started slipping off, causing him to rush two kick drum beats and the following snare hit. At Zoom preset 4, click with the Selector at the front of the kick at 2:35. SHIFT+click the hi-hat beat (2.35.9) after the rushed snare.

13. Separate the region, naming it **HEADPHONES,** and line it up with the click using the techniques you've learned. Save your session.

Introducing Batch Crossfades

Batch mode automatically creates crossfades across as many tracks as you want. This is a great time saver when crossfading edited drums.

1. Return to the session start and go to Zoom preset 1. Use the Selector to select across the entire song (don't include the Click track in your selection—hide it temporarily).

2. Press ⌘+F (CTRL+F) to bring up the Batch Fades dialog. Because these will be short crossfades, we'll use the default Equal Gain setting, with

standard curve shapes. We don't want to undo the fade-in we did at the drum entrance, so we'll uncheck the boxes titled Adjust Existing Fades and Create New Fade Ins & Outs. Set the fade length to about five milliseconds and click OK.

NOTE   *If you zoom in on some of your edits, you will see that Pro Tools has created a five-millisecond crossfade at each edit.*

3. Mute the Click track and listen closely through the edits you made to make sure the fades work.

Sometimes crossfades will allow unwanted sounds to "peek through." When this happens, it's usually the attack of a kick or a snare drum hit that is audible because you didn't completely cover it up when using the Trimmer. It can usually be fixed by moving the edit point slightly or by using a shorter fade (fades can be shortened or lengthened with the Trimmer). At times, an edit will sound better without a crossfade. To delete a crossfade, simply click the fade with the Grabber to highlight it, and then delete it. Use the TAB key to tab from one edit to the next. Pressing OPTION+TAB (ALT+TAB) will enable you to tab backwards. Save your session.

Fixing the Tom Track

Let's assume that the edit you did earlier at the beginning of Verse 1 is still unsatisfactory, despite all our crossfading efforts. It's the kind of thing that perhaps only the drummer would notice, but we want to keep him happy, because he's built like a gorilla. This time, we'll attempt to improve the sound of the edit by pasting in a tom hit from somewhere else in the song.

1. Go to Zoom preset 4 and click V1 in the Memory Locations window.

2. Take any soloed tracks out of Solo.

3. Use the vertical scroll bar if necessary to bring the Tom track into view.

4. Holding the CONTROL (START) key to temporarily suspend the group, Solo the Tom track and play the drum fill. You should be able to discern a sudden change in the sound of the tom hit at the edit point.

At the beginning of the solo section (1:29), we have a good tom hit we can use to replace the mangled one.

This is one situation where we can get away with suspending (turning off) the DRUMS group and making an edit on only one drum track. In this exercise, we'll be working with the Tom track only.

5. Press ⌘+SHIFT+G (CTRL+SHIFT+G) to suspend the DRUMS group.

6. Click Solo in the Memory Locations window to go to 1:29. On the Tom track, select across the tom hit and go to Zoom preset 5.

7. Using the Selector, SHIFT+click as close as possible to the front of the tom hit. Note that the front of the selection has moved to the new spot you just clicked.

8. Zoom in three more clicks of the T key and use SHIFT+click to move the selection even closer to the front of the tom. You want to get as close to the initial attack of the waveform as possible without cutting off any of it. The front of your selection should resemble the one shown in Figure 6-9. Don't worry about the tail end of the selection right now.

9. Press the C key to copy the tom. Go back to Zoom preset 3.

10. Go back to V1 and zoom in close to the front of the tom waveform at that location, as you did in Step 8.

11. Click with the Selector right at the front of the tom and press the V key to paste the good tom over the bad one. This method places the attack of the new tom exactly in the same spot as the old one and covers the old tom edit. Because you took the time to zoom in and place this region so precisely, there is no need to place a crossfade at the front of the tom hit.

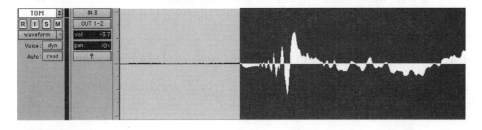

FIGURE 6-9   Tom waveform

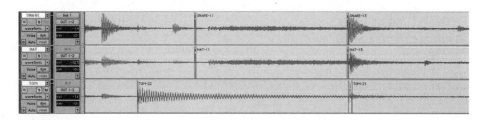

FIGURE 6-10   Tom edit

12. Go to Zoom preset 4 and press the RIGHT ARROW key to view the end of the pasted tom region. Trim the tail end of the pasted tom region to the point at which the next snare drum hit occurs.

13. Position the Smart tool cursor at the bottom of the edit so that the square Crossfade cursor appears, and then click and drag slightly to the right or left to create a crossfade at the edit point. The result should resemble Figure 6-10.

14. Once you have checked the edits and are satisfied with the results, save your session as **Love 5pre cons**.

Consolidating the Drum Tracks

Now that the drum tracks have been edited and crossfaded, we will clean up the tracks by consolidating them.

1. Press ⌘+SHIFT+G (CTRL+SHIFT+G) to reactivate the DRUMS group.

2. Click DRUMS IN in the Memory Locations window. With the Grabber, select the first drum region in the song on any drum track.

3. Press OPTION+SHIFT+RETURN (CTRL+SHIFT+ENTER). This is a useful shortcut that extends the selection to the end of the session. It's easy to remember because these three keys are all close to each other at the right side of many keyboards.

4. Press OPTION+F (ALT+F) and note that the entire song is selected.

5. Press OPTION+SHIFT+3 (ALT+SHIFT+3) or choose Edit > Consolidate.

Cleaning Up Auto-Created Regions

When Pro Tools finishes consolidating, open the Regions list. Scroll through the list and notice that all this drum editing has created a zillion Auto-Created Regions. Clearing these regions can speed up the screen redraw time and make the session run more smoothly. This time, we will use the shortcuts, instead of plowing through all those menus.

1. Click an empty space in the Edit window to make sure that no regions are selected.

2. Press ⌘+SHIFT+U (CTRL+SHIFT+U) to select the unused audio. The Auto-Created Regions in the list will become highlighted.

3. Press ⌘+SHIFT+B (CTRL+SHIFT+B) to bring up the Clear Audio dialog.

4. Click Remove in the Clear Audio dialog or press RETURN (ENTER). The Auto-Created Regions will disappear.

5. Close the Regions list.

Riding the Tom Track

Toms usually produce a rumbling noise during a performance. The tom mics can also pick up unwanted sounds, or *bleed,* from other drums and cymbals. Some people object to this sound; others like it. On this song, the tom rumble is not loud because it's a laid-back tune and there is only one tom. When recording a kit with three or more toms, the rumble becomes a lot more noticeable.

One method of reducing this bleed would be to insert a device called a *noise gate* on the Tom track to bring the volume of the tom down when it's not being played. Like many engineers, I don't like to use noise gates on drums because they have a tendency to cut off the attack of the drum, and they don't always behave predictably. If I want to reduce tom rumble, I prefer to use the automation to turn the Tom tracks down when the toms aren't being played. Performing this task with console-based moving fader automation is tedious and time consuming, but I have developed a method of "riding the toms" in Pro Tools that is not too laborious and produces much better results.

1. Press ⌘+SHIFT+G (CTRL+SHIFT+G) to disable the DRUMS group again.

2. Go to marker V1, where the first tom hit is located.

3. Scroll down (if necessary) to the Tom track, click its Track View selector, and change it from Waveform to Volume.

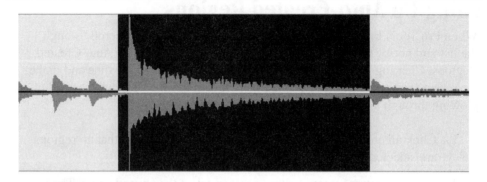

FIGURE 6-11   Selecting the tom

4. Solo the Tom track.

5. Go to Zoom preset 4. To reduce the rumble by 10 dB, set the Tom track's volume level at −10.

6. Select across the duration of the tom hit, starting the selection a little in front of the tom and ending where the tom fades out, as shown in Figure 6-11.

7. Position the Smart tool cursor in the middle of the selection (without clicking) and move it upward until the horizontal Trimmer appears.

8. When you click with the horizontal Trimmer, a display will appear with two numbers side by side. The number on the left tells you the overall volume (in this case −10 dB). The number on the right (in parentheses next to the little triangle) gives you the delta value. The *delta value* is the amount of increase or decrease in level in dB.

9. Click and drag the volume line upward until the volume level (*not* the delta value) is as close to 0 dB as you can get it. When you get close to 0 dB, press COMMAND (CTRL) for finer control. The result should appear as shown in Figure 6-12.

10. Click with the Selector on the front of the tom and go to Zoom preset 5.

A sudden volume change, such as the one at the front of this tom, can result in a popping sound. Therefore, we need to place a breakpoint in front of the tom that will cause the volume to fade in more gradually.

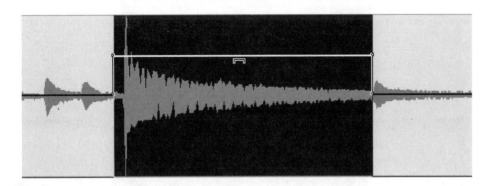

FIGURE 6-12   Trimming the volume level

11. Press F8 to select the Grabber tool. The cursor now looks like a hand with a finger extended.

12. Click the volume line about a half inch in front of the volume change you just made with the tip of the "finger." If you accidentally moved the volume line when doing so, Undo and try again. The breakpoints at the front of the tom waveform should look something like Figure 6-13.

13. With the Grabber, OPTION+click (ALT+click) on the breakpoint, shown by the arrow in Figure 6-14, to delete it. This will produce a more gradual fade in.

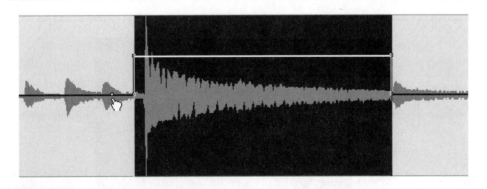

FIGURE 6-13   Setting breakpoints

OPTION+click (ALT+click) here to delete breakpoint

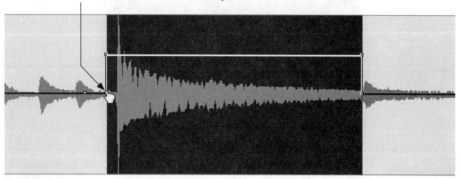

FIGURE 6-14   Deleting the breakpoint

14. We also need to fade the volume back down at the end of the tom hit. Go to Zoom preset 4, place another breakpoint in the middle of the tom waveform, and delete (OPTION+click / ALT+click) the next breakpoint to the right on the volume line. It should come out looking like Figure 6-15.

15. Drag with the Selector to select the volume automation you just created. Be sure to include all four breakpoints in your selection.

16. Go to Zoom preset 5 and nudge the automation to the right to tighten up the space between the volume rise and the tom's attack. The volume must be up to zero before the tom hit occurs, as shown in Figure 6-16.

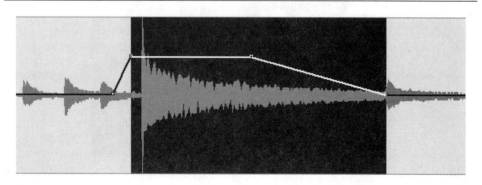

FIGURE 6-15   Fading the volume down

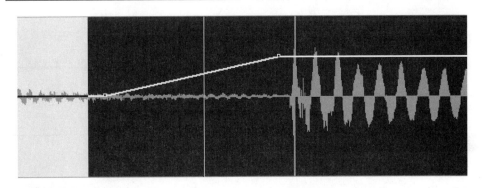

FIGURE 6-16   Tom attack

You're probably thinking, "This is way too much trouble!" Don't worry, you don't have to go through all these steps for each tom hit. Once you've done one tom hit, you'll just copy it and use it as a template to paste over the remaining tom hits. Once you're familiar with the procedure, you can do an entire song with three Tom tracks and an average number of tom hits in about ten minutes.

17. Play the tom hit and listen to your handiwork. The attack and fade of the tom should sound fairly natural.

18. Go to Zoom preset 4. The four breakpoints of automation data should still be selected. This will be our "volume template" for the rest of the tom hits.

19. Go to Zoom preset 3 and scroll to the right to find the next tom hit at the beginning of Verse 2.

20. Click with the Selector at the front of the tom hit and press the v key to paste the volume template over it.

21. Go to Zoom preset 4. Nudge the newly pasted volume template into place, so that the volume line is up to zero before the attack of the drum. This is a double tom hit, so the length of the volume template may need to be stretched out to accommodate the longer fill.

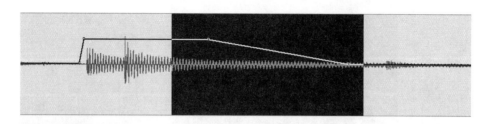

FIGURE 6-17   Stretching the template

22. To extend our volume template, make a selection that includes the third and fourth breakpoints, as shown in Figure 6-17.

23. Nudge the selected breakpoints to the right to extend the automation data until the fade-out of the tom fill sounds natural.

24. Click anywhere with the Selector to deselect the automation data.

25. Use Steps 19-21 to paste the automation data over the next three tom hits, adjusting the length of the template when necessary.

26. At 2:19, there is a long tom fill. It would take a lot of nudging to stretch the template all the way across this one with the nudge keys. A quicker way is to paste one volume template on the front of the fill and another one on the end. Then select and delete the breakpoints in the middle, so that only four breakpoints remain.

27. Finish the remaining tom hits and save your session, and then save it again as **Love 6drums**.

Using the Trim Plug-in

The rides on the Tom track are now complete. One problem remains, however. Because you have written automation to the Tom track, you can no longer change its *overall* volume by simply moving the volume fader. If you do, the automation will immediately snap the fader back to its former position. You could change the overall volume of the track by clicking with the Trimmer on the volume line (with Track view set to Volume) after the end of the song, where there are no more breakpoints, but that's somewhat inconvenient. A much easier way to make overall volume changes is to insert the Trim plug-in on the Tom track.

The Trim plug-in has a Gain control slider for adjusting the overall volume of a track without disturbing the automation data.

1. Click the Views icon under the Slip mode button and enable the Inserts view.

2. Insert Plug-in > Other > Trim (Mono) on the Tom track.

3. From now on, use the Gain slider on this plug-in to adjust the overall level of the Tom track. Save the session.

Chapter 7

Bass and Guitar Fixes

When working on basic tracks, I always try to sort out the drums first, because there's no point trying to build on a shaky foundation. If a Click track is involved, I tend to use that as a sort of yardstick to measure the tempo variations. If there's no Click track, I just use my ears to smooth out any rushed fills or sudden lurches in tempo (having gotten the best take possible during tracking, of course). Once the drums are sorted out, I tend to ignore the Click track and concentrate on making sure the other instruments are grooving with the drums.

In this chapter, the Doormats saga continues. We'll start with the Bass track first, and then move on to guitar. You'll learn some techniques for fixing common problems with bass and guitar, such as flying in parts to fix mistakes, nudging rushed or dragged notes, using plug-in automation to smooth rough spots, and using the Pencil tool to fix glitches.

Let's pick up where we left off at the end of Chapter 6, with Love 6drums.

Fixing the Bass Track

Now that the drum tracks have been cleaned up, we're going to solo the bass and drums to make sure they are solid and tight. I've found that the best way to accomplish this is to put the Bass track in between the Kick and Snare tracks. Let's get the Edit window set up for bass fixes.

1. Open the Tracks list in the Love 6drums session.

2. Mute the Click track and hide it.

3. Show the Bass track, and put it between the Kick and Snare tracks.

4. Press ⌘+SHIFT+G (CTRL+SHIFT+G) to enable the DRUMS group.

5. Set the Bass track to the Large Track Height setting.

6. Solo the Bass and drum tracks, and turn the bass up to around –8 dB.

7. Close the Tracks list, disable the Inserts view, and close any plug-in windows that are open.

8. Click V1 in the Memory Locations window.

It's time to put yourself in the producer's seat and listen for anything that doesn't sound quite right. There is a slight timing problem on the Bass track in the first verse. Play the first verse and try to find it by using your ears rather than your eyes. Listen for places where the bass and kick drum don't hit together.

9. You may have noticed that the bass player dragged a note at 26 seconds, causing it to hit after the kick drum. Zoom in on this note until you can plainly see the timing discrepancy, as shown here:

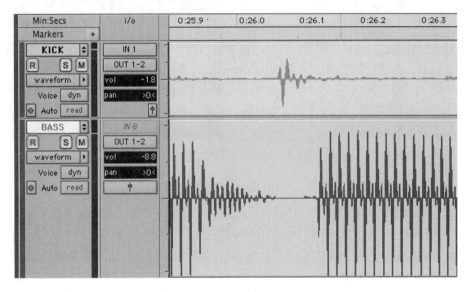

10. Select the late bass note and separate it.

11. Nudge the region to the left until the bass note lines up visually with the kick drum.

Crossfading with the Smart Tool

When crossfading edits, I usually prefer to do each crossfade individually, instead of using Batch mode, because different edits often require different types of crossfades. The easiest way to perform these crossfades is with the Smart tool.

1. Choose the Smart tool (F6+F7) and position it between the two regions at the bottom of the first edit on the Bass track, so the Crossfade cursor appears, as shown here:

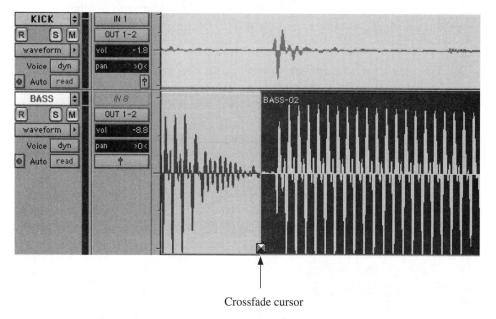

Crossfade cursor

2. Click and drag the Crossfade cursor to the left or right to determine the length of the crossfade (keep it short).

3. Attempt to use the Smart tool Trimmer to close the gap in the audio at the end of the bass note.

As you will no doubt find, no matter where you put the edit point, unwanted audio will be present. This is a case where you're better off with a gap in the audio. To make sure there are no pops as Pro Tools plays over the gap, we will use the Fade tool to avoid sudden changes in volume.

4. Use the Undo command (⌘+Z / CTRL+Z) to get back to the point where there is a gap in the audio.

5. Position the Smart tool at the top of the bass region to the left of the gap. The Fade tool (a box with a diagonal line) appears. Use this tool to fade out the end of the note on the left and fade in the note on the right, as shown here:

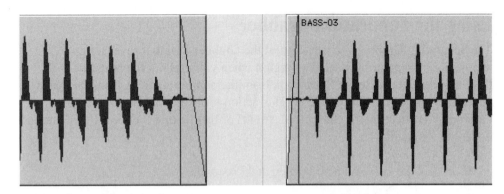

6. As always, check your edit to make sure it sounds good.

At 37.2 seconds, there is a rushed bass note. This one is a little tricky, because it is really a double note, or one note plucked twice, and the second pluck is not rushed. There's not much space between the notes. What we're going to do in this case is shorten the first note, hopefully without disturbing the second.

7. Find the double note at 37.2 seconds, zoom in, and select only the first note, as shown here:

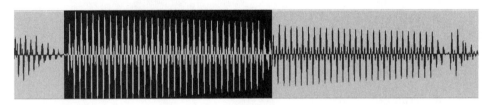

8. Separate the note and nudge it to the right until it lines up with the kick.

9. Use the Fade tool as before to smooth the gap in the audio created by moving the note.

10. Use the Trimmer to trim the end of the note so that the edit point lines up with the snare hit.

11. Place a crossfade at the edit point.

TIP

Placing an edit point at the exact moment that a loud drum hit occurs is a good way to hide an edit that might otherwise be audible.

Using the Separation Grabber

 The Separation Grabber is a variation of the Grabber tool that saves a step by automatically separating a selected region when you grab it. To choose it, click the Grabber icon and select Separation from the pop-up menu. A pair of scissors appears as part of the Grabber icon. This action turns the Smart tool off, so turn it back on by reselecting the Smart tool (F6+F7) or by clicking the Smart Tool button under the tool icons.

1. Select the late bass note located at 47 seconds.

2. Position the Smart tool cursor in the lower half of the selection so that the Separation Grabber appears. Grab the note and slide it to the left until it lines up with the kick. If necessary, fine-tune the placement of the region with the nudge keys.

3. Use the Fade tool to crossfade the edit at the front of the note and use fades to smooth the gap in the audio as before.

4. The bass note at 54 seconds is rushed and has a little noise in front of it. Using the techniques you have learned, use the Smart tool to align the note with the kick drum and silence the Bass track during the stop. The following lists the abbreviated steps:

    - Select the note
    - Grab and slide
    - Nudge
    - Trim
    - Fade

    The finished edit should look like Figure 7-1.

5. As always, listen to the edit and save the session.

NOTE   *You may not realize it, but you can save during playback.*

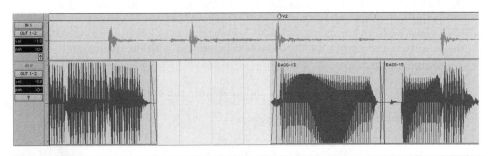

FIGURE 7-1   Finished edit

Flying In a Missing Part

Listen to the dropout at 1:03. The bass player apparently nodded off for a moment, leaving a gaping hole in the Bass track. No problem for us Pro Tools wizards. If you listen to the pattern of the bass line, it's pretty easy to figure out which notes are missing. We'll find a similar phrase elsewhere in the song and "fly it in."

1. Scroll a little to the left. At 58.9 seconds, you will find the five notes you need to fill in the gap. Select the five notes starting at that point and copy them (C key).

2. Scroll a little to the right (if necessary) to view the dropout.

Using Auto Region Fade In/Out (HD Systems Only)

In HD systems, it's not necessary to manually write a fade-in at the front and back of every region where gaps occur in the audio. Pro Tools can be configured to do this automatically. Go to Setups > Preferences > Operations. Next to Auto Region Fade In/Out Length, you can type in a value in milliseconds (10 msec is a good length). This will automatically place a fade-in and fade-out on every region in the session at the length you specify. One word of warning, however—when you consolidate a track, these invisible automatic fades are *not* incorporated into the new file with the manual fades. Therefore, you might experience some unexpected pops and clicks where the fades used to be when you play back the consolidated track.

3. Use the Selector to click at the front of the dropout and paste in the replacement phrase (v key).

4. Zoom in and nudge the region until it lines up with the drums and sounds right.

5. Close up the gaps in the audio and crossfade the edit points.

6. Check the edit, and save the session.

Using the AudioSuite Gain Plug-in

At 1:16, a note was played too quietly. For the purposes of this exercise, let's pretend this note doesn't occur anywhere else in the song. One solution is to use the automation to determine how much the note needs to be turned up, and then use the AudioSuite Gain plug-in to permanently turn the note up by that amount. Here's how:

1. Click the Bass track's Track View selector (currently set to Waveform) and select Volume.

2. Making sure the Smart tool is still selected in the toolbar, use the Selector to make a selection across the quiet note.

3. Move the cursor to the upper half of the waveform until the horizontal Trimmer appears. Click and hold the mouse button.

4. Still holding the mouse button down, move the Trimmer upward, while keeping an eye on the delta value (on the right, next to the little triangle). When the delta value gets to about +8 dB, release the mouse button (remember, you can use the COMMAND / CTRL key for finer control). When you play back the track, the automation will now turn the note up 8 dB.

Play across the quiet note. It's loud enough now. Why not just leave it this way? Because you don't want to get into automation until it's time to mix. As you learned when automating the Tom track, once you write automation data to a track, it's not as easy to change the overall level. What you want to do is incorporate the volume change permanently into the Bass track, so you don't have to think about it anymore. Now that you know the note needs to be turned up 8 dB, you can create a new audio file for the quiet note with the AudioSuite Gain plug-in.

5. Select and Delete the automation breakpoints you just created. Make sure you get rid of all the breakpoints.

6. Set the Bass track's Track view back to Waveform.

7. Select the quiet note again.

8. Under the AudioSuite menu, select the Gain plug-in. The Gain plug-in window appears.

9. In the Gain plug-in window, enter a value of **8** in the Gain field, and then press RETURN (ENTER).

10. Click the Process button. Close the plug-in window.

11. A new audio file has been created by the Gain plug-in. When you attempt to crossfade the edit points, a dialog will pop up asking permission to adjust the boundaries. As you learned earlier, that's because the computer must have some overlapping audio to accomplish the crossfade, so it wants to move the crossfade over a little bit. Click Adjust Boundaries or press RETURN (ENTER).

12. Listen to check the edit. Save the session while you listen.

Region vs. Audio File

Do you recall the difference between a region and an audio file? This is such an important point, it bears repeating. Remember, whenever you record anything in Pro Tools, you create an *audio* file—a whole, contiguous (uninterrupted) chunk of audio data that resides on your hard disk. A *region* is a user-defined area within an audio file.

When you separated the quiet bass note in the previous exercise, you created a region. When you used the Gain plug-in, a new audio file was created and placed in the same location. The original file was unaltered and can be easily restored via Undo or, days later, by simply deleting the Gained region, and then closing the resulting gap with the Heal Separation command (⌘+H / CTRL+H).

Pitch Shifting a Note

At 1:29.5, the bass player got excited and gripped the neck of the bass too tightly, pulling the note sharp. This kind of thing happens all the time. You probably won't notice it now, but it will become obvious once you've overdubbed a few guitars and keyboards. We can fix the note by adjusting its pitch.

1. Select the bass note at 1:29.5.

2. Under the AudioSuite menu, choose Pitch Shift.

3. In the plug-in window, click the Reference Pitch button. Turn the Level control up to about –10 dB. Move the Accuracy slider all the way over to Sound. Time Correction should remain checked.

4. The note in question is an F note, so click in the Note field and type F3. (The number 3 represents the octave.) Press RETURN (ENTER).

NOTE

Unlike some of the fancier pitch-shifting plug-ins, the AudioSuite Pitch Shift plug-in can't tell you how far off pitch the selected note is. Instead, it provides a reference tone you can compare with the audio you're pitch shifting.

5. Click the Preview button (lower left, in the plug-in window).

6. The plug-in loops the selected region along with the reference tone. Move the Fine control around until the pitch of the bass note matches the reference tone. If F3 doesn't work well for you, try an octave down at F2 or an octave up at F4. You should find that it sounds best when you pull the pitch down about 12 or 13 cents (a *cent* is a measure of pitch) with the Fine control. Use the Level control near the bottom of the plug-in window to adjust the volume of the reference pitch.

7. Click the Process button and close the plug-in window. The Pitch Shift plug-in has created a new region named BASS-Pish.

8. Crossfade the edit points. A dialog will pop up again asking permission to adjust the boundaries. Press RETURN (ENTER).

9. Listen to the edit and move on. Save the session.

NOTE

You may be wondering why I'm asking you to crossfade this note, since the crossfades occur during the silence between notes. While you could probably get away with not crossfading this note, I want you to get into the habit of crossfading regions automatically. There have been times when I got in a hurry and didn't bother to crossfade an edit, only to discover an audible glitch later on. Don't put off crossfading until later—it'll never happen. When you get to the end of the Bass track, all edits should be complete, or I'll give you a big fat zero.

Using the Pencil Tool

The *Pencil* tool is the only tool that permanently alters audio files. It enables you to repair a click or pop in a waveform by redrawing it. At 1:36.7, a pop can be heard on the Bass track. The bass player did not make this sound; it's a digital glitch. These things appear from time to time in Pro Tools and can often be fixed using the Pencil tool. Because redrawing the waveform will permanently alter the audio file, it's a good idea to make a backup of the file first.

1. Select the note containing the glitch and copy it.

2. Go to Zoom preset 1.

3. Scroll out past the end of the song and paste the note somewhere in the empty space at the end of the Bass track.

4. Press OPTION+SHIFT+3 (ALT+SHIFT+3) to consolidate the copy. Now you have a safety copy in case you mangle the original.

5. Go back to the glitch at 1:36.7 and zoom in until the waveform becomes a single line, as shown here:

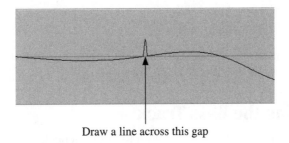

Draw a line across this gap

This is known as viewing a waveform at the *sample level.*

6. Select the Pencil tool. If you click and hold on the Pencil tool icon, a drop-down menu reveals several variations of the Pencil tool. The default Free Hand Pencil tool is the one most often used for repairing waveforms. Carefully use it to reconstruct the original shape of the waveform by drawing a short line across the gap created by the glitch. Don't draw any more than is absolutely necessary. If you make a mistake, press Undo and try again. The end result should resemble this:

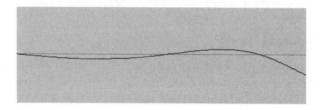

7. Go back to Zoom preset 3 and the Smart tool, and play the edit to make sure the glitch is gone. Save your session.

8. At 1:51, there are three rushed notes. Zoom in on the three notes. Grab and drag them to the right.

9. Nudge them around until they sound right. Crossfade the edit points, listen, and save.

10. At 1:56, the bass player tripped over his cord, causing a pop and another dropout. Listen to the dropout and think about which notes would normally go there. Two notes need to be replaced. A replacement can be found at 1:47.9.

11. Select the two replacement notes and copy them.

12. Scroll back to 1:56 and click with the Selector at the beginning of the note before the gap.

13. Paste in the replacement notes.

14. Nudge the notes into place, trim the edit points, and crossfade. Check the edit and save the session as **Love 7bass**.

Consolidating the Bass Track

Listen to the Bass track all the way through to double-check the edits. If you're satisfied with the bass, you should duplicate and consolidate the Bass track to preserve all your hard work.

1. Click the Bass track's Playlist selector (the pop-up menu next to the track name) and select Duplicate.

2. Name the new playlist **Bass backup** and press RETURN (ENTER). You are now viewing the new playlist.

3. Click the Bass track's Playlist selector once again and select Bass (1). Now you're back to the original Bass track. If you ever need to get back to the edited Bass track to change something, you can return to the Bass backup playlist.

4. Go to Zoom preset 1. Here's a new and convenient way to select all the audio regions on a track: triple-click with the Selector anywhere on the Bass track.

5. When all the audio is selected, press OPTION+SHIFT+3 (ALT+SHIFT+3) or choose Edit > Consolidate. Save the session.

Guitar Fixes

Luckily, the Guitar track is in pretty good shape. Just a few things need cleaning up.

1. Use the Tracks list to show the Guitar track, and set its Track Height to Large.

2. Turn up the Guitar track until you can hear it clearly, and then turn the Bass track down, so it is in the background.

3. Hide the Bass track and close the Tracks list.

4. Place the Guitar track between the Kick and Snare tracks.

5. Press RETURN (ENTER) to rewind to the beginning of the song.

6. Go to Zoom preset 3.

7. Use the Trimmer to remove the extraneous strums at the beginning of the song. The first sound you want to hear is at 3.62 seconds.

8. Solo the Guitar track and go to Zoom preset 1.

9. Locate the minor chord at 1:04.3 (hint: watch the numbers in the Cursor display as you move the Selector) and listen for a tapping sound made by the pick hitting the top of the guitar. This sound occurs here and there throughout the song (no big deal, really) but it kind of sticks out here. This same minor chord appears a few seconds earlier at 56 seconds, and the tapping is less pronounced. We'll "fly it in" to cover the errant chord.

10. Locate the good minor chord at 56 seconds and go to Zoom preset 4. Select the chord from "valley to valley," as in the following illustration, so the edit points will be in the quietest part of the waveform:

11. Copy the selected chord.

12. Scroll back to 1:04.3.

13. With the Selector, click the beginning of the chord to be replaced and paste the good chord over the bad one.

14. Take the Guitar track out of Solo and nudge the region around until it sounds in time with the drums.

NOTE *If the current nudge value isn't right for the job at hand, you can enter your own value in the Nudge field.*

Once you've lined up the guitar waveform visually with the drums, you should close your eyes and use your ears as you nudge the region into place. Try a three-second pre-roll, so you can hear how the pasted audio flows with the track. You may be surprised at the difference a ten-millisecond nudge can make in the way a pasted region feels.

15. Acoustic guitars are trickier to edit than bass and drums because the sound is more complex. Take some time to move the transition points around and experiment with different crossfade lengths. Solo the guitar again and listen to make sure the edit sounds natural. Save the session.

16. At 1:08.5, a chord is slightly muffled. A cleaner one is located at 1:35.6. Use the procedure outlined in Steps 11 through 15 to fix the muffled chord.

17. At 1:44.0, the guitar player muffles the same chord again, and the chord after it is dragged. You can use the same chord you used in the last edit. When you copy something, it is placed in the *clipboard* (held temporarily

in RAM) and remains there until you copy something else. Because the chord is still in the clipboard, you don't have to copy it again. You can paste the chord as many times as you want. Click with the Selector at 1:44.0 and paste the copied chord over the muffled one. Nudge the new chord into place.

18. Use the Trimmer to extend the end of the new chord region over to the downbeat of the third verse (at 1:46.14). Trim and crossfade the edit points as usual. This effectively fixes both chords.

19. Listen, save, and move on.

20. At 1:52.4, the guitar player muffles the same chord yet again. Evidently, his fingers were getting tired at this point. Paste the same chord onto this spot also. You should be getting the hang of it by now. See if you can remember how to do it without consulting Steps 11 through 15.

Squeak Removal

One problem you will often encounter when recording guitars is finger squeaks. At 2:28, a finger squeak can be heard on the acoustic guitar track. As finger squeaks go, it's not a particularly loud one, but because this is a common problem with acoustic guitars, you should learn how to fix it. We'll start by sweeping the AudioSuite EQ (equalization) plug-in's Frequency control to find the resonant frequency of the squeak. Then, we'll filter out the squeak with a notch.

1. Locate the squeak and go to Zoom preset 5.

2. Choose the Scrubber tool (the one that looks like a speaker). Click on the squeak and scrub back and forth to hear exactly where the squeak begins and ends.

3. Zoom in two or three more clicks for a closer look.

4. Select the squeak, leaving some space on either side for a crossfade, as shown here:

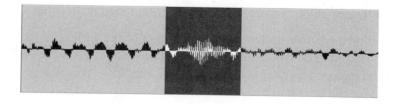

5. Select the 1-Band EQ 3 plug-in from the AudioSuite menu.

6. Turn the Gain knob all the way up.

7. Enter **10** in the Filter field (for the highest Q, or narrowest bandwidth). This will give us a nice sharp peak.

8. Click Preview to hear a loop of the squeak. (You might want to turn down your speakers a bit.)

9. Move the Frequency control (labeled FREQ) back and forth to find the spot that makes the squeak as loud and obnoxious as possible (probably about 2.5 kHz). This is a good way to find the frequency we need to cut.

10. Turn the Gain knob all the way down to create a *notch,* or very narrow EQ cut. This should get rid of most of the squeak.

11. Click the Process button and close the plug-in window.

12. As with all AudioSuite plug-ins, processing the squeak has created a new region on the Guitar track. Use the Smart tool to crossfade the new region's edit points. A dialog will pop up asking permission to adjust the boundaries to complete the fade. Press RETURN (ENTER). Listen to your edit. Save the session.

Whew! That's a lot of work just to reduce one little squeak, but sometimes noises like that will drive you nuts when you're mixing. This is a good technique to learn because it can be used to deal with a wide variety of problems, such as vocal sibilance and breath pops.

The final fix on the Guitar track is to fade out the very end. The guitar player breathed a sigh of relief as the last chord died out, plus you can hear some air-conditioner noise.

1. Zoom out, go to the end of the song, and Solo the guitar.

2. Use the Smart tool Trimmer to trim off most of the breath noise.

3. Position the cursor in the upper-right corner of the region, so that the box-shaped Fade tool appears, and put a one-second fade-out on the end of the region. The Length display in the Event Edit Area will give you the fade length.

4. Listen back to check all the edits in the song. When you're satisfied, duplicate the playlist to create a backup, and then select and consolidate the Guitar track the same way you did the Bass track.

5. Save the session as **Love 8gtr**.

Finishing Touches

The Doormats have just phoned you from a truck stop in Tulsa. They've been listening to the rough mix in the van (another common problem), and they've decided they want to go straight from the solo to the third chorus because they couldn't come up with any poignant lyrics for the third verse. Also, they think the first drum fill is lame and they want you to replace it with the one from the Outro. (So much for all the time you spent trying to salvage that first fill.)

Flying In the Drum Fill

For this edit, we'll be copying the drum fill that leads into the Outro and flying it into the Intro.

1. Make sure the DRUMS group is still active.

2. Make only the drum tracks visible in the Edit window, and then close the Tracks list.

3. Set the Track Heights to Medium, and the Track views to Waveform.

4. Go to Zoom preset 3 and click Outro in the Memory Locations window.

5. The fill leading into the Outro starts with a kick and snare that hit at the same time. Find this spot (2:19.5) and zoom in on the front of the kick waveform. Click with the Selector at the front of this kick beat.

6. Go back to Zoom preset 3 and SHIFT+click one bar later on the first kick drum beat of the Outro (2:21.6). Your selection should match Figure 7-2.

7. Copy the selection.

8. Click V1 in the Memory Locations window.

9. Locate the first kick drum beat of the Intro fill (:18.5) and zoom in close.

10. Click with the Selector as close as possible to the front of the kick waveform.

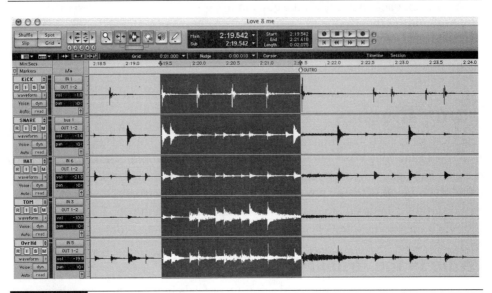

FIGURE 7-2   Selecting the Outro fill

11. Paste the Outro fill into this location.

12. Show and unmute the Click track, and listen back to make sure the fill is in sync. Nudge, if necessary.

13. Go back to Zoom preset 5 and trim the edit point at the front of the fill a dozen or so milliseconds to the left and crossfade.

14. Click with the Grabber on the fill region on the right to select it.

15. Press the RIGHT ARROW key to go to the end of the fill.

16. Trim the fill region to the right up to the next kick.

17. Trim the edit point back to the left to cover up the early kick and leave room for a crossfade.

18. Place a crossfade at the edit point.

19. Go to Zoom preset 3 and check your edit, and then check it again with the drums soloed. Save your session, and then save it again as **Love 9pre v3 edit**.

Taking Out the Third Verse

In this part of the tutorial, you will learn to use the markers to help make edit selections. Because we're about to change the structure of the song, we must make edits across all the audio regions in the session (even the Click track). Anytime you're about to attempt something big like changing the structure of a song, you should first save the session, giving it a new name that includes something like "preedit" in case you change your mind and want to return to the previous song structure. (That's why you were instructed to do this at the end of the previous exercise.) Then, you should always save the session again with a new name, such as putting the word "edit" at the end of the title. In the following steps you'll learn an editing technique using the memory locations to make edit selections. In order for this to work, we have to make sure the marker locations are extremely accurate.

1. Save the session as **Love 10edit**.

2. Open the Tracks list and show all the tracks in the session. Set the Track Heights to Medium.

3. Mute the Click track.

4. Use the Grabber to select the Click track's audio region, and press LEFT ARROW to view the front of the region.

5. Check to see if the Click track's audio region is still locked (look for the padlock icon at the front of the region). If so, you must unlock it to edit it. Choose Edit > Lock/Unlock Region (or press ⌘+L / CTRL+L).

6. Click All under Edit Groups in the Tracks list, and then close the list. All the tracks are now grouped together.

7. Go to Zoom preset 5 and click V3 in the Memory Locations window.

8. Click the yellow V3 marker in the Markers ruler and line it up with the very front of the first kick drum beat of Verse 3 (1:46.15).

9. Zoom in a few more clicks and make sure the V3 marker is as close as possible to the front of the waveform.

10. Go to Zoom preset 4 and click CH 3 in the Memory Locations window.

11. Line up the CH 3 marker with the front of the first kick drum beat of the third chorus (2:02.8). Zoom in a few more clicks and align the marker as closely as possible with the kick.

12. Click with the Selector anywhere in the Edit window to clear any current selections.

13. Go to Zoom preset 1 and click V3 in the Memory Locations window.

14. SHIFT+click on the CH 3 marker in the Memory Locations window. Look at the markers and notice that the area between these two markers (Verse 3) is now selected. This is the part of the song we are about to delete. The easiest way to accomplish this is by switching to Shuffle mode.

Using Shuffle Mode to Delete the Third Verse

Shuffle mode is the least commonly used of the four editing modes in Pro Tools. This is the mode that causes regions to act like magnets. The following steps will show how it can be used when removing parts of a song.

1. Select Shuffle mode in the upper-left corner of the Edit window (or press F1).

2. Watch the screen as you press DELETE (BACKSPACE). Note that the third verse disappears and the remaining regions snap together like magnets. This is the main feature of *Shuffle mode*. *Slip mode* enables you to have unfilled spaces between regions, but Shuffle mode pushes everything together.

3. Go back to Slip mode (F2).

4. Click V3 again in the Memory Locations window and go to Zoom preset 5. Open the Tracks list and deselect the All group. The DRUMS group should still be active.

Listen to the edit. You may have noticed that the edit works timing-wise, but there's something missing. (If you're a drummer, you'll probably notice it right away.) A drum fill is normally followed with a cymbal crash, but the edit has removed it. You'd better fix this, or you're gonna hear about it from you-know-who.

5. Go to Zoom preset 3 and trim the edit point on the Kick drum track to the right to uncover the cymbal crash. You'll have to move the edit at least an entire bar to avoid cutting off the sustain of the crash cymbal. Because the DRUMS group is active, the other drum tracks will follow suit.

6. Solo the drums and check the edit for glitches, and then crossfade.

TIP

This brings up an important point—when editing across all the tracks in a song, the edit point for the drums is not always the best edit point for the other instruments. The other instruments should be trimmed and crossfaded individually (with the All group disabled) to make the overall transition smoother.

7. Solo the Guitar track and listen to the edit. The strum is a little chopped off by the edit. Zoom in and trim the edit a little to the left to uncover the beginning of the strum and crossfade.

8. Check the edit on the Bass track and crossfade.

9. Check the edit on the Guitar track. The edit might sound better if the guitar edit were trimmed a little to the left to avoid cutting off the early part of the strum.

10. Crossfade the guitar edit.

11. Now that you've shortened the song, the marker placement is incorrect from this point on. Because there is no longer a third verse, delete the V3 marker by dragging it downward. The cursor will turn into a trashcan, indicating that the marker has been deleted. Go to Zoom preset 1 and drag the CH 3 marker over to the new edit point. Drag the Outro marker to the relocated start of the Outro (2:04.8). Save your session.

Now it's 2 A.M., and the Doormats have just phoned from Biloxi to inform you that they've decided to dump this version and recut the song with a reggae beat. Oh, well . . . you're still getting paid, right?

Great Job...Now Do It Again!

Congratulations! This concludes the Doormats session. I'm sure your head is probably reeling right about now. You've had to absorb a lot of new information to make these drum, bass, and guitar edits happen and it probably seems like a daunting task, but don't worry. Most people find this type of editing a little bewildering at first. In reality, once you get the session set up for this activity and learn the necessary commands, you get into a rhythm and it goes pretty quickly. Unfortunately, the only way to become proficient is to do it over and over again.

If you plan, someday, to represent yourself as a Pro Tools operator, you'll be expected to know how to perform this sort of plastic surgery on drum and instrument tracks. If you want to retain what you have learned in this chapter, I strongly suggest you open the session titled **Love 3pre edit** and go through the procedure again starting with the Chapter 6 section "Aligning the Drums to the Click" so that you don't have to go through the setups again. When you can locate the problem areas and fix them without referring to this book, you'll have come a long way toward your goal.

Chapter 8

Audio Quality Issues

Do Pro Tools LE systems sound as good as the HD systems? I get this question a lot (usually from songwriters), and it can't be answered with a simple yes or no, because giving a short answer doesn't do justice to Pro Tools LE systems. If a quick answer is all I have time for, I usually tell them that it's much more important to make sure the sound is good before it ever gets into Pro Tools.

Two major issues affecting the quality of audio in digital recording are A/D (analog-to-digital) conversion and clocking. The Pro Tools software itself works similarly in the HD and the LE versions. A session can be recorded on a HD system, transferred to an LE system for editing, and then transferred back to the HD system later for mixing with no loss in audio quality (in fact, I do this quite a bit in my studio). The tricky part is getting good-sounding audio into the system in the first place.

A/D Conversion

As most folks who dabble in recording are aware, all analog audio has to be *digitized*, or converted to digital ones and zeroes, on the way into a digital recording system. The design of the A/D converters has a major impact on the sound quality and, as you might have guessed, the A/D converters in the Mbox 2 or Digi 003 aren't going to sound as good as the converters in the HD system. That said, the audio quality of the LE systems is quite good for the money, and many tracks recorded on these systems have found their way onto major releases.

I usually advise beginners to start with a basic system. If you're not a beginner, and you feel the desire to go to the next level of recording quality, a better microphone and mic preamp (often called a "mic pre") would probably make a more noticeable difference in your recordings than would a fancy converter. The mic preamp is the amplifier that boosts the tiny signal from the microphone up to line level, and it has a huge effect on the quality of the sound. A high-end stereo mic pre can easily cost more than an entire Pro Tools LE rig (computer included), but chances are it's going to sound a lot better than the built-in mic pres in an LE system.

The next logical step would be to try out some of the outboard A/D converters available from such companies as Apogee, Grace, Mytek, Benchmark, Presonus, and so forth. These units all have their own sonic characteristics, and they generally sound better than the stock converters in the LE systems, but they can also cost much more than your entire system.

Jitter

In the world of digital audio, timing is everything. One of the most important features of an A/D converter is its audio clock. Every digital device relies on an internal (or external) clock to regulate the comings and goings of bits of data. The stability of the digital audio clock is crucial to the sonic accuracy of the system. Therefore, the designers of high-quality converters have gone to great lengths to make their audio clocks as stable as possible to reduce a phenomenon called jitter.

Jitter is caused by variations in the timing of the audio clock, and it's one of the biggest problems we encounter in digital audio. A jittery clock will not accurately sample the incoming audio. It is often responsible for the "edgy" sound that has long been associated with digital recording. In stereo recordings, jitter can subtly alter the stereo field, making it sound less three dimensional. In extreme cases, jitter can cause clicks and pops, and other nasty splatty sounds. Once your audio is sampled using a jittery clock, the damage is done. I'm not trying to give the impression that the LE systems are jittery, but clock stability is one of the reasons why the high-end converters tend to sound better.

NOTE

If you want to learn more about jitter, buy Bob Katz's excellent book: Mastering Audio *(Focal Press, 2002). Bob is committed to helping people like you and me cut through the hype and understand what happens to audio in the digital domain, and his web site (www.digido.com) is a great source of information on all things audio.*

Clocking: LE vs. HD

Two major differences between the high-end Pro Tools HD systems and the less-expensive LE systems are in the way digital audio is transferred to and from the systems, and the number of options for syncing to an external clock.

Pro Tools LE

All Pro Tools LE systems reference their own internal clock (independent of the host computer's clock) when Pro Tools is set to Internal Sync mode in the Hardware Setup window or the Session Setup window. If you want to use an outboard converter, this mode must be changed to reflect the type of I/O you want to use, whether it's S/PDIF (Sony/Philips Digital Interface Format) or Optical (if available), so that Pro Tools can reference the outboard converter's clock and input digital audio. This effectively bypasses the Pro Tools audio clock and converters. The Digi 002 and 003 uses the semipro two-channel S/PDIF (RCA connectors) and eight-channel ADAT (Alesis Digital Audio Tape) optical I/O (lightpipe) connections, while most members of the Mbox 2 family have only S/PDIF.

<table>
<tr><td>NOTE</td><td>While we're on the subject, you should know that the audio and the clock signal both pass through the same cable in this scenario. This is a less-than-ideal situation, but it's the only option with LE systems. Also, the only way to sync an LE system to a tape machine is via MIDI Time Code, which is also less than ideal, but it works well enough for some folks.</td></tr>
</table>

Pro Tools HD

HD systems are designed for the professional market and offer a great deal more flexibility than the LE systems in terms of interfacing with the outside world. In HD systems, the clock signal is normally routed separately from the audio, which is a big plus for keeping jitter to a minimum. Commercial studios often add Digidesign's SYNC I/O to their system, a peripheral device that allows Pro Tools to read and generate SMPTE (Society of Motion Picture and Television Engineers) time code and lock to every type of external clock signal available in the audio and film industry.

Using a Master Clock

Things start to get pretty complicated when you use several digital audio devices together in a studio. A typical midlevel Pro Tools studio setup might include multiple Pro Tools interfaces, a SYNC I/O, DAT machines, analog machines controlled by synchronizers, CD players, outboard converters, stand-alone digital recorders/CD burners like the Alesis Masterlink, samplers, and so forth. Trying to keep track of who's getting clock from whom can be a real nightmare. To make matters worse, external clock inputs seem to be vanishing from the back panels of new digital devices these days.

The best solution for keeping jitter and other bugaboos to a minimum is usually to have one stable clock source that feeds clock to all the digital devices, which are then configured to accept the external clock (with the shortest and highest-quality cables possible). Many studios are also using digital patch bays to transfer digital audio to and from their digital gear. If you're just a guy sitting in his basement with a guitar and an Mbox, you don't need to run out and buy all this stuff, but it's worthwhile going to web sites to learn about these products.

Chapter 9

Using a Click in Pro Tools

In many situations, it is desirable to use a click or a metronome for a timing reference when recording. Musicians often prefer to play along with a click when recording in the studio to keep the tempo from fluctuating. I think it's safe to say that the vast majority of popular music in the mainstream today is recorded to some type of timing reference. In this chapter, you will learn different techniques for creating a timing reference in Pro Tools and learn a little bit about Grid mode and using MIDI in Pro Tools.

Using the Click Plug-in

The easiest way to generate a click in Pro Tools is to use the Click plug-in. Although somewhat limited, it provides a fast and convenient way to get a basic click going. Let's take a look.

1. Create a new 24-bit 44.1 kHz session titled **Click.**

2. Make sure you are in the default Slip mode.

3. Choose Track > Create Click Track.

4. Set the Track Height to Medium.

5. Enable the Inserts view, and note that the Click plug-in has already been inserted on the track.

6. Press Play to audition the Factory Default click sound. Lovely, isn't it?

NOTE   *If you don't hear the click playing, make sure that Click is checked under the Options menu.*

7. Open the Click plug-in window and click the plug-in's Librarian menu (currently labeled Factory Default) to audition the other click sounds. Move the Accented and Unaccented sliders around, and note their effect on the sound. It is often advantageous to accent the downbeat of each measure, particularly during countoffs. While the click sounds presented here may not be inspiring, you can't beat the Click plug-in for sheer convenience. Beware of using the higher-pitched sounds in situations where the sound might bleed from headphones into an open microphone.

Up to this point in the book we have mainly been using Slip mode. Because the Click plug-in is always locked internally to the Pro Tools grid, it can be used in either Slip or Grid mode. That means you can record a song in Slip mode using the Click plug-in and then switch to Grid mode if you need to add MIDI tracks or loops later on. The other methods of generating a click presented in this chapter require switching to Grid mode.

What Is Grid Mode?

Grid mode will be familiar to anyone who has used the "snap to grid" function in a drawing program. *Grid mode* enables the user to create a visible grid in the Edit window that represents the bars and beats of the song. Regions will "snap" precisely to a specific beat, eliminating the need to nudge them back and forth to line them up. There's never a question of where the downbeat falls for a certain measure, because you can see the corresponding gridlines in the Edit window. In this mode, the counter is usually set to read bars and beats, rather than minutes and seconds, which can make song navigation easier. Automation events, such as panning, can be placed exactly in tempo. MIDI notes can be quantized to correct timing issues. Songwriters can easily try different arrangement ideas by dividing a song into sections that can be moved around like building blocks.

Working in Grid mode normally necessitates the use of a Click track or loop for use as a metronome. Even if the concept of dividing music into neat little blocks doesn't appeal to you, I suggest you do not skip these tutorials. A great deal of important information is disseminated in this chapter that will be relied on in the remainder of the book. If you are a beginner and hope, someday, to work in a professional studio situation, you will be expected to know these techniques.

The most important concept in this entire chapter is as follows: Grid mode can be useful in situations where music is played to a click, *especially if the click is locked to or generated by Pro Tools.* Trying to create a grid after the fact from a song that was not recorded this way can be both difficult and time consuming.

At the outset, it may seem much simpler to just put down a drum machine track in Slip mode, and then play along with it, as the Doormats did on the earlier demo. However, this approach made the session much less flexible, because the Click track was a recording of a drum machine that was not locked to Pro Tools. Even if you don't anticipate using Grid mode for a session, any time you record using a click, the best approach is to generate the click from Pro Tools. If you want to use an external MIDI device, such as a drum machine, for a click, that device should not be running on its own; it should instead be triggered by Pro Tools via MIDI. Why? When the click is generated by Pro Tools, the click will always stay in sync with the grid, even if your session was initially recorded in Slip mode. *This means you can always pop into Grid mode later.* This opens up a lot of editing possibilities and makes adding loops or MIDI tracks a snap. Once you get the hang of it, it's more convenient than using a stand-alone click.

The point here is, you never know where a session is going to take you, and you can't always predict what will happen to a project once it leaves your studio. If there is the remotest possibility that you or someone else may be adding MIDI tracks or rhythmic loops to the song, or if you might need to edit drums using Beat Detective, using the techniques in this chapter can save a great deal of time and frustration.

Not convinced yet? Read on. Once, when working on a record project for a prominent artist, I was given a home demo on an eight-track tape with instructions to transfer the song into Pro Tools. The artist liked the feel of the demo and wanted to use it as a basic track for the song. The demo consisted of a drum machine track, a couple of synth tracks, and a bass. The drum machine was one of those ancient pawn shop specials with push buttons for the different drum patterns with names like "Foxtrot," "Rock 1," and so on. I transferred the tracks into Pro Tools and the band began overdubbing additional parts. Two months later, nearly 50 tracks had been added to the song, including some expensive live strings. It was decided at that point that live drums would be added to the song. That's when we realized that something was wrong. No matter how hard the drummer tried, he was unable to stay in tempo with the song, and it was driving both the drummer and the producer crazy.

After listening closely to the drum machine track, we realized it was fluctuating slightly in tempo over the course of the song. Because of the dreamy, ethereal nature of the song, no one had noticed this at first, but now it was causing a real problem. It was clear that we were never going to be able to put live drums on the song until the tempo was evened out, so I bravely (foolishly?) volunteered to remedy the situation. The solution was to take one measure of the drum machine track at its "average" tempo and loop it in Grid mode for the duration of the song. Then, I nudged, edited, and crossfaded every single track to get everything back into the groove. Because of the complexity of the session, it took me two solid weeks of work to get the song "gridded out," so that we could then overdub drums to the track.

I think it's safe to say I learned that lesson the hard way. I could have saved myself two weeks of work by spending a couple of hours conforming the demo tracks to a grid before the overdubs started. In an ideal situation, the artist would have had a Pro Tools rig at home and looped the drum pattern in Pro Tools from the beginning.

You might think that if you use a modern digital drum machine for a click, it will line up just fine with the grid later on because it's digital, right? Not necessarily. If a drum machine is running on its own clock, it will *never* line up perfectly with the grid in Pro Tools. The drum machine must be triggered by Pro Tools via MIDI, or it will inevitably drift over time, just like the drum machine in the aforementioned example.

Setting Up for Grid Mode

To prepare the session for Grid mode, we need to make some changes in the Edit window.

1. Go to View > Rulers and select None. Close the Tracks list.

2. Referring to Figure 9-1, click the pop-up menu for the Main counter and select Bars:Beats.

3. Click the Grid pop-up menu and select 1 bar.

4. Enable Grid mode by pressing F4 (or click the Grid button in the toolbar). Note that the Timeline is now labeled Bars:Beats instead of Min:Secs.

5. Click the blue Bars:Beats label (as shown in Figure 9-1) and note that it turns the gridlines on and off. Leave them on.

6. Zoom in until you only see a few gridlines in the Edit window, as shown in Figure 9-1.

7. Press RETURN (ENTER) to rewind to the session start, and press Play. As you watch the cursor and the Main counter, you can see that each gridline represents one bar. The Main counter displays the location in bars, beats, and ticks (there are 960 ticks to a quarter note).

Turn gridlines on or off   Select Bars:Beats

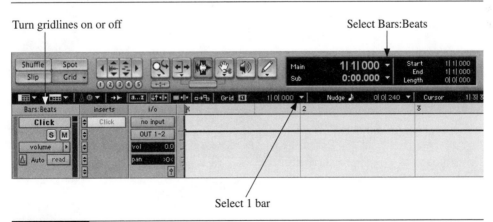

Select 1 bar

FIGURE 9-1   Setting up the Edit window for Grid mode

Viewing MIDI Controls in the Transport Window

As you have seen in previous chapters, the Transport window can be expanded to include controls for several basic MIDI functions. To view these controls, go to View > Transport > MIDI Controls, or ⌘+click (CTRL+click) the Expand/Collapse button in the Transport window. The names of the more commonly used controls are shown in Figure 9-2.

Although the Click plug-in doesn't have anything to do with MIDI, it does respond to these controls, so now would be a good time to see what these buttons do. If you have the Click plug-in active, the Metronome Click button will toggle it on and off. The Countoff button should be turned off most of the time. The purpose of the Countoff button is to enable the user to specify a certain number of measures to use for a countoff before recording begins. Therefore, if the Countoff button is accidentally engaged, it will cause a two-bar pause every time you press Record. The following steps will demonstrate how these MIDI controls are used to set up a session for Grid mode.

1. Locate the Conductor button and click to turn it off. This will place the session in Manual Tempo mode. Note that the Tempo slider is no longer grayed out, and the Tempo field becomes active. This means that you can now manually change the tempo by either moving the Tempo slider or typing a number into the Tempo field.

2. Press Play, click the Tempo slider, and change the tempo value. Note how the gridlines shift to match the new tempo. Changing this setting after

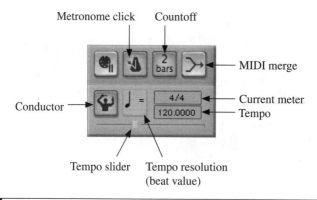

FIGURE 9-2   MIDI controls

recording audio can definitely get you into trouble. Any MIDI notes in the session will move with the changing tempo. The grid will change, and your audio will no longer be aligned with it. If this happens, you'll need to quickly change it back to the original tempo (if you can remember what it was) before you go any further.

3. You can "tap in" a tempo by clicking in the Tempo field and tapping the T key at the desired tempo. Give it a try, and then press RETURN (ENTER) to enter the tempo.

4. If you have a specific tempo in mind, you can enter it by typing a number into the Tempo field. Click the Tempo field and type in **120** to return to the default tempo of 120 bpm, and then press RETURN (ENTER).

5. Pro Tools defaults to what's known as a *quarter note click*, which means four clicks per measure. For slower tunes, the clicks may be too far apart, in which case an eighth note click may be preferred. This can be changed by double-clicking the Current Meter field (currently labeled 4/4), which opens the Meter Change dialog. Click the quarter note icon and choose the 1/8 note setting, click OK, and then press Play to hear the difference. Click all the different meter settings during playback to hear their effect on the click.

6. Open the Meter Change dialog again, enter 3/4 in the Meter field, and click OK. Press Play and watch the Main counter. Note that there are now three beats per measure.

7. Change the meter for the session back to 4/4. With the Selector, click anywhere in the Click track. Note that the cursor snaps to the nearest bar. The main feature of Grid mode is that your selections are restricted to the specified grid.

8. It is often desirable to divide the grid into smaller increments, such as quarter, eighth, or sixteenth notes. Click the Grid pop-up and select 1/4 note (quarter note). Note that each bar is now divided into four sections, or quarter notes. Click anywhere in the Click track and the cursor now snaps to the nearest 1/4 note. The bold gridlines represent bars, and the thinner gridlines represent the 1/4 notes within each bar. Any selection made in the Edit window will snap to the nearest quarter note. This setting can be changed at any time without fear of moving your audio around.

9. Save the session. We'll use it for the next tutorial.

Generating a Click Using Reason Adapted

Reason is a popular piece of music software invented by the folks at Propellerhead Software. Every Pro Tools system comes with a free copy of Reason Adapted for Digidesign, which is a feature-limited version than can be accessed within a Pro Tools session via the ReWire plug-in. Even if sequenced electronic music is not your thing, Reason Adapted is definitely worth exploring. If someone dropped a free drum machine, synthesizer, sampler, digital delay, reverb, compressor, and mixer on your doorstep, would you bring them into the house and play with them? Of course you would! That's part of what you get with Reason Adapted, but many Pro Tools users fail to make use of it, probably because the last thing they want to do is tackle another computer program.

Installing Reason Adapted

If you haven't installed your copy of Reason Adapted, I urge you to do it now and go through the following tutorials. Before you can use Reason Adapted in Pro Tools for the first time, you must quit Pro Tools and run Reason Adapted in stand-alone mode to set a few presets and enter the serial number. Reason Adapted expects you to connect a master keyboard to the computer, and presents dialogs asking you to designate a master keyboard. A keyboard is not necessary for this tutorial, and Reason Adapted will run without it. If you have a keyboard, by all means go ahead and connect it to your system. Otherwise, tell Reason Adapted you're not using a keyboard when the dialogs pop up.

Trash the Reason Adapted Prefs

These tutorials are designed to work with the default settings in Reason Adapted. If you have been playing around with Reason Adapted since we trashed the Reason Adapted Preferences in Chapter 2 and have made changes to Redrum (the drum machine), you must quit Reason Adapted first, then Pro Tools (Reason Adapted doesn't like it when you quit Pro Tools first). Then navigate to the Reason Adapted Prefs and trash them. Macintosh users will find the Reason Adapted Prefs in the same folder as the Pro Tools Prefs (if you don't recall the path to that folder, refer to Chapter 2). In Windows, the Reason Adapted Prefs are in Documents and Settings > (User's Name) > Application Data > Propellerhead Software > Reason Adapted for Digidesign.

Introducing Redrum

Redrum is Reason's virtual drum machine. In the following steps you'll learn how to program a basic pattern to use for a click.

1. Open the Click session from the previous tutorial (if it's not open already), and mute the Click track. Close the Click plug-in window if it is open, and hide the Click track.

2. Create a new stereo instrument track and name it **Drums**.

3. Click a plug-in insert and choose Multichannel Plug-in > Instrument > Reason Adapted for Digidesign (Stereo). (Users of HD systems choose Multi-channel RTAS Plug-in.) The ReWire window appears. ReWire is a DigiRack RTAS plug-in that allows Pro Tools to communicate with ReWire-compatible software such as Reason Adapted and Ableton Live. It will automatically open Reason Adapted (if it's not already running). In the ReWire plug-in window, you can choose which of Reason Adapted's outputs to use. Leave it at the default setting of Mix L-Mix R, and close the window.

4. Make Reason Adapted the active window on your screen. You can switch quickly between running applications by pressing ⌘+TAB (ALT+TAB). The top section of this window displays Reason Adapted's virtual studio rack.

5. Scroll down until you see Redrum. Across the top you will see modules numbered 1 through 10, which are the available drum sounds. The default sound for module 1 is kick drum (BD1 1 OHS). Click the Trigger (arrow) button in the upper-right corner of module 1 to trigger the kick drum sound. Click the Trigger buttons in the other modules to hear the sounds available in this particular "kit."

6. The modules are selected via the Select button at the bottom of each module. Select module 8, which is the hi-hat.

7. Below the modules is a row of 16 Step buttons for programming drum patterns. At the current default resolution of 1/16, each button corresponds to a sixteenth note. This row of buttons displays the pattern for whichever module is currently selected. Click all the odd-numbered step buttons (1, 3, 5, etc.) and press the SPACEBAR to start playback. You should be hearing an eighth note hi-hat pattern. If you don't hear anything, make sure the Pattern button is on.

8. Select module 1 (kick drum) and click Step buttons 1 and 9.

9. Select module 2 (snare drum) and click Step buttons 5 and 13. You now have a basic drum pattern playing.

10. Go back to the Pro Tools Edit window. If the Conductor button is lit, turn it off to switch to Manual Tempo mode. Move the Tempo slider around and note that Reason Adapted changes tempo as well.

That's pretty much all there is to programming a basic pattern into Redrum. Now you need to save your Reason file.

Saving the Reason Adapted File and Bouncing the Loop

The patterns you create in Reason Adapted won't necessarily be there every time you open your Pro Tools session unless you name and save the Reason file and put it somewhere safe, like the current session folder. The next time you open the Pro Tools Click session, Pro Tools will automatically launch Reason Adapted, but Reason Adapted won't remember which Reason file goes with this song—you will have to navigate to the correct Reason song file (having saved it ahead of time) and open it manually. Therefore, it behooves you to save the Reason file. If you don't want to bother with opening Reason Adapted every time you open the current Pro Tools session, you should bounce the drum pattern to an audio track before you close the session. I usually bounce one or two bars to a track and then use the Repeat command to loop the pattern for the duration of the song. Then I deactivate the Reason instrument track so I don't have to worry about opening Reason Adapted and navigating to the file every time I open the session.

Here's how to save the Reason file:

1. Return to the Reason window and choose File > Save As (do not choose Save).

2. Name the Reason file **Click**, navigate to the Click Pro Tools session folder on your audio drive, and click Save.

Bounce the Reason loop as follows:

1. Create a new mono audio track named **DrumLoop**, and set its input to Bus 1 (Mono).

2. Set the output of the Drums instrument track to Bus 1 (Mono).

Exploring Redrum Further

I suggest you spend some time playing around with this marvelous free toy. Obviously, there's a lot more to Redrum than what we've done in this exercise. You can get the full story in the *Operation Manual* in the Reason Adapted folder on your computer. Here are a few fun things you can do with Redrum:

■ Check out Redrum's variety of drum sounds—just click the current filename in the module (such as BD1 1 OHS) and choose another file in the Reason Sample Browser window.

■ Play any drum sound from any module.

■ Trigger sounds that you make yourself (woo hoo!).

■ Use Reason Adapted's virtual mixer to put reverb and delay on the drums (just scroll up to the mixer and turn up aux 1 and 2 on the Redrum channel).

■ Alter drum dynamics for a more human feel.

■ Store up to 32 different drum patterns.

■ Play Redrum with a MIDI keyboard instead of using the step buttons.

3. Put the DrumLoop track into Record Ready and select the first bar.

4. Record one bar of the loop.

5. While the loop is still selected, press OPTION+R (ALT+R) to bring up the Repeat dialog, type in **100**, and click OK. Now you have 101 bars of your loop.

At this point I would normally deactivate the Reason track (Track > Make Inactive), but we're going to use this track for the next tutorial.

Using MIDI with Redrum

You've learned a fast and easy way to get a drum pattern going for a session with no tempo or meter changes, but what if you need to change tempo or meter within a piece of music? This happens quite a bit in film-scoring applications. A way to accomplish this is to use MIDI notes on an instrument track to drive Redrum. That way, most of the work is done in Pro Tools, and you're using Redrum the way you would use an external drum machine.

As you may know, *MIDI* is basically a system for transmitting performance information between electronic instruments. It's important to realize that MIDI information is not audio. It is simply data that tells the receiving MIDI device what notes to play, and when, like a piano roll on a player piano. Although it is beyond the scope of this tutorial to fully explain MIDI, many excellent books have been written on the subject. My favorite is *Basic MIDI,* by Paul White (Sanctuary, 2004). It's a straightforward, easy-to-understand, pocket-sized reference that can be read in a matter of hours.

Drawing MIDI Notes on an Instrument Track

The instrument track is a fairly recent addition to Pro Tools. As we found out in the previous exercise, it is capable of playing the audio from a virtual instrument like Redrum. It is also capable of recording and displaying MIDI information. A common application would be to route a keyboard to the track and play the instrument as you would any sound module. Since you may or may not have a MIDI keyboard available, we will instead use the Pencil tool to draw the notes directly on the track. In the following exercise you will learn how to use the Pencil tool to draw MIDI notes on an instrument track to create a drum pattern.

1. First, we must disable the pattern we created in the previous exercise. Make the Reason window active and click the Pattern button in Redrum to turn off the pattern.

2. Go back to Pro Tools and set the output of the Drums track back to OUT 1-2. Delete the DrumLoop track (Track > Delete > Delete).

3. Note that the instrument track is grayed out. That's because no instrument has been assigned yet. Click the View Selector icon (or go to View > Edit Window) and select Instrument view. This view shows the MIDI input (currently set to All) and the MIDI output (currently set to None). Click the MIDI output selector and select Redrum from the list of Reason virtual instruments.

4. Zoom in on the first bar and set the Drums Track Height to Jumbo (use the Track Height selector button next to the Track View selector). Set the Grid selector pop-up to 1/16 note.

NOTE

Take a look at the part of the track that resembles a vertical piano keyboard. Clicking in this area will not change the Track Height. The little arrows at the top and bottom of the keyboard enable you to scroll up or down to access all 88 keys. The numbers on the keyboard correspond with the different octaves, which makes it easy to locate MIDI notes.

5. Position the cursor to the right of the keyboard, and move it up and down. Notice that the corresponding keys on the keyboard are highlighted. If you're not familiar with keyboards and don't know which keys play which notes, watch the Cursor display for note values.

6. Somewhere on this keyboard are the ten notes that trigger the Redrum sounds. The easiest way to find them is to choose the Pencil tool and click just to the right of the keyboard anywhere within the first 1/16 note to create a MIDI note, as shown here:

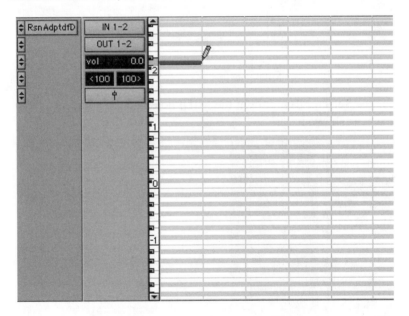

7. Choose the plain Grabber and drag the MIDI note up and down the keyboard. As you drag the note, you will hear the different drum sounds being triggered by the note. Place the MIDI note at the closed hi-hat sound, which is G1.

8. Click the MIDI Zoom button to expand the MIDI note to the height shown in the following illustration. You may need to use the scroll arrows to bring the note back into view.

MIDI Zoom button

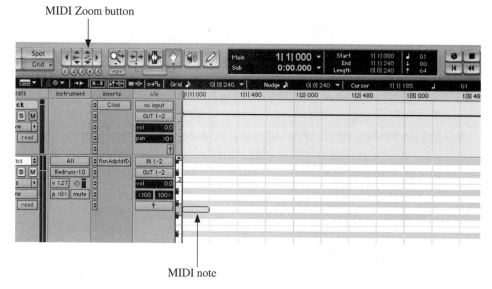

MIDI note

9. Use the Selector to highlight the MIDI note and the adjacent 1/16 note space, as shown here:

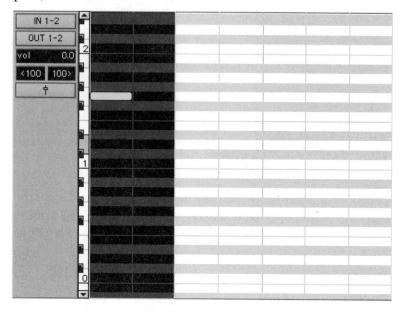

10. Press OPTION+R (ALT+R) to bring up the Repeat dialog, type in **7**, and click OK. Now you have a one-bar 1/8 note hi-hat pattern.

11. Using the following illustration as a guide, use the Pencil tool to add MIDI notes for a kick and snare pattern on C1 and C#1, and use the Grabber to move the last hi-hat note to G#1 for an open hi-hat.

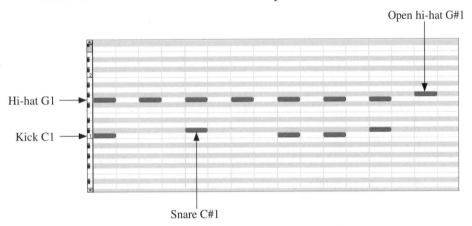

Open hi-hat G#1

Hi-hat G1

Kick C1

Snare C#1

12. Let's play our drum pattern in a loop. Enable the Loop mode by CONTROL+clicking (START+clicking or right-clicking) the Play button, or by pressing 4 on the numeric keyboard. Note that the Play button icon changes to show that you are in Loop mode. Then use the Selector to select Bar 1, and press Play to hear your drum pattern in a loop.

13. Here is where the Link Edit and Timeline Selection button (shown here) comes in handy. While your loop is playing, click this button and note that the blue border disappears to show that this feature is disabled.

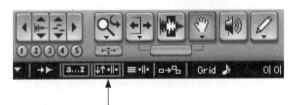

Link Edit and Timeline Selection

14. Click anywhere in the Edit window to deselect Bar 1. You can see that the timeline is still selected because it is no longer linked to the edit selection. This means that the transport will continue to play the loop regardless of any selection you might make in the Edit window. Now you can add and

delete MIDI notes from the loop without having to constantly reselect the loop for playback.

15. Use the Pencil tool to add a grace note to the snare pattern while the loop is playing. Use the soft snare hit on E1, and place it on the beat before the second kick drum hit, as shown here:

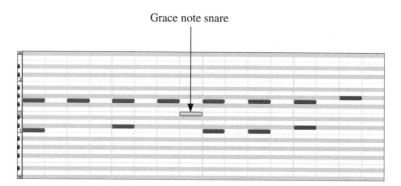

Grace note snare

At this point I suggest you play around with the loop, adding different drum sounds in different places until you get the hang of it. When you're done, return your loop to the pattern shown previously with Step 15 and Save the session as **Click 2**. Also, go to Reason Adapted and save the Reason song file as **Click 2** and put it in the Click Session folder with the Pro Tools files.

Adding Tempo and Meter Changes

Let's say you're using the drum pattern from the previous exercise for a film score. In the film, the protagonist is cruising down a city street at night, minding his own business while our drum pattern plays in the background. Little does he know things are about to change. You'll need to make some changes in the drum pattern to follow the action. To aid in this endeavor, we need to make a few changes in the Edit window.

1. To unclutter the window, turn off the Instruments and Inserts views and make sure the Tracks and Region lists are closed.

2. Go to View > Rulers and enable the Tempo ruler. It appears as a pink strip under the Timeline.

3. At the moment, the Tempo ruler is telling you that you are in Manual Tempo mode. This means that only one tempo is available for the session, and the Tempo ruler is disabled. Click the Conductor button in the Transport window to disable Manual Tempo mode. The Conductor button lights up and the Manual Tempo slider is grayed out. The tempo is now controlled by the iron fist of the mighty Tempo ruler.

4. Change the Drums Track View selector from Notes to Blocks. This view prevents accidental changes to the MIDI notes, and makes it easier to move chunks of MIDI data around.

5. We need eight bars of this loop, so use the Smart tool to select the loop and press OPTION+R (ALT+R) to bring up the Repeat dialog. Add 7 repeats and click OK. Zoom out so you can see all eight bars.

6. The default tempo is 120 bpm. That's a little too fast for cruising down the street. Let's knock it down a bit. Go to View > Rulers and enable the Tempo Editor. In this part of the Tempo ruler, a horizontal line across the top of the green-shaded area represents the tempo for the session. Click on this line and pull the tempo down to 88 bpm. (Hint: the tempo is displayed at the left edge of the Tempo ruler and also in the MIDI Functions section of the Transport window.)

7. Click the Link Edit and Timeline Selection button to reenable that feature.

8. At Bar 4, a Hummer full of thugs appears out of nowhere and rams our hero from behind. Quite naturally, he floors it. CONTROL+click (START+click) the Tempo ruler (anywhere in the pink-shaded area). This brings up the Tempo Change dialog. Enter **4| 1|000** in the Location field, and **140** in the BPM (Tempo) field. Click OK. You have just instructed Pro Tools to speed up to 140 bpm at Bar 4.

9. The Tempo Editor now reflects the new tempo change at Bar 4. Listen to the tempo change. It's not fast enough for a good car chase, so click on the Tempo line after the Bar 4 tempo change and jack it up to 155 bpm. Now we're moving.

10. At Bar 9, the bad guys run our hero off a bridge and into the river. As he hits the water, we need to change the meter to 6/8 time. Go to View > Rulers and enable the Meter ruler.

11. CONTROL+click (START+click) anywhere in the Meter ruler.

12. This brings up (you guessed it) the Meter Change dialog. Enter **9| 1|000** in the Location field, **6/8** in the Meter field, and click OK. As you might expect, the meter change shows up in the Meter ruler.

13. We need a new pattern at Bar 9 for this meter, so click the Track View selector (currently set to Blocks) and choose Notes. Use the Pencil tool to create the two-bar pattern shown here:

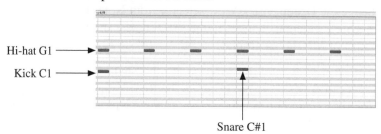

14. Select the two-bar 6/8 pattern and use the Repeat command as before to create three repeats for a total of eight bars.

15. As the car fills with water and sinks, we want the tempo to gradually slow (*ritard*). With the Selector, click on the horizontal dividing line between the Tempo Editor and the Meter ruler and drag downward an inch or so to expand the Tempo Editor.

16. Click and hold the Pencil tool, and choose Line from the drop-down menu.

17. In the Tempo Editor, click and hold on the Tempo line at Bar 9, and drag the Pencil tool to Bar 19, pulling the tempo down to about 80, as shown next. (Hint: watch the Cursor display for the tempo value.) Pro Tools creates a series of small tempo events in the Tempo Editor, each step slightly reducing the tempo.

18. Rewind and listen to your handiwork. Save the session.

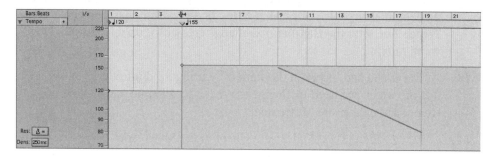

Creating the Shaker Track

In this tutorial, we'll create a separate percussion track using a shaker sample from the Reason Factory Sound Bank. At the moment, all the Redrum sounds are routed through the Drums instrument track. We want the shaker on a separate instrument track to make it easier to manipulate. To make this happen we'll need to open a new instrument track and do some rerouting in Reason Adapted.

1. Close the Tempo Editor by clicking the triangle next to the word "Tempo" at the left edge of the Tempo ruler.

2. Change the Drums Track Height to Medium.

3. Create a new mono instrument track named **Shaker**, and set the Track Height to Large.

4. Enable the Inserts and Instruments views.

5. Insert the Reason Adapted plug-in on the Shaker track. When the ReWire plug-in window appears, set the Reason Adapted output to Channel 3, and close the ReWire plug-in window.

6. Make the Reason window active and scroll to the Redrum section.

7. Go to drum module number 6, which is currently set to play a tom sample. Click the folder-shaped Browse icon to open the Sample Browser and follow this path: Reason Factory Sound Bank (under Locations) > Redrum Drum Kits > Xclusive Drums Sorted > Percussion-Hi > SH_Jeepkeys.wav. Click OK. Module 6 will now play the Jeepkeys sample instead of the tom.

8. To make the shaker play through the shaker track we'll have to use Reason Adapted's virtual patch bay. Press the TAB key to view the rear of the Redrum unit. Virtual patch points and cables appear.

9. Click and hold on the Left (Mono) output of Module 6 (the topmost connector), drag upward until you reach the Hardware Interface at the top of the rack, and plug the virtual patch cord into Audio In 3.

10. Go back to Pro Tools and set the Shaker track's input to Bus 3 (Mono).

11. In the Shaker track's Instruments view, change the MIDI output from None to Redrum. Now the shaker sound is no longer routed through the Reason Adapted's virtual mixer with the rest of the drums—it has been routed directly to the Shaker instrument track in Pro Tools, where its volume and panning can be controlled separately.

12. Go back to the Pro Tools Edit window. Position the cursor inside the vertical keyboard at the left edge of the Shaker instrument track. The cursor changes to a horizontal I-beam. Click and drag the cursor up and down to play the different Redrum sounds until you hear the shaker sound. The Shaker track's meter will jump when you arrive at the correct note to trigger shaker sound in Module 6, which is F1.

13. Choose the Pencil tool (it should still be set to Line).

14. Position the Pencil tool over the first F1 note in Bar 2. Click and drag to the left to create a row of 1/16 notes in Bar 1. The results should appear as shown here:

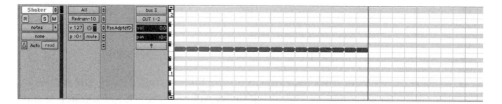

Working with the Velocity View

Solo the Shaker track, select Bar 1, and play the shaker (you should still be in Loop mode). It sounds more like a water sprinkler than a musical instrument because every note is played at the exact same volume or velocity. A human could never make a shaker sound like that. In this exercise we'll the use Shaker track's Velocity view to vary the velocity of the sample for a more human feel.

1. With Bar 1 still selected, turn off the Link Edit and Timeline Selection button so you can work on the loop without changing its starting point.

2. Click the Shaker track's Track View selector (currently labeled Notes) and select Velocity. In this view, the velocity (volume) of each note is represented by a "velocity stalk" with a diamond at the top. In the world of MIDI, velocity values can be anywhere between 0 and 127. When you use the Pencil tool to write a MIDI note, Pro Tools sets it to a default value of 80.

3. Click with the Selector somewhere in Bar 1 to deselect it. With the Grabber, click the first 1/16 note, then SHIFT+click on the 5th, 9th, and 13th notes to select them.

4. Choose the Trimmer and drag the velocity stalks of these four notes all the way up to the maximum velocity of 127. Listen to the difference in the loop.

5. Use the Grabber to SHIFT+click the even-numbered notes (2, 4, 6, and so on) to select them, and then click and hold somewhere in Bar 1 with the Trimmer. Notice the number zero in the upper-left corner of the track. This is the delta value, or starting velocity.

6. Drag downward to lower the even-numbered notes for a delta value of –25. Bar 1 should now appear as shown here. Listen to the loop. The variation in velocity helps the loop sound more human.

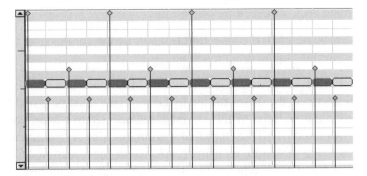

7. Click the Shaker track's Track View selector and select the Blocks track view. This is the best view to use when cutting and pasting chunks of MIDI data.

8. Select the loop and use the Repeat command to loop the shaker for 13 more repeats.

9. Enable the Link Edit and Timeline Selection button.

10. Take the Shaker track out of Solo and listen to the entire piece. The advantage of having the shaker on a separate track is that you can easily adjust its volume and panning without disturbing the Drums track.

Using Pro Tools with a Drum Machine

In the introduction of this chapter, I mentioned triggering a drum machine with Pro Tools. Some Pro Tools users find it easier to compose their drum patterns on a drum machine and then transfer them into Pro Tools. There's no problem with this approach as long as the MIDI Beat Clock feature in Pro Tools is enabled. *MIDI Beat Clock* is a timing reference transmitted via MIDI that most drum machines will lock to.

Suppose someone shows up at your studio with a drum machine that she has meticulously programmed an entire song into for use as a basic track. Are you going to try to recreate that entire sequence on an instrument track in Pro Tools? Only if you're a glutton for punishment, because there's no reason to—MIDI Beat Clock will come to the rescue.

To use MIDI Beat Clock, the following steps must be taken:

1. The drum machine in question must have its external clock enabled. You can usually find this control by pressing the MIDI button on the drum machine and looking through the menus. Turn on anything that says External Clock, or Clock In, or the like.

2. There must be a MIDI connection from either the computer or the Pro Tools interface to the drum machine.

3. If your Pro Tools system doesn't include MIDI ports and you're using a MIDI interface, the driver for the MIDI interface must be properly installed in the computer. If the MIDI interface is connected to a Mac, you have to tell AMS (Audio MIDI Setup) that a drum machine is connected to the interface. For more info on using AMS, see the next section, "Configuring AMS in Mac OSX." Windows systems don't require configuration for MIDI interfaces. If the driver is properly installed, the interface will automatically show up in Pro Tools.

4. Pro Tools must be told to transmit MIDI Beat Clock, and to whom. (MIDI Beat Clock defaults to On in Windows systems.) To do this, go to Setup > MIDI > MIDI Beat Clock. In the dialog that appears, enable MIDI Beat Clock and select the drum machine to receive it. Press RETURN (ENTER) to close the dialog.

5. Pro Tools must be set to the desired tempo of the song.

That's pretty much all there is to it. As soon as you start Pro Tools, the drum machine will start whatever song or pattern is programmed into it. The drum machine will ignore its own clock and follow the tempo information it receives from Pro Tools. The main drawback of this method is that you will always have to start at the beginning of the song. In this scenario, the drum machine is not receiving time code, so it has no idea where you are in the song. It will start the sequence from the beginning whenever and wherever you start playback in Pro Tools.

The way to work around that would be to record the output of the drum machine into Pro Tools, preferably with each sound on a separate track. If the drum machine only has stereo out, do multiple passes and record two sounds at a time with the other sounds muted until you have them all recorded. If there's no countoff, just start recording at Beat 1, Bar 3, and paste one in later.

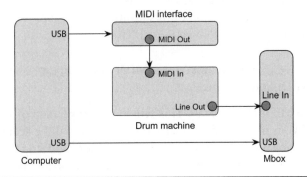

| FIGURE 9-3 | Connecting a drum machine to an Mbox Mini |

Figure 9-3 illustrates how a drum machine would be connected to a Pro Tools interface with no MIDI ports such as the Mbox Mini. In this case an external MIDI interface must be used.

Figure 9-4 illustrates how a drum machine would be connected to a Pro Tools interface with MIDI ports, such as the Digi 003.

Configuring AMS in Mac OS X

Mac OS X users will use Apple's AMS utility to configure their MIDI setup. AMS runs in the background and serves as the liaison between Pro Tools and any connected MIDI devices. Because it's not a Digidesign product, you won't find

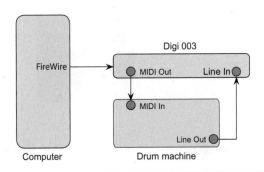

| FIGURE 9-4 | Connecting a drum machine to a Digi 003 |

much information about AMS in the Pro Tools documentation. The Mac Help Center provides a basic description of this utility, but it's so easy to use, you don't need a manual.

1. To open AMS, go to Setups > Edit MIDI Studio Setup. This opens the Audio MIDI Setup dialog.

2. Click the MIDI Devices tab. This window shows a map of your MIDI setup. If your interface is properly connected, it will be scanned by AMS and will show up in this window. Digi 003 users will find that AMS has already detected the interface's built-in MIDI ports, and is displaying its icon. Figure 9-5 shows an example of an Mbox system with a MOTU Micro Express USB interface.

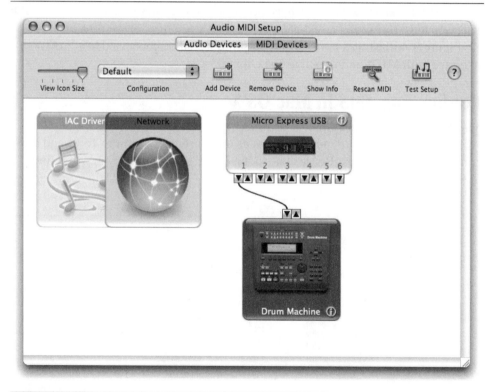

FIGURE 9-5   AMS Audio MIDI Setup window

3. Now you have to tell AMS which MIDI device you have and how it's connected. To do this, click Add Device.

4. The New Device icon appears. Drag this icon to a convenient spot within the window. Double-click the icon. In the window that appears, type in a name for your MIDI device. Choose or enter the name of the manufacturer and the model number for the device.

5. Click the More Information button. The window expands to show the MIDI channel assignments for the device.

6. Make sure the device is set to receive channel 1 (it doesn't matter which channel you use, as long as it's not already being used by another device). Click Apply and close the window.

7. The interface and device icons have triangular black arrows representing the input and output ports. To show how your MIDI cables are connected, simply click an interface port and drag to the appropriate MIDI device port. To disconnect, click a cable to select it and press DELETE. In the example shown in Figure 9-5, only one cable is connected because there is no need to send MIDI data from the drum machine back to the interface in this particular setup.

8. Close the Audio MIDI Setup window.

Conclusion

Congratulations on completing Chapter 9. Feel free to experiment further with the Click 2 session. (Hint: Try using the Reason Adapted's virtual mixer to put digital delay on the drums. The delays are automatically timed to match the tempo, and the delay settings change when the tempo changes.) Don't worry about mangling the session, you won't be needing it in the following chapters.

Part III

The Honeywagon Session

Chapter 10

Working with Loops

Pro Tools is the workstation of choice for many world-renowned artists who rely heavily on loops in their music. In this chapter, we will explore some of the looping features Pro Tools has to offer.

In the remaining chapters, we will simulate a demo session for a loop-based version of the traditional hymn "Wayfaring Stranger," as performed by the (imaginary) band Honeywagon. In this scenario, the group has provided you with some loops to provide the basic tracks for the song. We will import the loops and conform them to the desired tempo using the Time Compression/Expansion feature in Pro Tools.

Using Time Compression/Expansion

The capability to compress and expand audio is essential in situations where loops of various tempos must be made to work together. The files you'll be importing for the following exercises can be found on your audio drive in the Session Disc folder > Honeywagon folder.

1. You should have copied the Session Disc files to your audio drive in Chapter 6. If not, put in the Session Disc CD-ROM and copy the Honeywagon folder onto your audio drive.

2. Launch Pro Tools. The session you'll be using for this chapter is titled W.Stranger 1. You'll find it in the Honeywagon folder that now resides on your audio drive. The path is Honeywagon > Wayfaring Stranger > W.Stranger 1.

3. Double-click the W.Stranger 1 session to open it.

4. Because this session was not created on your computer, you're going to see the usual warning dialogs about the Disk Allocation, the I/O, and so forth. Ignore them, and keep pressing RETURN (ENTER) until the session opens. You'll need to resize the Edit window to make it fill the screen.

Importing Audio Files with the Workspace Window

You may have noticed that there are no tracks or audio in this session. That's because we're going to import everything we need from outside the session. There are a few different ways to import audio into Pro Tools. We'll start by using the *Workspace window*. Pro Tools can import a wide variety of audio files (a full list can be found in the *Reference Guide*) and allows you to convert them to the session's native file type. The conversion process creates a new file and allows you to put it in a folder of your choice. The default location is the Audio Files Folder for the current session, which is usually the best place for it.

1. Choose Window > Workspace (or press OPTION+; / ALT+;) to open the Workspace window.

2. Navigate to the Honeywagon folder on your audio drive and locate the V loop and C loop WAV files. These are the verse and chorus loops, respectively, for the session. You can audition the loops by clicking and holding on the speaker icons on the right side of the Workspace window.

3. To import these files, drag them from the Workspace window into an empty space in the Edit window. Pro Tools will create a stereo audio track for each loop. Close the Workspace window if it is still visible.

Setting Up the Session for Grid Mode

Before you can begin working with these files, you must first set up the session to work in Grid mode, and enter the correct tempo for the session.

1. Drag the files all the way to the session start.

2. Set the Track Height of these two stereo tracks to Large.

3. Drag the V loop track to the top of the Edit window, and mute the C loop.

4. The members of Honeywagon have determined that the tempo should be 70.19 bpm. Because we're not going to program any tempo changes, we will use Manual Tempo mode. Check in the Transport window's MIDI Controls section (Display > Transport Window Shows > MIDI Controls) to make sure the Conductor button is unlit, and the tempo is set to 70.19 in the Tempo field.

5. Make sure the Main counter is set to Bars:Beats.

6. Create a new mono audio track titled **Grid**, set its Track Height to Small, and drag it to the top of the Edit window. This track is just a visual reference to make it easier to see the gridlines when you're zoomed in.

7. Choose Grid mode (F4) and set the Grid pop-up to 1 bar.

8. Select the C loop audio region and press OPTION+F (ALT+F) to zoom in for a better look at the loops. If you've followed the steps correctly, your Edit window should look like Figure 10-1.

Tracks to Large height

Grid mode   1 Bar   Bars:Beats   Grid track

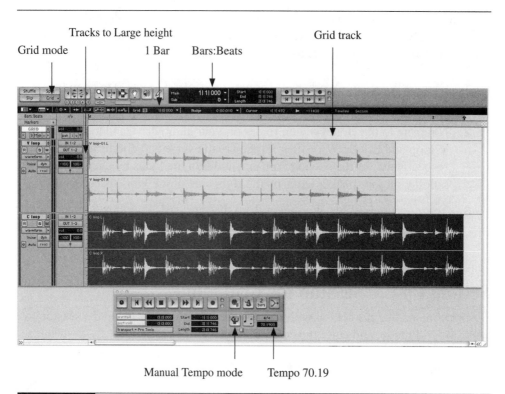

Manual Tempo mode   Tempo 70.19

FIGURE 10-1   Grid setup

The loops you have imported are both about two bars long. As you can see by comparing them to the gridlines, neither of these loops is at the desired tempo. The V loop is too fast and the C loop is too slow.

9. Select the V loop audio region with the Grabber and zoom in on the front of the loop, as shown in Figure 10-2.

10. Switch to Shuffle mode, and use the Trimmer (the regular one, not the Time Trimmer) to trim the loop as close as possible to the front of the first beat. Because you're in Shuffle mode, the region snaps to the session start, as shown in Figure 10-3.

Trim to here in Shuffle mode

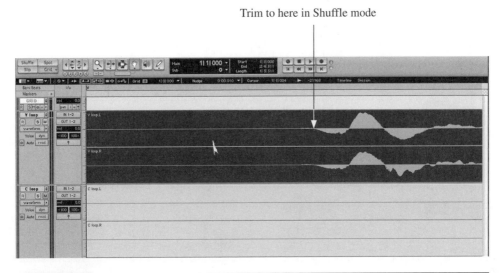

FIGURE 10-2   Zoom in on the front of the V loop

11. The V loop region has an extra kick drum beat at the end that must be trimmed off to shorten its duration to exactly two bars. Press the RIGHT ARROW key to go to the end of the V loop region, and zoom out slightly to see the beat, as shown in Figure 10-4.

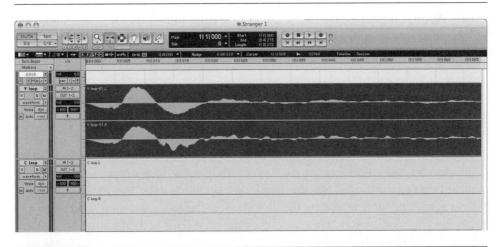

FIGURE 10-3   Trimming the front of the V loop

Trim off the extra beat

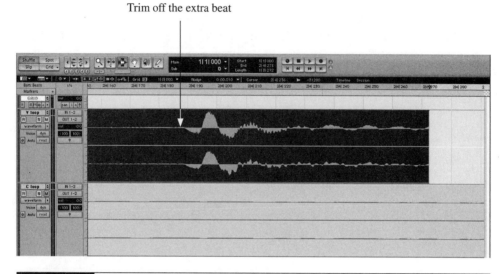

FIGURE 10-4   Trimming the end of the V loop

12. Go to Slip mode, click with the Selector at the front of the kick, and zoom in close.

13. Use the Trimmer to trim the end of the region back to a point right before the attack of the drum, as shown in Figure 10-4.

14. At this point, we have to use our ears to determine if this region sounds good as a loop. Go to Zoom preset 3, enable Loop Playback, and press Play to start the loop.

This is a critical point in the loop-making process. Turn up the speakers and listen closely to the loop, especially at the loop point. The rhythm should sound even and smooth across the loop point, with no pops. You should be able to close your eyes and listen, and not be able to hear any sort of tempo or groove variation. If it seems to rush or speed up at the loop crossover point, it means you've trimmed it too short and the loop needs to be lengthened. If you hear a pop or double attack on the kick drum at the loop crossover point, you haven't trimmed enough from the end of the loop. This is the foundation of the song, and it has to feel right.

15. Mute the V loop, unmute the C loop, and trim the beginning and end using Steps 9–14.

16. When you're satisfied with the loops, it's time to expand/compress them to make them play at the selected tempo. Save your session, and then save it again as **W.Stranger 2loop**.

17. Before we alter this loop, we should make a safety copy. Click the V loop track's Playlist pop-up and choose Duplicate.

18. Name the new playlist **V loop safety**, and press RETURN (ENTER).

19. Click the V loop safety track's Playlist pop-up again and choose V loop (1) to return to the original playlist. Now you can switch to the safety playlist whenever you want to hear the original loop. While you're at it, make a safety copy of the C loop track in the same way.

Time Shift vs. the TC/E Plug-in

Unlike pitch-shifting plug-ins, time compression/expansion plug-ins can change the length of a region without changing the pitch. At the time of this writing, Pro Tools systems include two different AudioSuite plug-ins that can accomplish this: the older TC/E (Time Compression/Expansion) plug-in and the newer and better-sounding Time Shift plug-in. I imagine the older TC/E plug-in will be phased out in future versions of Pro Tools.

It's worth mentioning that every time you compress or expand an audio file, some audio quality is lost; therefore, you should avoid processing a file more than once unless you're purposefully trying to grunge it up. If you make a mistake, select File > Undo and go back to the original file each time. The higher-end plug-ins like Digidesign's X-Form, Serato's Pitch'n Time, and Wave Mechanics' Speed do a much better job of keeping the audio pristine but, of course, you have to pay for them.

The Time Trimmer

The easiest way to compress and expand loops is via the *Time Trimmer*, which is a variation of the Trimmer. The Time Trimmer may be currently set to use the default Digidesign TC/E plug-in, but it can be configured to use Time Shift or third-party time compression/expansion plug-ins. Let's change the Preferences to specify Time Shift.

1. Go to Setup > Preferences > Processing, and select Time Shift from the TC/E Plug-in pop-up menu.

2. In the Default Settings pop-up, choose Drums Rhythmic to optimize Time Shift for the type of audio we will be processing, and then click OK.

3. To select the Time Trimmer, click the Trimmer tool icon in the toolbar and hold down the mouse button until the drop-down menu appears. Select TCE from the menu, and then release the mouse. The Trimmer icon changes to the Time Trimmer icon, which includes a clock symbol.

4. Select the C loop and zoom to fill the window (OPTION+F / ALT+F)

5. Select Grid mode.

6. Because both the V loop and the C loop are two bar loops, we want them both to end at the beginning of Bar 3. You can tell that the V loop is faster than the session tempo, because it's a two-bar loop and it doesn't quite extend to Bar 3. Use the Time Trimmer to stretch the V loop to the Bar 3 line. The region is automatically expanded to the correct tempo, using the Time Shift plug-in.

7. The C loop is slightly slower than the session tempo. Use the Time Trimmer to shorten (compress) the C loop to the Bar 3 line.

8. Save your session, and then save it again as **W.Stranger 3loop**.

The Time Trimmer can get you into a lot of trouble. Like any dangerous toy, you should put it away when you're not using it, to avoid accidentally mangling your audio files. Pressing F6 will cycle through the various Trimmer tools. Go back to the regular Trimmer before you break something.

Fine-Tuning Your Loops

You should now have a V loop and a C loop of equal length. To avoid clipping, turn both tracks down to about −4 dB and play both loops at the same time. If you have looped them correctly, they should sound fairly good together. You will probably notice that the drums in the V loop don't always hit precisely with the drums in the C loop. This double attack you're hearing is generally referred to as *flamming*. It's pretty rare that two rhythmic loops imported from different sources will match up perfectly without some tweaking. The loops will sound much better together when we get the drums hitting at the same time.

The C loop came from a drum machine, and the V loop was made from a live performance, therefore the C loop is more likely to line up with the grid. If you listen closely, you'll notice that the low hand drum at 1|2|480 on the V loop is flamming with the corresponding kick drum on the C loop.

In the following steps we'll move the hand drum slightly to tighten up the timing discrepancy.

1. Change the Grid pop-up to 1/16th note.

2. Click with the Selector at 1|2|480 and zoom in, as shown in Figure 10-5.

3. A visual comparison reveals that the hand drum is behind the kick drum on the C loop. Switch to Slip mode and select the hand drum hit (but not the drum hit directly after it).

4. Separate the selected region (use the B key with Commands Focus enabled).

5. Drag the newly separated region, so that the hand drum lines up with the C loop kick, as shown in Figure 10-6.

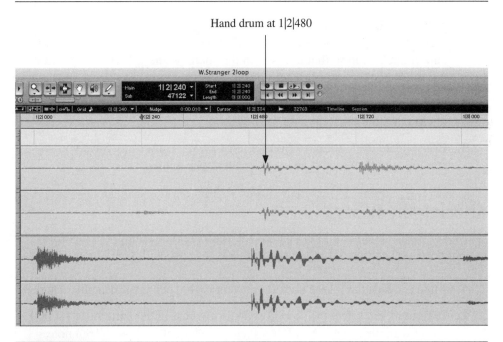

FIGURE 10-5   Fine-tuning the V loop

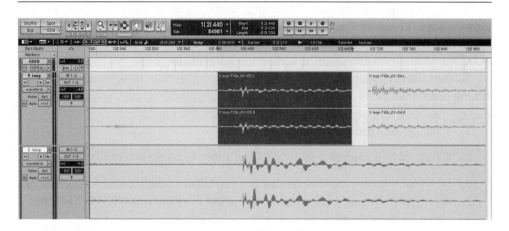

FIGURE 10-6 Lining up the hand drum with the C loop kick

6. Use the Smart tool Trimmer to close the gap in the audio, and then crossfade the transition points.

7. Solo the V loop to check your edit, and then listen to the two loops together. The two loops should sound tighter now. Fix the snare hit at the end of the V loop so that it hits with the snare on the C loop. Just be sure not to change the overall length of the loop.

8. When you're satisfied with the V loop, select the entire loop by triple-clicking within the loop with the Selector.

9. Consolidate the V loop (OPTION+SHIFT+3 / ALT+SHIFT+3). Save your session, and then save it again as **W.Stranger 4cons**.

Altering the Beat

Often, you will encounter a loop that has the right feel and sound, but the drum pattern needs to be altered. Let's suppose this is the case with the C loop.

1. Mute and hide the V loop track (to prevent it from being accidentally mangled).

2. In Grid mode, select the second snare drum beat in the pattern (at 1|4|000) along with the hi-hat beat after it (selecting a total of three 1/16th note sections), as shown in Figure 10-7. (Hint: when I ask you to make a

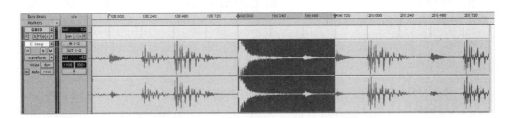

FIGURE 10-7   Selecting the snare and hi-hat

selection at a specific bar location, watch the Event Edit Area to the right of the Main Counter display while making the selection—it will tell you exactly which bars you are selecting.)

3. Copy the selected region.

4. Paste the copied region over the first snare beat in the pattern at 1|2|000.

5. Select and copy the first kick drum beat of the C loop and the hi-hat beat after it (a total of two 1/16th note segments), as shown in Figure 10-8.

6. Paste the region at 1|2|720.

7. Now listen to the entire C loop and note the difference between the first bar and the second.

FIGURE 10-8   Copying the first kick drum beat

8. Zoom out and use the Trimmer to trim off the entire second bar of the C loop (trim back to 2|1|000).

9. In Slip mode, crossfade the transition points between the regions (using very short crossfades), and consolidate the C loop.

10. Press ⌘+D (CTRL+D) to duplicate the loop.

11. Unhide and unmute the V loop track and listen to the combination of the two loops. If you followed the steps correctly, they should sound pretty good together.

12. Save the session, and then save it again as **W.Stranger 5cons**.

Checking Your Work

Because you're going to build an entire song using these loops as the foundation, it's important to make sure everything has been done correctly up to this point. In the Honeywagon folder, a session titled WS Tracks has been provided, which contains tracks that you'll be instructed to import into your session from time to time throughout the chapter. You'll place these tracks next to yours and compare them visually to make sure you've performed the steps correctly. If your tracks don't match the imported ones, you'll have to go back and repeat the steps to find out where you went wrong. Remember, you have safety copies of the original loops for just such an occasion. The imported tracks are mainly for visual reference—if you play them along with your edited tracks, there will inevitably be some "flanging" because of slight variations in timing.

Importing Tracks from Other Pro Tools Sessions

It's important to understand the difference between importing audio and importing tracks. Audio files can be imported from a variety of sources, but tracks can only be imported from other Pro Tools sessions. When you import a track from another session, the entire track arrives complete with all regions, edits, crossfades, automation, and plug-ins intact, unless you specify otherwise. If the session you're importing tracks from has the same session start time and contains the same song as the current session, the imported track will be in sync with the tracks in the current session, providing you have not offset the track when importing it. As you can imagine, this is a useful capability. If you want to clear unused tracks from a session, you can save the session under a new name, and then delete the unused tracks, secure in the knowledge that you can always import them from the old session if you ever need them again. Tracks are imported via the Workspace window.

1. Press OPTION+; (ALT+;) to open the Workspace window.

2. Find your audio drive and navigate to the Honeywagon > WS Tracks folder > WS Tracks session icon.

3. Drag the WS Tracks session icon into an empty white space in the lower right corner of the Edit window. The Import Session Data dialog appears.

4. Check the Track Offset Options field to make sure it is set to 1|1|000. If a different number appears in this field, the audio regions in the imported track will not be in sync with the current session.

5. In the lower half of this dialog, you can see a list of the imported session's tracks. Click the pop-up for the track titled VL-1 (Stereo Audio) and change it from (None) to New Track. Do the same for CL-1, and click OK to import the tracks. Ignore any disk allocation dialogs that may pop up.

6. Close the Workspace window.

Check these imported tracks against your own. If you have done the exercise correctly up to this point, the VL-1 track should match your V loop track, and the CL-1 track should match your C loop track. If there are noticeable differences, go back and try the exercise again using the safety copies of the original loops. When you're finished, select the VL-1 and CL-1 tracks, and delete them from your session (Track > DELETE). Then continue with the rest of the tutorial.

NOTE   *You can use this process to import any track from any session into another session.*

Setting Up the Song Structure

Because the V loop runs throughout the song, it will serve as our basic track after a few alterations.

1. To make navigation easier, song markers have been provided. Go to View > Rulers, and select both the Meter and Markers rulers for display.

2. Select Grid mode and set the Grid pop-up to 1 bar.

3. Select the V loop region and press OPTION+R (ALT+R) to bring up the Repeat dialog.

4. Type in **35** for the number of repeats, and click OK.

Adding a Two-Beat Rest

The song starts with an instrumental Intro, and the first two bars will serve as a countoff. The band wants the rhythm track to stop (rest) for two beats at the end of the Intro, so that the Intro melody can fade out before the verse starts. Because a bar is four beats long, we can't simply remove part of a bar. If we did, we'd be starting back up in the middle of the loop, instead of on the downbeat. The best solution is to insert a meter event at Bar 11, switching to 2/4 for one bar, and then change back to 4/4 for the rest of the song. (It'll make more sense once you've done it, I promise.)

1. Here is yet another way to bring up the Tempo/Meter Change dialog. Click the Add Meter Change button on the left side of the Meter ruler, as shown here:

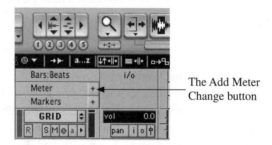

The Add Meter
Change button

2. Type **11|1|000** in the Location field and **2/4** in the Meter field(type a 2 in the top box to replace the default number 4), and then click OK.

3. Zoom in on the meter change shown in the Meter ruler at Bar 11. If you look closely at the gridlines, you can see that all the bars after the meter change are now only two beats long, but the audio remains unchanged.

4. Click the Add Meter Change button again and type **12|1|000** in the Location field and **4/4** in the Meter field, and then click OK. A glance at the Meter ruler shows that we're back to 4/4 at Verse 1.

We're not out of the woods yet, however. We still need to create a space for the stop. The V loop regions need to be moved over two beats to create a rest and to realign the loop with the grid.

Using the Extend Selection to End of Session Command

Quite often, you'll be working your way through a song chronologically from left to right, and find it necessary to select a region and all the regions after it to the end of the song. The Extend Selection to End of Session command provides an easy way to accomplish this. This useful command is easy to memorize, because the keys are right next to each other on most keyboards. You can invoke it with a well-placed Karate chop.

1. With the Grabber, select the V loop region at Bar 11.

2. Press OPTION+SHIFT+RETURN (CTRL+SHIFT+ENTER) to select all the regions that follow.

3. Drag the selected regions to the right until they snap to Bar 12.

The band wants the region at Bar 9 to stop a little early, so we need to shorten it with the Trimmer and put a kick drum beat at the stopping point.

4. Set the Grid pop-up to 1/16th note.

5. Trim the end of the region at Bar 9 back to 10|2|720 (watching the cursor display as you trim to the left).

6. Select and copy the kick drum beat at 9|1|720 (and the following sixteenth note), as shown in Figure 10-9, and paste it at 10|2|720.

7. We need to create another stop in the first chorus. Set the Grid pop-up to 1/2 note.

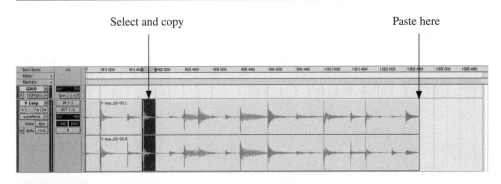

Select and copy   Paste here

FIGURE 10-9   Copying and pasting the kick

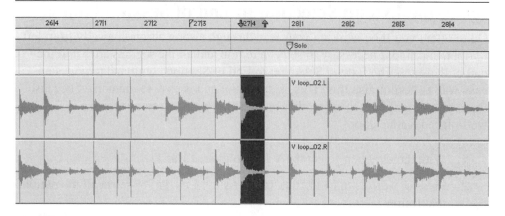

FIGURE 10-10   Copying the snare hit at Bar 27

8. Trim off the second half of Bar 23 and use the Smart tool in Slip mode to put a short fade at the end of it.

9. Go back to Grid mode.

10. At Bar 27, you need to create another stop with a snare accent. Set the Grid pop-up to 1/8 note.

11. Select and copy the last snare hit of Bar 27, selecting only a single 1/8 note, as shown in Figure 10-10.

12. Change the Grid pop-up to 1/16th note and trim Bar 27 back to 27|3|000.

13. Paste the snare hit at 27|3|000 and use the Smart tool in Slip mode to fade the end of the pasted snare.

Chorus 2 is similar to Chorus 1, so we'll copy Chorus 1 and paste it to save the trouble of trimming and crossfading the stops again.

1. Go back to Grid mode and change the Grid pop-up to 1 bar. Zoom out so you can see Chorus 1 and Chorus 2.

2. We're going to use the Memory Locations window to select and copy sections of the V loop. To do this, you must first click with the Selector anywhere in the V loop track, and then press ⌘+5 (CTRL+5) on the numeric keypad to bring up the Memory Locations window. (On Windows machines, the NUM LOCK key on the numeric keypad must be engaged for this to work.)

Laptop users without numeric keypads can select Memory Locations from the Window menu.

3. In the Memory Locations window, click Chorus 1, and then SHIFT+click on Solo to select all the regions in the first chorus.

4. Copy the selected regions, and then click the Chorus 2 memory location and paste the chorus regions.

5. Chorus 2 is a little different from Chorus 1—the stop needs to be moved to make room for a repeat of the last vocal line in the song. Select and copy the last two bars of Chorus 2 (from Bar 46 to Bar 48).

6. Click on Bar 48 with the Selector and paste the two bars.

7. Zoom in and select the two-bar region between Bar 44 and Bar 46.

8. Press ⌘+D (CTRL+D) to duplicate the region and remove the stop.

9. Set the Grid pop-up to 1/16 note.

10. Scroll to Bar 57 and trim it back to 57|2|240.

11. Use the Smart tool in Slip mode to put a short fade at the end of the trimmed region.

12. This is the end of the song, so select and delete the audio after Bar 58 using the Extend Selection to End of Session command—OPTION+SHIFT+RETURN (CTRL+SHIFT+ENTER).

By now, you've probably figured out that it pays to get your loops and fades absolutely correct before you copy and paste them into other parts of the song. It makes for a lot less work in the long run. Hang in there, you're almost through with the V loop track. You just need to import a track to check your work. Your V loop track has to match the imported track perfectly, because it's the foundation for the lessons that follow.

13. Press OPTION+; (ALT+;) to open the Workspace window, and import the track titled VL-2 from the WS Tracks session in the Honeywagon folder as before to check to make sure everything is in the right place.

14. Select and delete the VL-2 track from your session when you're done (File > Delete Selected Tracks).

15. Triple-click with the Selector in the V loop track to select all the audio, and press ⌘+L (CTRL+L) to lock all the regions in the track.

16. Save your session, and then save it again as **W.Stranger 6vloop**.

Moving On to the Chorus Loop

Now that we have the song structure mapped out, we can work on the choruses, where we will be adding the C loop for a different feel.

1. In Grid mode, select the two C loop regions at the song start and copy them. While the regions are still selected, press ⌘+M (CTRL+M) to mute them.

2. Click Chorus 1 in the Memory Locations window and paste the C loop regions at the Chorus 1 marker.

3. Press ⌘+D (CTRL+D) to duplicate the two-bar region. The results should appear as shown in Figure 10-11.

4. Press ⌘+D (CTRL+D) twice more for a total of eight bars of C loop, spanning the length of Chorus 1.

5. Select the fourth C loop region at Bar 23 and trim the end of it back to 23|3|000 to match the stop on the V loop track.

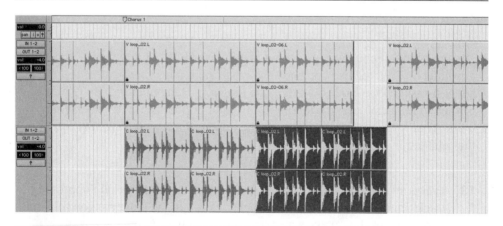

FIGURE 10-11   Pasting the C loop into Chorus 1

6. In Slip mode, put a short fade out on the end of the trimmed region, and then return to Grid mode.

7. We need some accented kick drum beats at the end of Chorus 1. Make a selection in the last C loop region from 27|1|720 to 27|2|720.

8. Switch to Shuffle mode and delete the selection. Then switch back to Grid mode.

9. Listen to the end of Chorus 1. You'll hear a couple of extra hi-hat beats. Trim them off and fade the end of the region. The first chorus is now complete, and should appear as shown in Figure 10-12.

10. In Grid mode, select the entire eight bars of the first chorus on the C loop track and copy them.

11. Click the Chorus 2 memory location and paste the regions.

12. Set the Grid pop-up to 1 bar.

13. Select and copy the second group of regions in the chorus (after the stop), as shown in Figure 10-13.

14. Paste the regions at Bar 46.

15. Paste the regions again at Bar 50, Bar 52, and Bar 54.

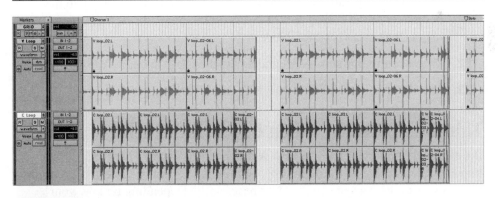

FIGURE 10-12   Chorus 1 is now complete

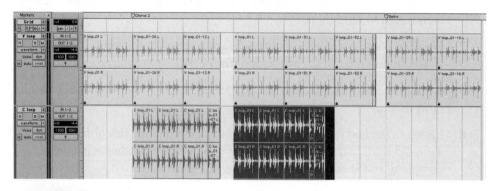

FIGURE 10-13 Selecting the regions after the stop

16. Set the Grid pop-up to 1/16 note.

17. Select and delete the snare hit at 57|3|000.

18. In Slip mode, fade the end of the last kick beat to get rid of the hi-hat.

19. Delete the C loop regions from Bar 58 on.

20. Select and lock all the regions in the C loop (⌘+L / CTRL+L).

21. Import CL-2 from the WS Tracks session and compare it to your C loop track. Make sure all the regions and edits match. If not, go back to the beginning of the C loop part of the exercise and go through the steps again using CL-2 as a visual reference.

22. When you're through, select and delete the CL-2 track.

23. Save the session, and then save it again as **W.Stranger 7Cloop**.

Things to Consider When Importing Tracks

It's extremely important for you to understand exactly what's happening when you import audio tracks. Are the audio files on these tracks being copied to the Audio Files Folder of the current session? Not necessarily. Depending on how your Preferences and Audio Media Options are configured, Pro Tools may be simply referencing them from wherever they happen to be.

Here's what this means to you: if you're importing files or tracks from your buddy's hard drive into a session on your hard drive, you'll want to make sure those files are copied to the Audio Files Folder on your drive, so they'll be available to your session after your buddy takes his or her drive home. Otherwise, the next time you open your session, the "borrowed" files will appear as grayed-out *ghost regions*—editable, but not playable. You'll be on the phone, yelling, "Bring that drive back over here!"

The first time this happened to me, I was not a happy camper. By the time I figured out what had happened, the drive I had imported the tracks from had been erased. This is why I don't like having elements of a session scattered about. I want every sound file associated with a session kept in the Audio Files Folder for that session and, believe me, so do you.

Before I explain how to avoid this scenario, let me put another happy little thought into your head. Suppose you import a track from a session on your buddy's hard drive, and then decide to record something on that track, or perform some sort of file-based process on the audio—consolidation, time compression/expansion, duplication, or the like (using AudioSuite plug-ins, for example). Where do you think those new audio files are going to end up? On your buddy's hard drive, not yours!

That's because the tracks you import will retain their original disk allocation unless you change the disk allocation for that track after importing it. To change a track's disk allocation, go to Setup > Disk Allocation, scroll down to the track in question, and choose your own disk from the pop-up menu for that track. Many coffee mugs have been hurled across the room as a result of lack of attention to these details.

The Automatically Copy Files on Import Preference

Go to Setup > Preferences > Processing and find the Automatically Copy Files on Import Preference. This Preference is disabled by default. When it's enabled, any files you import by dragging and dropping will be copied to the Audio Files Folder for the current session. If you're adding loops and samples from other sessions that you want to keep, this Preference will ensure that they are all copied to your hard drive. Leave it unchecked for now.

The Import Sessions Data Dialog

This dialog should be familiar to you by now. It's the one you see when importing tracks from another session. The Audio Media Options pop-up in this dialog is where you specify how imported data is handled. Let's take a closer look.

1. Press OPTION+; (ALT+;) to open the Workspace window.

2. Locate the WS Tracks session icon and drag it into the Edit window, as if you were going to import a track. The Import Session Data dialog appears.

In this dialog, click the Audio Media Options pop-up. There, you will find four options for handling imported media. The following is an explanation of each option:

- **Link to source media (where possible)**   This is the default option. Imported files will not be copied if this option is selected. (This option is grayed out when the Automatically Copy Files on Import Preference is enabled. It's also grayed out when importing from sessions whose bit depth and sample rate do not match the current session, or when importing from unsupported playback media such as CDs or DVDs.)

- **Copy from source media**   This is the default setting if Automatically Copy Files on Import is enabled in the Preferences. With this option, you're going to be copying all the audio associated with the imported track. Therefore, if you're importing a track that was heavily edited and comped from several performances, you could be copying a lot of unused audio. This option also automatically converts imported files to the correct format for the current session, if necessary.

- **Consolidate from source media**   If you don't want to copy unused audio, this option will automatically consolidate the track while it's being copied, while converting the files to the correct format for the current session, if necessary.

- **Force to target session format**   This option only copies files that don't match the current session's file format. Files that do match aren't copied. This option is grayed out when the Automatically Copy Files on Import Preference is enabled.

NOTE   *Personally, I prefer to enable the Automatically Copy Files on Import Preference and use either the second or third option in the preceding list. You can also manually copy files when importing by OPTION+dragging (ALT+dragging) them from the Workspace window and dropping them in the Edit window.*

3. Close the Import Session Data dialog and close the Workspace window.

Beefing Up the Drums

After listening to the drum loop track, the band has decided that the kick and snare aren't punchy enough, so they have given you the following directive:

"Make it rock, dude." One way to beef up the drum sound is to import drum samples and fly them in.

Using the Import Audio to Track Command

We could use the Workspace browser to import the samples but, this time, we're going to do it a different way, using the Import Audio to Track command. This command enables you to import sound files in a variety of formats. Pro Tools converts the files to the current session's file format (if necessary) and places them on a track.

1. Go to File > Import > Audio. The Import Audio dialog appears.

2. Navigate to the Honeywagon folder and choose the kick drum sample titled K Smp.

The dialog tells you that the sample is a 16-bit, 44.1 kHz WAV file, and that it can be added directly to the session (which is the same sample rate and bit depth). You can audition the sample by clicking the triangular Play button.

3. Click Add. The file shows up in the Regions to Import window.

4. Choose the snare drum sample titled Sn Smp and add it as well.

5. Click Done to close this dialog, and the Audio Import Options dialog appears, asking whether you want to place the file on a new track or put it in the Regions list. Leave it at the New Track default and click OK.

6. Go to Zoom preset 3 and rewind to the session start. As promised, the samples appear in your session, each on its own track.

7. Mute the Sn Smp track and hide the C loop and Grid tracks.

Flying In the Kick Sample

In this exercise, you will paste the newly imported kick drum sample onto a new track and align it with the kick drum in the V loop.

1. Turn the K Smp track's volume down to about −10 dB, and set the Track Height to Medium.

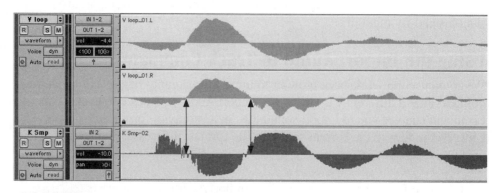

FIGURE 10-14 Align the zero crossing points as much as possible

2. Zoom in, and then trim the front of the kick sample in Shuffle mode, so the waveform's zero crossing points line up with the ones on the V loop kick, as shown in Figure 10-14.

3. Return to Slip mode.

Phase Cancellation

In comparing the waveforms of these two kick drums, you can see that the V loop kick's waveform begins in a downward direction, while the kick sample's waveform begins in an upward direction. This tells you that these two kick drums are "out of phase" with each other. When two similar, out-of-phase waveforms are combined, they have a tendency to cancel each other out. This phenomenon is known as *phase cancellation*. Think of it this way: the waveforms are pulling in different directions like a tug of war. Compare the sound of the first kick on the V loop with and without the sample. Now you know what phase cancellation sounds like. If your kick sample is aligned as shown in Figure 10-14, the kick sample will partially cancel out the V loop kick, resulting in a mushy kick sound—exactly the opposite of what you are trying to accomplish. It's one of the risks of combining drum sounds. You hope that the combination of two drum sounds will result in a bigger sound, but you have to keep an eye (and an ear) out for phase cancellation. We can fix this by inverting, or *flipping*, the phase of kick sample.

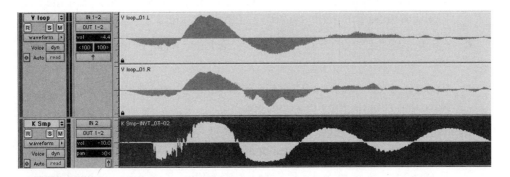

FIGURE 10-15   Inverting the phase of the kick sample

4. Select the K Smp region, go to AudioSuite > Other > Invert, and click the Process button to flip the phase.

5. Close the plug-in window. The kick sample should now appear as shown in Figure 10-15, with the peaks and valleys of the waveform aligned.

> Now, listen to the first beat of the V loop with and without the sample. The addition of the in-phase sample should result in a punchier kick drum sound.

6. Copy the kick drum sample.

The Tab to Transients Option

When the Tab to Transients option is enabled, the Tab button moves the cursor to the next transient peak in the waveform. This is handy for the present task, as it takes us to the next drum hit without zooming or scrolling.

1. Click the Tab to Transients button, as shown here. Note that the button lights up when selected.

The Tab to Transients button

2. Go to Zoom preset 4 and switch to Slip mode.

3. With the Selector, click to place the cursor in the V loop track after the first kick and press TAB until you arrive at the next kick.

4. Click with the Selector in the K Smp track and paste in the sample at that location.

5. Zoom in a few more clicks and line the sample up with the V loop kick. Save that zoom setting to Zoom preset 5.

6. With the Selector, click in the V loop track again and press TAB until you arrive at the hand drum located at approximately 1|3|480.

7. Paste a kick sample in the K Smp track and line it up with the hand drum, as shown here:

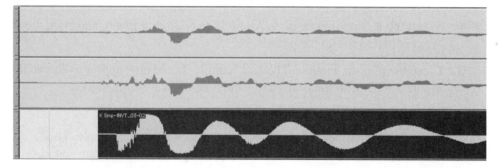

8. Click with the Selector in the V loop track, press TAB to go to the next kick (at Bar 2), and paste in another sample on the K Smp track, aligning it as usual.

9. Click with the Selector in the V loop track, press TAB to go to the next kick (at approximately 2|1|740), and paste in another sample on the K Smp track, aligning it as usual.

10. Click with the Selector in the V loop track, press TAB to go to the hand drum at approximately 2|3|480, and paste a kick sample.

11. The hand drum at this spot is out of phase with the kick sample. Use the Invert plug-in as before (choose AudioSuite > Other > Invert, click the Process button, and close the plug-in window) to flip the phase of the kick sample and line it up with the hand drum.

12. Zoom out until you can see the entire V loop region, as shown in Figure 10-16. There should be a total of six kick samples pasted into the K Smp track.

13. Save your session.

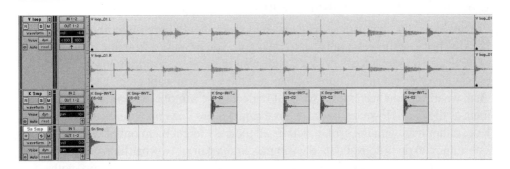

There should be six kick samples pasted with the V loop region.

Flying In the Snare Sample

Now we'll use the snare sample to add impact to the snare hits in the V loop.

1. Rewind to the session start and unmute the Sn Smp track.

2. Turn the track's volume down to about −5 and drag it upward to place it beneath the V loop track.

3. In Slip mode, drag the snare sample to align it with the first snare hit on the V loop (approx. 1|4|000) and line it up with the V loop snare, as shown here:

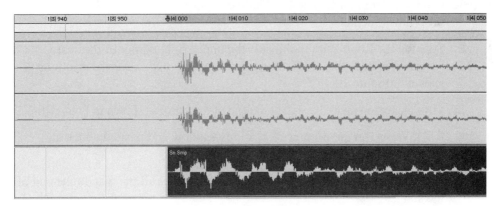

4. Copy the sample and paste it at the next snare hit on the V loop track.

5. Save your session.

Consolidate the Sample Regions

Listen to your two-bar pattern. The kick and snare should have more impact now. Luckily, because this session is based on a grid, you are saved from the tedious task of pasting in a sample for every kick and snare in the song. Working in Grid mode usually involves getting a couple of bars just the way you want them, and then pasting them wherever you need them. We could select these samples in Grid mode and paste them as they are. However, because these samples are lined up with the drums in the loop, rather than with the grid, it will be all too easy to get them out of whack. The safest thing to do is consolidate the samples into a pair of two-bar loops. The resulting regions will be exactly two bars long, which will make them easier to work with.

1. Select the K Smp and Sn Smp tracks and group them (⌘+G / CTRL+G), naming the group **Smp**.

2. In Grid mode, select the two bars you've been working on and consolidate them (OPTION+SHIFT+3 / ALT+SHIFT+3).

3. Copy the consolidated kick and snare regions.

Use the Loop Trim Tool to Extend the Sample Loops

The Loop Trim tool is a variation of the Trimmer. To see how it works, we'll use it to extend our sample loops instead of using the Repeat command.

1. Click the Trimmer icon and select the Loop Trim tool from the drop-down menu.

2. Position the Loop Trim tool inside the upper-right corner of the snare sample region so that the Trimmer icon appears with a curved arrow, as shown in Figure 10-17.

3. Trim the region up to the stop at the end of the Intro, as shown in Figure 10-17.

4. Click Verse 1 in the Memory Locations window and paste the kick and snare loops.

5. Use the Loop Trim tool as before to trim the loops all the way to the end of the song.

6. Unhide the C loop track and turn it down to −6.

7. We don't need the sample tracks where the C loop is playing, and we also need to clear them out of the stops. Click with the Selector anywhere in one of the sample tracks.

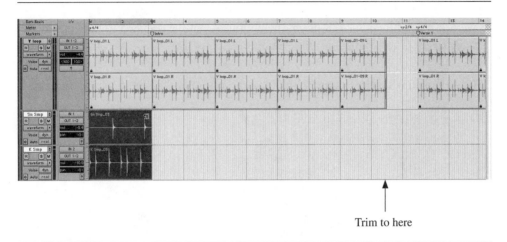

Trim to here

FIGURE 10-17   Using the Loop Trim tool

8. Click Chorus 1 in the Memory Locations window, and then SHIFT+click Solo to select the sample tracks in the first chorus. Delete the selected audio.

9. Click Chorus 2 and SHIFT+click in one of the sample tracks in the space after the end of the song. Delete that audio as well. Your Edit window should now look like the one shown in Figure 10-18. Save the session.

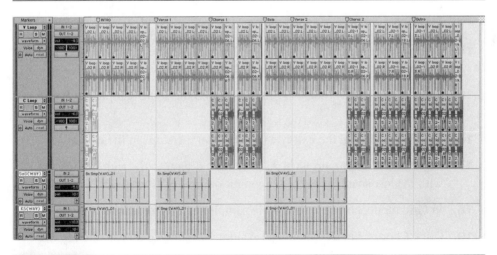

FIGURE 10-18   Your completed chorus loops should look like this

We don't need the kick sample in the choruses, but we do need to beef up the snare in the C loop with the snare sample.

10. Open the Tracks list and click the Smp group to disable it, as shown here:

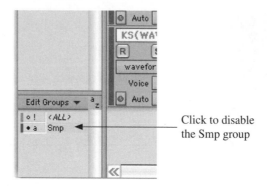

Click to disable
the Smp group

11. Copy the first snare sample on the Sn Smp track (at 1|4|000).

12. Paste the snare samples at the two snare hits in the first bar of Chorus 1. Zoom in and line them up with the C loop snare in Slip mode.

NOTE   *The snare hits in the C loop have a lot of noise mixed in, which makes it harder to determine the phase visually. Just use your ears and place the snare where it sounds best.*

13. Set the Grid pop-up to 1 bar.

14. In Grid mode, select the first bar of Chorus 1 on the snare sample track and consolidate it (OPTION+SHIFT+3 / ALT+SHIFT+3).

15. Press ⌘+D (CTRL+D) seven times to extend the snare sample track to the end of the chorus.

16. In Slip mode, trim the extra snare hits from the stops in the chorus.

17. Separate the snare sample at 27|2|000 and drag it to the right to line it up with the last snare hit in the C loop (at the end of Chorus 1).

18. In Grid mode, copy the first snare sample region from Chorus 1.

19. Click Chorus 2 in the Memory Locations window and paste the region.

20. Press OPTION+R (ALT+R) to bring up the Repeat dialog, enter 16 repeats, and then click OK or press RETURN (ENTER).

21. Set the Grid pop-up to 1/8 note and clear the snare samples from the stops in the remainder of the song.

22. In Slip mode, drag the snare sample at 49|2|000 to the right to line it up with the C loop snare at 49|3|000.

23. Import KS-1 and SS-1 from the WS Tracks session and compare them to your drum sample tracks. Make sure all the regions and edits match. If they do not, go back through the steps to find out where you went wrong, using these tracks as a visual reference.

24. When you're through, delete the KS-1 and SS-1 tracks from the session.

25. Save the session, and then save it again as **W.Stranger 8smp**.

Submixing the Drums

Now that we have a few loops going, we are in danger of overloading the stereo bus. Even if it's not clipping now, we still need to alter the gain structure (in other words, turn some stuff down) to make room for the other instruments that will be added later. The best solution is to create a submix by bussing the drums to a stereo aux channel. This will enable us to adjust the overall drum level with a single fader.

1. Make sure the Grid track is hidden and only the four audio tracks are showing.

2. Holding down the OPTION (ALT) key, change all the Track Heights to Medium and assign their outputs to Bus 1-2 (Stereo).

3. Create a new stereo aux input track labeled **Drum Bus**. To avoid confusion, it will now be referred to as an aux channel instead of a track, because it contains no audio.

4. Set the Drum Bus channel's Height to Medium and assign the inputs to Bus 1-2 (Stereo).

As you learned earlier, aux returns should always be put in Solo Safe, so they won't be muted when other tracks are soloed.

5. ⌘+click (CTRL+click) on the Drum Bus aux channel's Solo button. It becomes grayed out to show that it has been put in Solo Safe. The following flow chart shows the signal flow for the current setup:

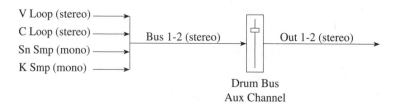

Fine-Tuning Volume Levels in the Mix Window

You have, no doubt, discovered how difficult it is to set volume levels at a precise value in the Edit window. It's a little easier in the Mix window, where all the faders are showing and volume levels can be adjusted in .1 dB increments by holding down ⌘ (CTRL) while adjusting the fader.

1. Press ⌘+= (CTRL+=) to toggle to the Mix window. Resize the window, if necessary, so that you can see all the faders.

2. Set the volume levels of the four drum tracks using the following table:

V loop	−4
C loop	−6
Sn Smp	−5
K Smp	−16

TIP

Move the fader close to the desired value, and then press ⌘ (CTRL) for finer control.

Play back the mix and listen to the balance. The kick drum in the verse is too loud and boxy sounding, and the V loop is the culprit. We need to make the kick drum quieter without changing the overall level of the loop. One simple way to do this is to use the EQ plug-in to reduce the bass frequencies in the V loop.

3. If it's not already showing, enable the Inserts view (View > Mix Window Shows > Inserts).

4. Insert the EQ 3 plug-in on the V loop track—Multi-Mono Plug-In > EQ > 1-Band EQ 3 (Mono)—and set the parameters as follows:

Input	0.0 dB
Type	Peak
Q	1.3
Frequency	100 Hz
Gain	−6 dB

The verse sounds better now, but that tinny little snare drum in the C loop is starting to drive everyone in the band nuts. We can't fix this by EQing the loop, but we can do some volume rides to lower the offending snare hits.

5. Close the EQ 3 plug-in window.

6. Switch to the Edit window (⌘+= / CTRL+=).

7. Change the C loop's Track Height to Jumbo and change the Track View selector to Volume.

8. Click Chorus 1 in the Memory Locations window.

9. In Slip mode, zoom in on the first C loop snare beat in Chorus 1.

10. With the Grabber, place three break points—two before the snare hit, and one before the following hi-hat beat, as shown here:

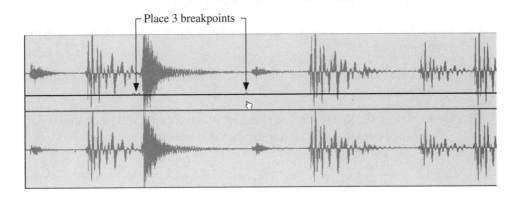

11. Holding down the SHIFT key to keep the breakpoint on a vertical axis, and ⌘ (CTRL) for finer control, pull the middle breakpoint down to about −10, as shown here:

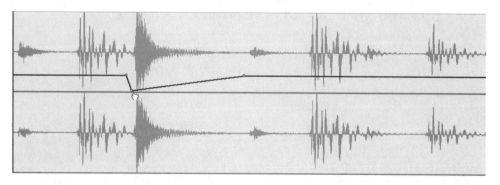

12. Use the Selector to select and copy the volume automation data, and then paste it over the next snare hit in the C loop.

13. Go to Grid mode and change the Grid pop-up to 1/2 note.

14. Zoom out and select the volume data over the entire bar, as shown here:

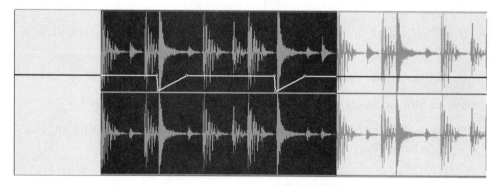

15. Press ⌘+D (CTRL+D) six times to paste the volume data over the rest of the snare hits.

16. Change the Nudge pop-up to Min:Secs, and then click the pop-up again and set the Nudge value to 10 msec.

17. Go to Slip mode, locate the last snare hit in the chorus, and paste the volume data over it, nudging it into place if necessary.

18. Go back to Grid mode and zoom out to view the entire chorus.

19. Select and copy the automation data for Chorus 1.

20. In the Memory Locations window, click Chorus 2 and paste the automation data.

21. Select and copy the automation data between Bar 45 and Bar 48, and paste it at Bar 47.

22. Select and copy the automation data across the first seven bars of Chorus 2.

23. Paste the data at Bar 50. Save your session.

Now that the C loop snare drum is taken care of, one problem remains: the V loop needs to be turned down in the choruses to make room for the C loop.

24. Change the V loop's Track Height to Jumbo and change its Track View selector to Volume.

25. Click with the Selector anywhere on the V loop track, and then click on Chorus 1 in the Memory Locations window.

26. SHIFT+click on Solo in the Memory Locations window to select the entire chorus on the V loop track.

27. Use the Trimmer to pull down the volume to −8 dB (when you get close to −8, press ⌘ [CTRL] for finer control). The result should appear as shown here:

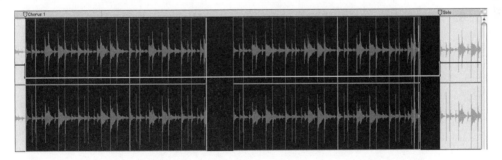

28. Select and copy the volume automation and paste it at the beginning of Chorus 2.

29. Select and delete the last two automation breakpoints, so that the volume will stay at −8 dB for the rest of the song.

30. Return all the tracks to Medium height.

31. Save the session.

Adding the Shaker Track

Now that the drum loops are arranged, we have one more concern: there is no timing reference during the stops in the song. A stop that lasts for a full measure will often cause musicians to come in early or late when the song resumes; therefore, we need a sound that will play through the stops to keep the musicians on track.

1. Import the Shaker track from the WS tracks session in the Honeywagon folder.

2. Set the output of the Shaker track to Bus 1-2 (Stereo) to add it to the drum submix.

3. In Grid mode, use the Grabber to select the Shaker audio region.

4. Press OPTION+R (ALT+R) to bring up the Repeat dialog, enter 54 repeats, and press RETURN (ENTER) to close the dialog.

5. Select the shaker region at Bar 11 and press OPTION+SHIFT+RETURN (ALT+SHIFT+ENTER) to select the remaining regions.

6. Copy the regions and paste them at Bar 12.

7. Hide the Shaker track.

8. Save the session, and then save it again as **W.Stranger 9shkr**.

Congratulations! Your basic track is now finished and ready for overdubbing.

Chapter 11

Bring on the Band

I n this chapter, you will learn how to set up multiple headphone mixes for a tracking session. While this scenario normally requires the use of a Pro Tools system with more than two outputs, this exercise can be done on a stereo-only Pro Tools system such as an Mbox. Later on you'll do some editing on the guitar and shaker tracks and learn how to work with MIDI files.

Setting Up a Cue Mix

Now that the rhythm loops are complete, it's time to bring in the remaining members of Honeywagon for overdubbing (the drummer was fired a while back). The band members have reluctantly agreed to occupy the same room long enough to put down their parts as a group. While lead singer (Medusa) would prefer to remain in rehab until the other tracks are finished, you have convinced her that her presence is essential for the vibe of the session (in other words, the other band members are unlikely to make it through the song without her vocal cues).

To keep everybody happy, you need to set up four cue (headphone) mixes for the musicians: Lars (bass), Jimbo (acoustic guitar), Otis (steel guitar), and Medusa (lead vocal). Luckily, you had the foresight to spring for the Digi 002, whose multiple outputs make this scenario possible (unlike the guy next door with the Mbox). While it's true that you could just feed everybody the same stereo mix you're listening to in the control room, you know from experience that if you do, everyone will be griping about the headphone mix (turn me up!). In addition, you know that Medusa and Jimbo refuse to listen to each other ever since the divorce.

At this point, there should be six audio tracks and one aux channel in the session titled W.Stranger 9shkr:

- Grid

- V loop

- C loop

- K Smp

- Sn Smp

- Drum Bus

- Shaker

Using the Tracks List Pop-Up Menu

The Tracks list pop-up menu has many handy shortcuts for showing and hiding groups of tracks.

1. Open the Tracks list and click the Tracks list pop-up, as shown here:

2. Choose Hide All Tracks from the pop-up menu that appears, and close the Tracks list.

3. Make sure the I/O view and the Sends A-E view are enabled, and the Inserts view is disabled.

4. Import these four tracks from the WS Tracks session in the Honeywagon folder:

- Lars.bass

- Jimbo.gtr

- Otis.steel

- Medusa.voc

5. Set their Track Heights to Medium.

NOTE *Owners of one- or two-channel interfaces like the Mbox should skip the next step*

6. Holding the ⌘+OPTION keys (CTRL+ALT), set the input of the Bass track to IN 1. Note that the inputs of the remaining tracks are automatically numbered sequentially (hidden tracks are not affected). This trick works for the outputs, too. It's a real godsend for those live 48-track HD recordings. For this session, however, we want to leave the outputs at the default setting of OUT 1-2.

Assigning the Sends

Pro Tools provides a total of ten sends in two separate views: A through E and F through J. This makes it is possible to have ten separate headphone mixes. In our example, each headphone mix will be sent to an output on the Digi 002. Because we are already using OUT 1-2 for the main mix, the headphone mixes will be assigned as follows:

Lars.bass	a (Output 3)
Jimbo.gtr	b (Output 4)
Otis.steel	c (Output 5)
Medusa.voc	d (Output 6)

The flow chart in Figure 11-1 shows how the signals would be routed to and from the Digi 002 interface in our imaginary session.

Because you probably don't really have four headphone amps and four sets of headphones hooked up to a Digi 002, you're going to have to use your imagination a bit. Instead of routing the headphone mixes to Outputs 3 through 6, we're going to route them to *busses* 3 through 6 so that we can listen to the cue mixes in the stereo bus.

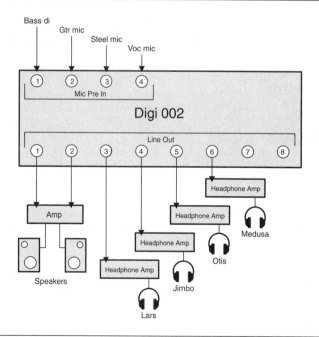

FIGURE 11-1   Cue mix flow chart

Pre- and Post-Fader Sends

The aux sends on most modern recording consoles feature switches for pre- and post-fader operation. This switch determines whether the aux send is inserted *before* or *after* the fader in the signal chain.

Post-Fader Operation

When using aux sends for effects such as reverb, the send is normally inserted post-fader (after the fader). As the fader is turned up or down, the volume of the reverb changes with it, maintaining the ratio of reverb to dry signal. When the track is muted, you hear no reverb at all.

The aux sends we used earlier with D-Verb were post-fader, which is the default setting. The flow chart in Figure 11-2 illustrates this configuration.

Pre-Fader Operation

When using sends for headphone cue mixes, the post-fader configuration is undesirable. You need to be able to adjust levels in the main mix without affecting

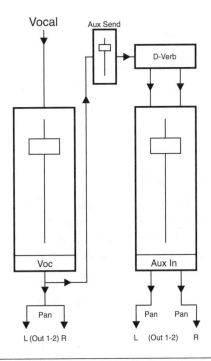

FIGURE 11-2 Post-fader effect send

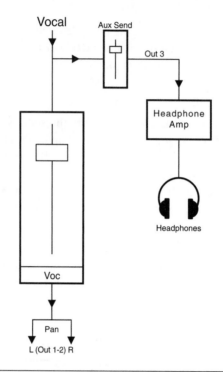

FIGURE 11-3　Pre-fader cue send

the artist's headphone mix. To accomplish this, the sends are set to pre-fader, in which case the send is inserted *before* the fader in the signal path, as shown in Figure 11-3.

1. Unhide the Drum Bus channel.

2. OPTION+click (ALT+click) the first send on the Drum Bus channel (Send selector A) and assign it to Bus 3 (Mono). (Busses 1 and 2 are already in use.) Note that a send assigned to Bus 3 appears on each visible track in the Edit window. This will be Lars's headphone mix.

3. This action brings up the Send window for the Drum Bus channel. OPTION+click (ALT+click) on the Pre button to set all the Bus 3 sends to pre-fader.

4. OPTION+click (ALT+click) the second send on the Drum Bus channel (Send selector B) and assign it to Bus 4. This will be Jimbo's headphone mix.

5. OPTION+click (ALT+click) the Pre button in this Send window to set all the Bus 4 sends to pre-fader.

6. OPTION+click (ALT+click) the third send on the Drum Bus channel (Send selector C) and assign it to Bus 5. This will be Otis's headphone mix.

7. OPTION+click (ALT+click) the Pre button in this Send window to set all the Bus 5 sends to pre-fader.

8. OPTION+click (ALT+click) the fourth send on the Drum Bus channel (Send selector D) and assign it to Bus 6. This will be Medusa's headphone mix.

9. OPTION+click (ALT+click) the Pre button in this Send window to set all the Bus 6 sends to pre-fader and close the Send window.

Relabeling the Send I/O

To keep confusion to a minimum once the session starts, let's relabel the busses with the musicians' names.

1. Go to Setup > I/O > Bus.

2. Before you change anything, a good idea is to save your current I/O settings. Click the Export Settings button and save the settings as Normal. This will save your settings to a folder on your startup drive.

3. Click the Expand/Collapse triangle next to Bus 3–4 (on Windows systems, it's a square box with a + sign) to reveal the mono Bus 3 and Bus 4 subpaths. Do the same for Bus 5–6.

4. The Bus 3 mono send is Lars's headphone mix, so double-click the Bus 3 label and rename it **Lars**. Press the TAB key and change Bus 4 to **Jimbo**. Tab down to Bus 5 mono and change it to **Otis**, and then change Bus 6 to **Medusa**.

5. Click the Export Settings button again and save these settings as **Honeywagon Cue Mix**. Click OK to close the dialog.

6. Your Sends view should appear as shown in Figure 11-4. Save the session.

In a real-life tracking setup with live musicians, there would be no audio on the players' tracks yet. The tracks would be in Record-Ready and the musicians would be playing together and telling you what they want to hear in their headphones.

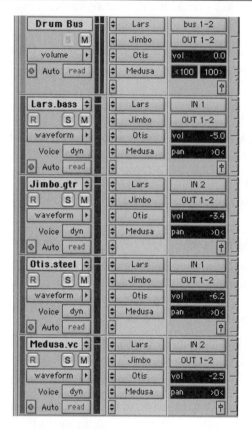

FIGURE 11-4   Relabeled send assignments

For the purposes of this exercise, however, we are going to use aux returns instead to listen to the cue mixes.

1. Press ⌘+= (CTRL+=) to open the Mix window.

2. Go to View > Mix Window and turn off all the views except for Sends A-E.

3. Mute all five tracks. Note: Do not use OPTION+click (ALT+click) to mute these tracks—we don't want the hidden tracks to be muted.

4. Create four new Mono Aux Input channels. Name them and assign their inputs as follows:

Lars mix	Set input to Lars (Bus 3)
Jimbo mix	Set input to Jimbo (Bus 4)
Otis mix	Set input to Otis (Bus 5)
Medusa mix	Set input to Medusa (Bus 6)

5. Mute these new aux return channels.

6. Go to Views > Sends A-E > Send A.

In this view, you will see a row of small faders representing Lars's cue mix, as shown here:

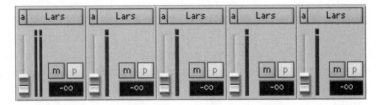

7. Unmute the Lars mix fader.

8. Rewind to the session start and press Play. Because the instrument channels are muted, you won't hear anything at first.

9. Bring up the small send faders one by one to create a cue mix for Lars. Because Lars is the bass player, he's going to want a mix that is bass- and drum-heavy. Make sure you don't clip the aux return channel by bringing the faders up too high.

> While you're listening to the cue mix, there's an important concept to be grasped here. You can see that the session's tracks are muted. Move the big faders up and down and note that Lars's cue mix doesn't change. That's because the little faders are getting their signal *pre-fader*.

10. Mute Lars's mix return.

11. Go to Views > Sends A-E > Send B to display Jimbo's cue mix.

12. Unmute Jimbo's mix return.

13. Bring up the small faders to create a mix for Jimbo. He needs to hear his guitar over the other instruments but, for reasons explained earlier, he wants Medusa completely out of his mix.

14. Mute Jimbo's mix return, go to Views > Sends A-E > Send C, and show Otis's cue mix. Unmute Otis's mix return and set up a mix with plenty of steel guitar.

15. Mute Otis's mix return and unmute Medusa's. Show the Sends view for Send D and set up a mix for Medusa. She wants to hear everyone but Jimbo.

Play the song and listen to the different mixes, one at a time. Watch for a couple of things here. You can only listen to one mix at a time or it won't make sense. The audio tracks have to stay muted so that you will only hear the cue mixes.

As I mentioned earlier, these mix returns were created solely for demonstration purposes. In a real recording situation with just a Digi 002, you can set up multiple cue mixes as we did in this exercise, but there's no easy way for you to monitor the different mixes within Pro Tools because the mixes would be routed to line outputs, not busses. You would have to put the musicians' headphones on to check their cue mixes.

Take your time exploring this setup until you're confident that you understand what's going on. Are you confused yet? You should be. Setting up multiple cue mixes during a tracking session is a complicated business. In commercial studios, it's not unusual to assign an assistant to the sole task of keeping up with the cue mixes, so the engineer can concentrate on recording the sounds.

16. When you're through playing with the cue mixes, the tracking session is complete. Delete the four mix return channels.

17. Go to View > Sends A-E > Assignments.

18. On the Drum Bus aux channel, OPTION+click (ALT+click) each Send button and choose No Send from the pop-up menu to clear the cue mix sends.

19. Now we need to change the I/O labels back to normal. Go to Setup I/O and click the Import Settings button. Choose Normal from the list and click Open.

20. A dialog will appear asking if you want the unused paths deleted. It's referring to the cue mixes you deleted from the session. Click Yes, and then click OK to close the dialog.

21. Save the session, and then save it again as **W.Stranger 10cue**.

Doubling the Acoustic Guitar

Some time after Jimbo's rapid departure from the tracking session, it was decided that the acoustic guitar ought to be doubled for a fuller sound. *Doubling* is the technique of recording the same instrument or vocal part twice with the idea of making the two performances as similar as possible. Although Jimbo's not around to record another take, we can create this effect by copying pieces of the existing performance and pasting them onto another track.

While it might not be common to double a guitar part in this way, the purpose of this exercise is to familiarize you with the concept of moving audio around within a song. The ability to do this is one of the main advantages Digital Audio Workstations have over tape machines, and it's a very common practice. I also want you to get used to switching frequently and rapidly between tools and editing modes. This exercise is fairly complex, and it's crucial that you change edit modes when instructed to do so or you will end up with a mess. Therefore, the edit mode changes in this exercise will be printed in **bold** type to get your attention.

I'm assuming that you are familiar enough with zooming to be able do it on your own without being prompted, so there won't be any specific zooming instructions in the remaining exercises.

In addition, we're going to try a different editing procedure in this exercise. We will make all the edits first, and then do all the crossfades at the end. Some prefer this method over the crossfade-as-you-go technique we have used so far, because there's less switching between tools and modes. You be the judge.

Setting Up the Edit Window

Whenever starting a complex editing procedure, it always helps to prepare the Edit window.

1. Press ⌘+= (CTRL+=) to toggle back to the Edit window. The tracks should still be muted.

2. Unmute the bass and drums, and turn the bass down to about −8 dB.

3. Hide all tracks except for the guitar.

4. Close the Tracks list, and disable the Send and Insert views.

5. Unmute the guitar and set its Track Height to Large.

6. Rename the Jimbo.gtr track **Gtr 1**, and pan it all the way to the left.

7. Create a new mono audio track titled **Gtr 2**.

8. Set its Track Height to Large, and pan it to the right.

9. Set the volume of both guitar tracks to about –5 dB.

10. In **Grid** mode, set the Grid pop-up to 1/2 note.

11. Set a short pre-roll value, such as **0|1|000**, and a long post-roll value, such as **99|0|000**.

12. If Loop Playback is on, disable it.

Searching for Repeated Sections

Beginners are sometimes under the impression that they can double a track by simply duplicating the track and then panning the two tracks left and right. Wrong! You'll end up with the exact same thing you started with, except you will have unnecessarily used up an extra track. A real double track consists of two separate performances. Therefore, you need at least two occurrences of each part of the song to double the guitar part from a single track. It would be simpler if you had multiple takes to choose from, but this song is repetitious enough to make a double from one performance. We'll accomplish this by copying bits from the Gtr 1 track and pasting them onto the Gtr 2 track. If you listen to the Outro, you'll find it very similar to the Intro, so we'll start building our fake double track by copying the Outro and pasting it alongside the Intro to see how well they match.

1. Click Outro in the Memory Locations window.

2. Select and copy the guitar in the Outro and paste it onto Gtr 2 at the Intro marker, as shown in Figure 11-5.

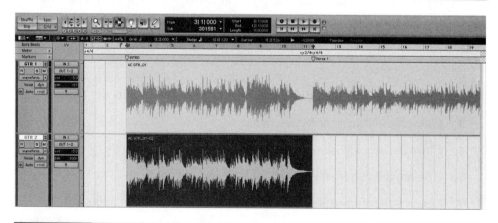

FIGURE 11-5   Pasting the Outro onto Gtr 2

Listen to the two tracks together. They work pretty well, except in a couple of spots. The F chords at the end of Bar 4 don't match, and the strum at the end of the Intro needs to be moved. For now, let's just fix the F chord, and come back later in Slip mode to fix the strum.

3. On the Gtr 2 track, select and copy the F chord between 6|3|000 and 7|1|000, and paste it at 4|3|000, as shown in Figure 11-6. (Hint: watch the Event Edit Area while making selections—it will tell you exactly which bars you are selecting.)

4. Now we need to double Verse 1 and Chorus 1. Click with the Selector anywhere on the Gtr 1 track.

5. In the Memory Locations window, click Verse 2, and then SHIFT+click on Outro and copy the selection.

6. Click with the Selector anywhere on Gtr 2, and then click Verse 1 in the Memory Locations window and paste.

Listen to Verse 1. The two guitar tracks work fine together until Bar 24, where a sloppy A minor chord on Gtr 1 track clashes with the one on Gtr 2. There's a better A minor chord at Bar 12.

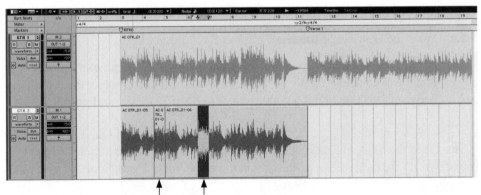

Paste it here   Copy the F chord

FIGURE 11-6   Pasting the F chord

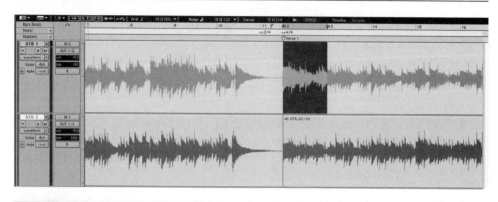

FIGURE 11-7   Copying Bar 12 on Gtr 1

7. Click Verse 1 in the Memory Locations window.

8. On the Gtr 1 track, select and copy the Am chord at Bar 12, as shown in Figure 11-7.

9. Paste the region at Bar 24 on Gtr 1. Check the edit, and then continue listening.

10. The Gtr 2 track needs to stop at the end of the first chorus to match Gtr 1. We'll fix that by shortening the chorus on the Gtr 2 track. Select the region between 27|3|000 and 29|3|000 on the Gtr 2 track.

11. Select **Shuffle** mode and press DELETE.

12. In **Grid** mode, select and copy the Outro on the Gtr 1 track again.

13. Paste the Outro onto the Gtr 2 track at the Solo marker.

14. As you can see, the Outro is longer than the Solo. It has an extra part that the Solo doesn't have, so let's remove it. On Gtr 2, select the region between 29|3|000 and 33|3|000, switch to **Shuffle** mode, and press DELETE.

That fixes the Solo, except that the strum at the end doesn't match. In the next edit, we'll take care of that problem when we use Verse 1 and Chorus 1 to double Verse 2 and part of Chorus 2.

15. In **Grid** mode, copy the region between Bar 10 and Bar 28 on Gtr 1 and paste it onto Gtr 2 at 31|1|000.

16.   On Gtr 2, make a selection between 32|1|000 and 32|3|000.

17.   In **Shuffle** mode, press DELETE. Return to **Grid** mode.

Listen to your handiwork. You should be okay until Bar 47, where the Gtr 2 track ends early because Chorus 1 is shorter than Chorus 2.

18.   On the Gtr 2 track, copy the region between Bar 45 and Bar 48, and paste it at Bar 47. This effectively stretches the Gtr 2 track to match Gtr 1.

19.   Now we'll use the Gtr 1 Intro for the Gtr 2 Outro. Select and copy the Intro on Gtr 1 (between 3|1|000 and 12|1|000) and paste it at the Outro on Gtr 2.

20.   It sounds pretty good, but we've got that problem with the F chord again. On the Gtr 1 track, copy the F chord between 53|3|000 and 54|1|000.

21.   Paste the F chord back onto the Gtr 1 track at 51|3|000.

22.   Take a look at the last strum at the end of the song, and you'll see that the guitar tracks don't match. We can fix it by moving the strum on Gtr 2 to line up with Gtr 1. Change the Grid pop-up to 1/16 note.

23.   On the Gtr 2 track, select the sixteenth note between 57|2|480 and 57|2|720.

24.   Switch to **Shuffle** mode and press DELETE.

25.   Switch to **Slip** mode and trim the edit point for the most natural-sounding transition (don't crossfade yet).

Congratulations! You've now created a double track all the way to the end of the song without having to drag Jimbo back into the studio. There are still a couple of spots that need work, however.

26.   On the Gtr 2 track, zoom in on the strummed chord at the end of the Intro (near 10|2|480). Click with the Selector at the front of the chord and press the B key to make a separation at that point.

27.   Drag or nudge the separated chord to the right, so it matches the chord on Gtr 1. This leaves a bit of a hole in the Gtr 2 track, but we'll fix that later.

28.   Switch to **Grid** mode. With the Trimmer, trim the edit at the downbeat of Verse 1 on the Gtr 2 track so that the transition is at Bar 12, as shown in Figure 11-8.

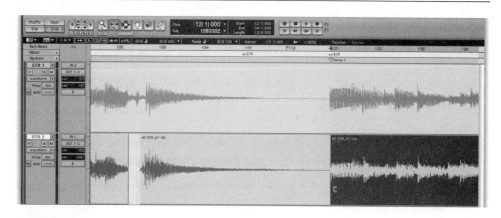

FIGURE 11-8   Editing at Verse 1

Fine-Tuning the Edits

Now that the copying and pasting is finished, it's time to polish those edits.

1. Go to the first edit on Gtr 1 and zoom in.

2. In **Slip** mode, trim the edit point to the left, so the transition is in the space between the chords, and then crossfade, as shown in Figure 11-9.

3. If the Tab to Transients button is on (beneath the Zoom preset buttons), turn it off.

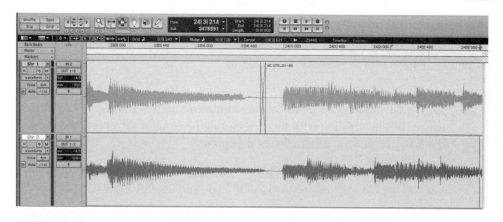

FIGURE 11-9   Place the transition in the space between chords

4. Click with the Selector anywhere on Gtr 1, and then press the TAB key until you reach the next edit point. Trim the edit point for the best-sounding transition and crossfade.

On the Gtr 2 track, the edits are pretty straightforward, except for the one at Bar 12. This edit is going to sound a little strange when you solo it, because the pasted region doesn't start from a pause, and therefore Jimbo is in the middle of a phrase at the edit point. Luckily, the edit falls right on a kick drum beat, so you'll probably never hear it in the mix. As I've mentioned before, whenever you have an edit that's going to sound weird, it's best to hide it behind something loud and percussive, like a kick or snare. The presence of a second guitar track will also help make the edit less noticeable. In this case, I would leave the edit as is.

5. You should be proficient enough at crossfading by now to do the crossfades on Gtr 2 on your own. Go through the edits from beginning to end, trimming and crossfading them with the Smart tool, and using the TAB key to go to the next edit. Try to place the crossfades at the quietest part of the waveform, and always listen to each edit before you move on to the next. Remember— OPTION+clicking (CTRL+clicking) on the Tab button will tab to the left. When you get to the end of the song, fade out both guitar tracks, as shown in Figure 11-10.

6. Save the session, and then save it again as **W.Stranger 11gtr.**

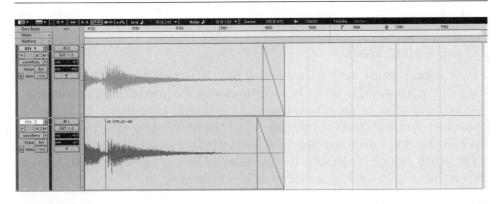

FIGURE 11-10   Fades at the end

Now you've got your doubled guitar. (Hey, I said it could be *done*—I didn't say it would be easy.) Try doing *that* with a tape machine! Luckily, you're getting paid by the hour and the band has plenty of money (Medusa's great-grandfather invented the marshmallow). If you'd like to see how I would have done the edits and crossfades on Gtr 2, you can import Gtr 2-edit from WS Tracks and see how it compares with your track. Delete Gtr 2-edit from the session when you're done.

Combine Two Mono Tracks to a Stereo Track

Now that the guitar tracks are finished, let's put them on a stereo track so we can process them together.

1. Select Gtr 1 and Gtr 2 and group them (⌘+G / CTRL+G). Name the group **Gtr**.

2. Create a new stereo audio track and name it **Gtr**.

3. Triple-click on one of the audio regions to select all the audio on both tracks.

4. Hold the CONTROL+OPTION (START+ALT) keys and use the Grabber to grab the audio regions and drag them down to copy them onto the stereo Gtr track. Holding CONTROL (START) keeps the regions on a vertical path so that you don't accidentally shift the audio in time. Holding OPTION (ALT) causes the regions to be copied instead of moved.

5. Consolidate the audio regions on the Gtr track.

6. Now that we don't need Gtr 1 and Gtr 2 anymore, let's deactivate them. Select the two tracks and go to Track > Make Inactive. The tracks will be grayed out and will not play or use any of the available voices unless you activate them again.

7. Hide the two inactive tracks.

EQ the Guitar Track

People sometimes ask me, "What does EQ do?" EQ stands for equalization. In the simplest terms, EQ is basically a way to change the tone of musical material. The bass and treble knobs on your car stereo are simple EQ controls. If the sound doesn't have enough bass for your tastes, you "equalize" the system by turning up the bass. The EQ 3 plug-in in Pro Tools has a dazzling array of knobs, but it's just a fancy tone control. It's a useful tool for learning how an equalizer works because the graphic display shows you exactly what is happening.

Now that the guitars are on a stereo track, we can process them with a single stereo plug-in. Lars has been complaining that "That wooly guitar is interfering with my bass." Acoustic guitars can be a little bass-heavy, especially when finger-picked. This makes Lars's bass harder to hear, an effect known as *masking*. We're going to remove some bass frequencies from the guitars to give the bass guitar more definition.

1. Enable the Inserts view and insert the 4 Band EQ 3 plug-in on the Gtr track—Multi-Mono Plug-in > EQ > 4-Band EQ 3 (Mono).

2. In the EQ 3 plug-in window, you will see that there are seven sections, but only four can be active at a time on the four-band version. Each section has its own IN button, which lights up blue when activated. Turn off all the IN buttons except for the section labeled HPF, shown here:

The high-pass filter (HPF) is useful for removing unwanted bass frequencies because it "lets the highs pass through," but not the lows (the low-pass filter [LPF] does the opposite).

3. Since this acoustic guitar doesn't produce much useful sound below 110 Hz, let's enter **110** in the Freq (cutoff frequency) field (you don't have to type in the "Hz"). Since this is a high-pass filter, all the frequencies below 110 Hz will be attenuated, or "rolled off" as the graphic display shows.

4. Solo the acoustic guitar and click the IN button on and off to hear the effect. If your speakers don't reproduce low frequencies very well, try using headphones instead so you can hear the difference.

5. The Q knob controls how sharply the lows are attenuated. At a higher setting, the effect is more noticeable. Turn the Q knob up to 24 dB/oct (dB per octave). The graphic display shows a much steeper rolloff curve, and you should be able to hear that the low frequencies are even more attenuated.

6. While the guitar is playing, turn the Freq (frequency) knob up and listen to the profound effect it has on the guitar, and then return to the 110 Hz setting.

The low-pass filter is helping, but the main problem with the guitar is the overabundance of lower midrange around 180 Hz, which is above the cutoff. We can help the situation by using the LMF (low mid frequency) control to get rid of some of the "mud."

7. Click the IN button in the LMF section and enter a Q of **4**, a frequency of **180**, and a Gain value of **–8**. Look at the graphic display. Now we're really carving a chunk of low end out of this guitar.

8. Take the Gtr track out of Solo and listen while clicking the plug-in's Bypass button on and off. You should be able to hear Lars's bass guitar more clearly with the EQ turned on.

9. This EQ setting might be useful in the future, so let's save it as a preset. Click the Settings menu button (to the left of the button labeled <Factory Default>) and select Save Settings As. Name the preset **Jimbo Gtr** and click Save. Now the Librarian menu shows the current preset as Jimbo Gtr, and that preset can be recalled at a later date by clicking the button and selecting Jimbo Gtr from the list. Sweet.

10. Turn the Gtr track down to about –5. Close the EQ plug-in window and save the session.

Editing the Shaker Track

The band has gotten used to hearing the Shaker track and decided to keep it in the song, but they want it muted at the stops. That's fine, but we need to keep a copy of the current Shaker track for overdubbing purposes. The solution is to make a duplicate playlist with the Shaker muted at the stops.

1. Unhide the V loop and Shaker tracks, and put the Shaker track under the V loop track.

2. Click the Playlist button on the Shaker track and select Duplicate. Name the new playlist **Shaker OD**, and click OK.

3. Switch back to the original Shaker playlist.

4. In **Grid** mode, zoom in on the first stop and select the area between 10|2|720 and 12|1|000 on the Shaker track.

5. Delete the selected regions.

6. Separate and mute the Shaker at the other stops in a similar fashion. Save the session.

Adding a D-Verb Channel

Medusa and Otis would like to hear their tracks with some reverb, so let's add a D-Verb channel.

1. Hide all the tracks currently showing in the Edit window.

2. Create a new Mono Aux Input track and label it **D-Verb**.

3. Insert the D-Verb (Mono/Stereo) plug-in on this track. Note that the D-Verb plug-in has converted the track to a mono in, stereo out track.

4. In the D-Verb plug-in window, select the Medium-sized Hall algorithm and turn the input up to 0.0 dB. Close the D-Verb plug-in window.

5. Put the D-Verb channel into Solo Safe mode by ⌘+clicking (CTRL+clicking) its Solo button.

6. Assign the D-Verb channel's input to Bus 3.

7. Unhide the Sn Smp, Otis, and Medusa tracks, and unmute them.

8. Enable the Sends A-E view, and insert a Bus 3 send at Send selector A on all three audio tracks.

9. Go to View > Sends A-E > Send A.

10. The inserts and sends in your Edit window should look exactly like the ones shown in Figure 11-11. Check the Sends, Inserts, and I/O views to make sure everything is configured correctly.

11. Play the song and bring up the small send faders on these tracks to put reverb on the snare drum, steel guitar, and vocal.

12. Save the session, and then save it again as **W.Stranger 12verb**.

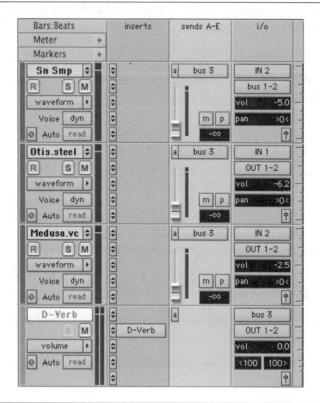

FIGURE 11-11   D-Verb Edit window

Using the Xpand! Plug-In

In order to do the next exercise, you need Xpand, a free sample-playback/synthesis workstation plug-in from Digidesign. As of this writing it has not yet been included with all Pro Tools systems. If you have Pro Tools 7.3 or higher, the installer can be found on the Pro Tools 7.3 installation DVD. If it was not included with your Pro Tools system, you'll need to download it (at no cost) from the Digidesign web site and install it in your system.

1.   Create a new stereo aux track and name it **Pad**.

2.   Insert the Xpand! Plug-in on the Pad aux track—Multichannel Plug-in > Instrument > Xpand! (Stereo)—and put the track in Solo Safe mode by ⌘+clicking (CTRL+clicking) its Solo button.

Importing MIDI Files

Jimbo has written a keyboard part for the song, which he composed on his laptop on the way to Amsterdam and e-mailed to your studio in the form of a MIDI file. You need to import the MIDI file and perform a few tweaks to clean it up.

1. Choose File > Import > MIDI.

2. Navigate to the Honeywagon folder, click Synth.mid, and click Open to import the MIDI file. When the MIDI Import Options dialog opens, click OK.

3. The MIDI file contains two tracks: Hi Synth and Lo Synth. On import, they will appear as two MIDI tracks in the Edit window. Group the two tracks, and name the group **Synth**.

4. Assign the output of both MIDI tracks to Xpand.

5. The Xpand plug-in is currently set to the factory default. Click the Librarian menu, shown here, and navigate to 01 Soft Pads > 14 X-Mas Pad:

6. Mute the steel and vocal tracks and listen to Jimbo's synth part. Close the Xpand plug-in window and save the session.

7. Disable the Inserts and Sends views and close the Tracks list.

Editing MIDI Notes

Jimbo has asked you to clean up the sloppiness in the MIDI tracks. As you listen to the playback, you notice that some notes are a lot louder than others.

We can change this by leveling out the note velocity, but before we start changing Jimbo's keyboard part, let's make a safety copy first.

1. Click the Hi Synth track's Playlist selector and choose Duplicate. Both synth tracks will be duplicated onto new playlists.

2. Name the new playlists **Hi Synth.safety** and **Lo Synth.safety**, and then switch back to the original playlists.

3. Switch from Notes view to Velocity view, and set the Track Heights to Large. Looking at the variation in velocity, you can see that Jimbo's playing is rather inconsistent.

4. With the Trimmer, click near the bottom of the Hi Synth track and drag upward until all the velocity stalks are at the max velocity of 127. Now that they are evened out, you can pull them back down to any desired velocity.

This method is useful when you want to change the velocity on only one MIDI track in a group. Notice that the velocity values for the Lo synth track remained unaffected, even though it was grouped with the Hi Synth track. When you want to change *all* the selected MIDI notes to the same velocity, you'll use the Change Velocity command.

5. Double-click with the Selector in either of the synth tracks to select all MIDI notes on both tracks.

6. Go to Event > MIDI > Change Velocity to bring up the Change Velocity dialog, where we are presented with several options for globally changing the velocity values of all selected notes.

7. Under Set All To, move the slider to the right to set the note velocity to 117 (or enter the value into the field), and click Apply.

8. Close the Change Velocity dialog and click anywhere in the Edit window to deselect the notes.

9. Zoom in on the first couple of bars, switch back to Notes view, and click the MIDI Zoom button, shown in Figure 11-12, to make the notes larger and easier to edit.

MIDI Zoom button

FIGURE 11-12   Click the MIDI Zoom button to make the notes easier to edit

Now the volume is consistent from note to note, but the *timing* leaves something to be desired. (There must have been some turbulence on Jimbo's flight.) When you visually compare the notes to the grid, you can see that some of the notes are rushing or dragging. With the Quantize command, we can automatically align the notes with the grid. Because there are chord changes that occur on offbeats, we'll specify a 1/16-note grid, in the hopes that the majority of the notes will be moved to the correct gridline. Notes that are very early or late might be moved to the wrong gridline, so we'll have to go through the song and check for stray notes.

10. Double-click with the Selector in either of the synth tracks to select all MIDI notes on both tracks.

11. Go to Event > MIDI > Grid/Groove Quantize to bring up the Quantize dialog.

12. Make sure Attacks and Releases are checked under What To Quantize, and the Quantize Grid is set to 1/16 note.

13. Click Apply and close the Quantize dialog.

14. The MIDI notes should now be aligned with the gridlines. Click anywhere in the Edit window to deselect the MIDI notes.

On listening to the synth part, we discover a problem in Bar 10. One of the notes on the Lo Synth track is changing early. This is the sort of thing you run into when quantizing tracks. The note was so rushed that Pro Tools quantized it to the wrong gridline. Also, the keyboard part plays through the stop in the next bar. To fix this, we'll trim the MIDI notes the same way we trim audio regions.

15. Zoom in on Bar 10. (Close the Sends and Inserts views to make room, if necessary.) The Grid pop-up menu should still be set to 1/16 note.

16. In Grid mode, use the Trimmer to change the duration of the notes on the Lo Synth track, so the notes change at the same time as the notes on the Hi Synth track, as shown in Figure 11-13.

The chord you just fixed is the last chord of the Intro. The synth parts sustain over the stop before Verse 1, but we want them to cut off at Bar 11.

17. SHIFT+click with the Grabber on the three notes at 10/2/720 to select them.

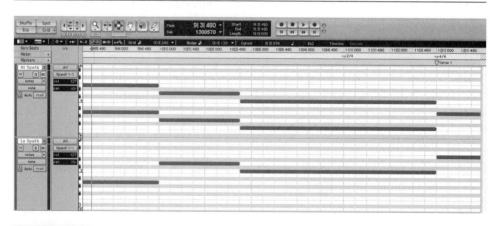

FIGURE 11-13   Trimming MIDI notes

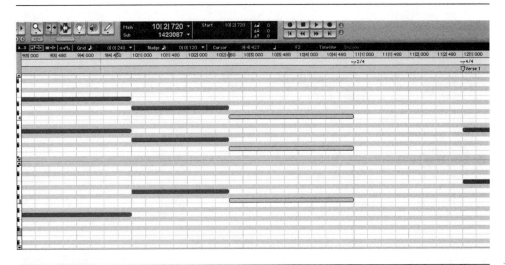

FIGURE 11-14   Trimming the stop

18. With all three notes selected, use the Trimmer to trim the ends of the notes back to Bar 11, as shown in Figure 11-14.

19. At 48|3|000, there is an A3 note on the Hi Synth track that shouldn't be there. Select the A3 note with the Grabber (click the different notes and watch the Event Edit Area display if you're not sure which note is an A3) and delete it.

20. At 55|3|000, there is a wrong chord. The highest note in the chord is an F4. Drag it down one semitone to change its pitch to an E4.

21. Two notes below that, there is an A3 note. Drag its pitch down to C3.

22. On the Lo Synth track, the bottom note of the chord is missing. Use the Pencil tool to place a C2 note at 55|3|000.

23. The Pencil tool created a 1/16 note because that's the current Grid pop-up setting. Use the Trimmer to extend the note all the way to the end of the bar. The resulting chord should appear as in Figure 11-15.

Add the missing C2 note

FIGURE 11-15   Fixed chord at 55|3|000

24. The C note you just created is not at the correct velocity. When MIDI notes are created with the Pencil tool, their default velocity is 80. Switch to the Velocity view and use the Grabber to pull the note's velocity stalk up to 115. Switch back to Notes view when you're done.

When you play the edited tracks over the phone for Jimbo, he informs you that this particular keyboard patch sounds an octave higher than the synth plug-in he used to write the part. We can fix this by using the *Transpose command*, which enables the user to shift selected notes to a new pitch. The Transpose command could be used to change the key of a MIDI track from A minor to E minor, for instance. The current situation calls for us to transpose down an octave.

25. Double-click with the Selector to select all the MIDI notes as before, and go to Event > MIDI > Transpose to bring up the Transpose dialog. You can transpose by octaves or semitones. Each semitone represents a note on the keyboard. An octave contains 12 notes (7 white ones, 5 black ones), so 12 semitones equals an octave. Therefore, you can either enter **−1** in the Octaves field or **−12** in the Semitones field. Choose either method, and click Apply.

26. Close the Transpose dialog and note that the selected MIDI notes have dropped an octave.

27. Let's tweak the sound of the synth a bit. Unhide the Pad aux channel (if necessary) and enable the Inserts view.

28. Click the Xpand plug-in to open the plug-in window.

29. There are six knobs across the top of the Xpand window that enable us to fine-tune the sound. Number four is the Cutoff control, which controls the point at which the high frequencies are filtered out. Solo the synth tracks and lower the cutoff to about −75% for a much mellower tone, and then close the plug-in window.

Exporting MIDI Files

Now that the MIDI tracks have been fixed, it's time to e-mail them back to Jimbo for final approval. MIDI files are easily e-mailed because they are tiny compared to audio files.

1. Choose File > Export > MIDI.

2. In the dialog that appears, make sure MIDI File Format is Type 1 (Multi-track) and click OK.

3. Name the file **Synth 2**.

4. Navigate to the Desktop and click Save.

5. Save the session, and then save it again as **W.Stranger 13midi**.

The new MIDI track is now sitting on your Desktop, waiting to be whisked away to Amsterdam via e-mail.

Chapter 12

Working with Vocals

Opinions and techniques abound when it comes to the subject of recording vocals. While my approach differs depending on the type of project I'm working on, it usually goes something like this:

- Once the singer's voice is warmed up, we'll record three or four takes from beginning to end. If the artist wants to keep going and the takes are getting better and better, I'll keep recording until they start to get worse. If the takes aren't getting better, I might stop and work on problem areas with the vocalist.

- I give the vocalist a break, pick out the best three or four takes, and do a vocal comp, combining the best parts of each take.

- If the vocal performance is fine but for a few small problems, we'll take a crack at punching in the trouble spots. If the performance is nowhere close to acceptable, we might try again in a day or two.

I recall recounting this procedure at a producers' panel at a major music seminar when a vocalist stood up and asked me how I recorded vocals. As I spoke, I watched her jaw drop in horror at the prospect of compiling a vocal take from different performances. She gasped, "There's no way I would *ever* allow anyone to record me in that manner!" I looked around at the other producers on the panel (some of whom were industry heavyweights). They all shrugged and basically said, "That's the way everybody does it in rock and roll."

I've found that most vocalists prefer to work this way because each take is a complete performance and, therefore, follows the natural dynamic changes in the song. It takes the pressure off—not many singers can deliver a perfect take in one pass. Many vocalists become disoriented when trying to punch in a phrase somewhere in the middle of the song because they have to think too much about what they're doing. Things can get stale in a big hurry and, once they do, you'll have to stop and come back to it later.

The great thing about Pro Tools is that you have unlimited tracks on which to record vocal takes. The bad thing about Pro Tools is that you have unlimited tracks on which to record vocal takes, and everybody knows it. That old lie, "I'm out of tracks" doesn't work any more. Lazy singers will want to do a bunch of takes, and then take off, leaving you instructions to "Just Pro Tools it."

When you get to the point where a vocalist has done the best they can and it's still not quite good enough, there are things you can do to make it sound better, providing it's not against your religion. Whatever your views on the subject might be, sooner or later, someone is going to say, "Please, can you fix my vocal track?"

In this chapter, we'll delve into the joys of comping and fixing vocals. You'll use some of the techniques learned in earlier chapters, and you'll learn a few new ones. In the scenario for the first exercise, you have four takes of Medusa (introduced in Chapter 11) singing the first verse and chorus, and it's your job to create a comp track and do some fixes.

Setting Up for Vocal Comping

Four different vocal performances have been provided in the WS Tracks session. In the following exercise you'll import some vocal takes and set up the Edit window for comping.

1. Open the session titled W.Stranger 13midi from the previous exercise.

2. Make sure the lead vocal track is muted and hide all the tracks currently showing in the Edit window.

3. Use the Workspace window to import the M1, M2, M3, and M4 tracks from the WS Tracks session.

4. Select Slip mode.

5. Create a new mono audio track titled **M.comp**.

6. In the Edit window, arrange the five tracks from top to bottom, as follows: M1, M2, M3, M4, and M.comp.

7. All of these vocal tracks should be muted except for the M.comp track.

8. Hide the Tracks list.

9. Go to the beginning of Verse 1 and zoom in until the four lines of Verse 1 fill the Edit window. Your Edit window should look like the one shown in Figure 12-1.

FIGURE 12-1   Edit window setup for comping

Comping with the One-Click Method

The Medusa.voc track that you've been listening to was comped from these four tracks, but we're going to pretend that the lead vocal has not yet been comped. The normal procedure here is to listen to the vocal tracks one at a time, separate the best parts, and drag them down into the Comp track. This involves quite a bit of muting and unmuting, which can be tiring after a while, especially in a situation where you have six or eight vocal tracks to comp. In these situations, I use what I call the one-click method of auditioning the tracks. Here's how it works:

1. ⌘+OPTION+click (CTRL+ALT+click) any track's Solo button. This places all the tracks in the session in Solo Safe mode, even the hidden ones. The Solo buttons are grayed out.

2. ⌘+click (CTRL+click) the Solo buttons of all five vocal tracks to take them back out of Solo Safe. Now, all the tracks in the session are in Solo Safe *except* for the vocal tracks.

3. Go to Options > Solo Mode and select X-OR (Cancels Previous Solo). Now the Solo buttons are "unlatched." This means that only one track can be soloed at a time.

4. Unmute M1 through M4.

5. Click the Solo buttons on the different vocal tracks and note the change in the way the Solo buttons operate when unlatched. Now you can switch instantly from one vocal track to another just by clicking that track's Solo button, and the instrument tracks in the session are not muted.

6. Play Verse 1 while soloing different vocal tracks. Pretty slick, huh?

7. CONTROL+click (right-click) the Play button to loop the playback.

8. Select the first line of the song, "I am a poor wayfaring stranger," on any of the tracks.

9. Solo the M1 track.

10. Press Play. After the first line has played through, solo M2.

11. After you've heard the first line of M2, switch to M3, and then to M4.

If you've followed the steps correctly, the selected line will loop continuously as you solo the different tracks. This is the fastest way I've found to compare several takes of a performance with the least amount of button pushing. It's probably overkill for a four-take comp, but it can save a lot of time when you're comping from several takes.

12. The Separation Grabber is another helpful tool for comping vocal tracks. Click the Grabber icon and hold until a drop-down menu appears, and then select the Separation Grabber. (The one with the scissors, remember?) You can also select it by pressing F8 until you see the Grabber icon with the scissors in the toolbar.

13. Use the Selector to select the first line on M2. Use the Separation Grabber to drag it down onto the M.comp track. (As you will see, this process involves a lot of switching between the Selector and the Separation Grabber. You can also use your left hand to switch between the two with the F7 and F8 function keys, or use the Smart tool instead.)

14. Select the second line, "travelin' through this world of woe," from M3 and drag it down onto the M.comp track.

15. Press OPTION+F (ALT+F) to fill the Edit window with the selection.

16. Solo the M.comp track and listen to the line. Let's say we're happy with "travelin through," but we prefer the rest of the line on M4.

The Constrain Command

When you drag these files vertically, there's always the danger of inadvertently moving them slightly to the left or right as you pull them down. If you press the CONTROL (START) key *before* you drag a selected region, the region will be constrained to vertical movement only. Digidesign calls this the Constrain Audio Region to Vertical Movement command—not the easiest group of words to remember. Therefore, I refer to it as the "Constrain command." Incidentally, a full list of all the Pro Tools keyboard shortcuts is available under the Help menu.

17. Select "this world of woe" from M4 and CONTROL+drag (START+drag) it onto the M.comp track. Trim the edit point, if necessary, for the smoothest sounding transition. The results should appear as shown in Figure 12-2. Don't worry about gaps in the audio before and after the vocal phrases—we'll come back later and smooth them out.

"this world of woe"

FIGURE 12-2   Waveform for "this world of woe"

18. Take the third line in Verse 1 from M3, and the fourth line from M1.

19. Take the first three lines of the Chorus from M4, and the fourth line from M3. Your M.comp track should now appear as shown here:

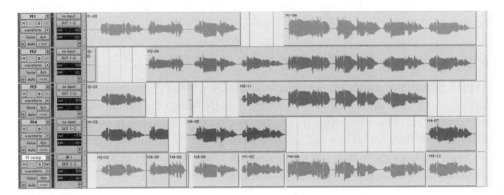

While the one-click method is helpful, it does have a drawback—there's no easy way to turn off the music and hear the vocal by itself. Now that the comp is finished, it's time to undo the setup.

20. ⌘+OPTION+click (CTRL+ALT+click) *twice* on any track's Solo button to take all the tracks in the session out of Solo Safe.

21. Unfortunately, your aux return channels are no longer in Solo Safe. Open the Tracks list.

22. Aux channels are designated in the Tracks list by a green, downward-pointing arrow. Click the D-Verb, Pad, and Drum Bus tracks to show them in the Edit window.

23. ⌘+click (ALT+click) their Solo buttons to put them back in Solo Safe, and then hide them again.

24. Go to Options > Solo Mode and select Latch.

25. Mute M1 through M4, and take the M.comp track out of Solo.

26. CONTROL+click (right-click) the Play button to get out of Loop Playback mode.

Tweaking Vocal Tracks in Pro Tools

Comping vocal tracks is just the beginning—there are all sorts of ways to enhance vocal tracks in Pro Tools. In the following exercises you'll learn several real-world techniques for cleaning up and manipulating vocal tracks. The first order of business is to make sure all the edits are correct.

Checking the Vocal Edits

In rock music, vocals are often subjected to quite a bit of compression and equalization (EQ) during mixdown, which usually brings the breathing sounds to the foreground. Therefore, you should listen closely to the transitions in your comp to make sure they sound natural. In particular, pay close attention to he breaths between the phrases. When I'm doing this, I usually slam the vocal with radical compression to exaggerate the breath sounds.

1. Enable the Inserts view (if necessary) and insert Plug-in > Dynamics > Compressor/Limiter Dyn 3 on the M.comp track.

2. Click the Librarian menu button (labeled <Factory Default>) and choose Vocal Levelor.

3. To bring out the breaths even more, insert the 1-Band EQ 3 plug-in on the M.comp track and set the parameters as follows:

   ■ **Input**   0.0 dB

   ■ **Type**   Peak

   ■ **Filter (Q)**   .32

   ■ **Freq**   5 kHz

   ■ **Gain**   5 dB

4. Click the Settings menu (the arrow button to the left of the words "Factory Default") and save the settings as **Medusa Voc**.

5. Close the plug-in window and hide the Inserts view.

6. Solo the M.comp track and go through the comp, trimming the gaps in the audio to close them, and crossfading the edit points. Pay particular attention

to the second line in the verse where an edit occurs in the middle of a phrase. A short crossfade like the one shown in the following illustration is usually best for this type of edit:

Stretching a Note

As you have seen, it's quite possible to have a fairly transparent edit in the middle of a vocal line, providing that the vocal tone and phrasing is consistent enough. If you are careful enough, it's also possible to have an edit in the middle of a sustained note. Often, background vocalists will hold out a note too long or cut it off too early. While it's possible to stretch notes with a time compression/ expansion plug-in, the process degrades the audio quality by putting in a zillion tiny crossfades when just one will do. Let's suppose that Medusa wants to hear what it would sound like if the word "home" were phrased differently.

1. Because we're going to alter this track, click the Playlist button and duplicate the M.comp track, naming the new playlist **Stretch**.

2. Switch to Grid mode and set the Grid pop-up to 1/8 note.

3. On the Stretch track, select the first line of Chorus 1 from 19|3|000 to 21|3|000 and press OPTION+F (ALT+F) to fill the Edit window with the selection.

4. Select the area from 20|2|000 to 21|3|000 and press the B key to separate the second half of the line, as shown here:

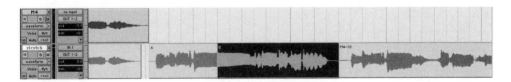

5. The line is now divided into two regions. For the sake of simplicity, rename the first region **A** and the second region **B**.

6. Drag the B region two 1/8 notes to the right, so that it starts at 20|3|000, as shown here:

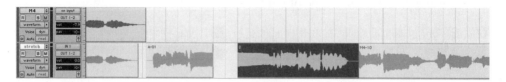

7. Trim the B region an 1/8 note to the left, so that it starts at 20|2|480, as shown here:

8. Trim the A region an 1/8 note to the right to close the gap in the audio, as shown here:

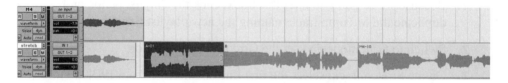

9. The word "home" is now a 1/4 note longer. Play the track and listen for the pop at the edit point.

10. Zoom in on the edit point until the waveform resembles the one shown here:

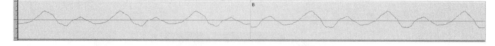

11. As you can see, the peaks and valleys in this waveform follow a pattern: tall, short, tall, short.

12. Switch to Slip mode and trim the B region to the right, as shown in the following illustration, so that the edit point is at the zero crossing point of the short peak.

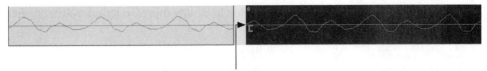

Trim to the zero crossing

13. Drag the trimmed B region to the left, until you reach the corresponding zero crossing of the short peak in the A region, as shown here:

14. Zoom out and listen to the edit.

If you followed the steps correctly, the edit in the middle of the word "home" should be nearly undetectable when listening to the whole mix. Because you took the trouble to make the edit by carefully matching the waveforms at the sample level, a crossfade is unnecessary. It was accomplished with a single edit, and without any processing or degradation of the audio signal.

15. Save the session as **W.Stranger 14voc1**.

Making Tracks Inactive

Deactivating a track frees up the Digital Signal Processing (DSP) used by that track and its plug-ins, while preserving the track's edits, automation, plug-in settings, and so forth. This is an extremely important feature for some LE users, as it enables them to open and edit sessions created on HD systems that exceed Pro Tools LE's track limit. It's important to realize that although inactive tracks won't play, they can still be edited, and then reactivated later.

I'm not a big fan of hanging on to tracks I no longer need, but I have learned from experience to always keep all the vocal tracks for a session in case I have to go back and fix something later. When I'm finished comping a vocal, I always deactivate the source tracks. Not only does it free up the DSP allocated to the track, it also prevents me from unmuting them all by accidentally OPTION+clicking a Mute button during mixdown. You haven't lived until you've experienced eight vocal tracks all slamming through the same output at once.

We don't need M2, M3, M4, or the Stretch track any more, so let's deactivate them.

1. Select M2, M3, M4, and Stretch.

2. Choose Track > Make Inactive. Note that the selected tracks are now grayed out, and their names are in italics in the Tracks list.

3. Hide the deactivated tracks, leaving only the M1 track showing in the Edit window.

4. Save the session.

Fixing Vocal Tracks with Auto-Tune

Pitch-correcting vocal tracks is nothing new. Ever since the invention of the Eventide Harmonizer (and probably before that), producers and engineers have gone to great lengths in their efforts to tune vocal tracks with various gizmos. When Auto-Tune came along, fixing off-pitch vocals got a whole lot easier for Pro Tools users. Lots of folks cried "No fair!" when this plug-in came out, but I wasn't one of them (the same hue and cry arose with the arrival of the Hammond organ, the multitrack tape machine, and the drum machine). I began using Auto-Tune shortly after it was introduced in 1997, and it has paid for itself many times over. I consider it a useful tool when used carefully. For me, it's a last resort—after I've tried everything else to get the vocal right. Many times, I have been able to salvage that one magical vocal performance that was perfect except for one or two off notes. In my humble opinion, it's only obtrusive when you go overboard with it.

Auto-Tune works on just about any monophonic sound that isn't full of harmonics or noise. I've used it successfully on bass, strings, horns, harmonica, electric guitar solos, theremin, and steel guitar. It can also be used to create some pretty wacky effects by drawing radical pitch changes over normal tracks.

This exercise requires the installation of the Auto-Tune demo (if you don't already own it). Don't install the demo until you are ready to do the exercise. The Auto-Tune demo will only run once, and it expires after ten days. If you have already run the Auto-Tune demo on your system in the past, you won't be able to run it again on the same computer. In this exercise, you'll learn a technique for tuning vocals with Auto-Tune that involves the least amount of processing and keeps your tracks organized.

Installing the Auto-Tune Demo

Take the following steps to install the Auto-Tune demo:

1. Quit Pro Tools if it is running.

2. Navigate to the Honeywagon folder and open the Auto-Tune folder. There are four different versions of Auto-Tune:

   - **Pro Tools LE on Mac OS X**   Auto-Tune RTAS OS X

   - **Pro Tools LE on Windows**   Auto-Tune RTAS PC

   - **Pro Tools TDM on Mac OS X**   Auto-Tune TDM OSX

   - **Pro Tools TDM on Windows**   Auto-Tune TDM PC

3. Choose the version that's appropriate for your system and run the installer. Follow the instructions for using the product in demo mode.

4. Start Pro Tools and open the session titled W.Stranger 14voc1.

5. Select the M1 track, choose Track > Duplicate, and then click OK to create a duplicate of M1.

6. We're going to do the pitch processing on the original M1 track, so change its name to **Pitch**.

7. Name the duplicate track **M.tune**.

8. The Auto-Tune plug-in window takes up a lot of space, so let's get rid of the rulers (View > Rulers > None).

9. We're going to bounce audio from Pitch to M.tune, so assign the output of Pitch to Bus 4.

10. Assign the input of M.tune to Bus 4.

11. Enable Inserts view and insert Plug-in > Pitch Shift > Auto-Tune (Mono) on the Pitch track. The tracks in your Edit window should be configured as shown in Figure 12-3.

Auto Mode vs. Graphic Mode

Auto-Tune has two main modes, Auto and Graphic. Auto-Tune defaults to Auto mode when it is first opened. This mode is for lazy folks who just want to set it and forget it. While this mode works well enough for simple things like vocal oohs

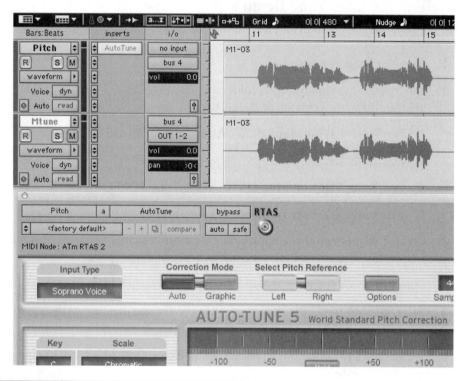

Input and Output assignments for bouncing tracks with Auto-Tune

and ahs that will be way back in the mix, I never use Auto mode on a lead vocal because Auto-Tune doesn't always behave itself.

Auto mode works something like this: Auto-Tune detects the pitch of a note. If the pitch is off, Auto-Tune pulls it to the nearest note that's in the correct scale for the specified key. It works most of the time, but if a vocalist bends a note or sings a smooth upward glissando from one note to another, Auto-Tune will attempt to hold the note to a constant pitch. As the sung note goes up in pitch, Auto-Tune will eventually snap up to the next note in the scale. If you've encountered "that Cher song," ("Real Love") you've heard an example of Auto-Tune (or something like it) used as an effect. Auto mode is also capable of removing vibrato if you set the

Retune knob to a fast setting. Because we're not going to use Auto mode in this exercise, there's no need to specify a key, so we'll leave it set to Chromatic.

1. In the Auto-Tune window, click Input Type and select Alto/Tenor Voice.

2. Under Correction Mode, choose Graphic.

3. Unmute the Pitch and M.tune tracks and select the first audio region on Pitch, which contains the first three lines of Verse 1.

4. Put the M.tune track into Record-Ready and Input mode (OPTION+K / ALT+K).

5. Click the Track Pitch button near the bottom of the Auto-Tune window. It flashes red to show that it is active.

6. Turn off any pre- or post-roll.

7. Click the Auto Scroll button to the left of the pitch graph to turn that feature off.

8. Press Play and let Pro Tools play through the entire audio region.

9. Click the Track Pitch button to turn it off.

When you played the region, Auto-Tune created a graphic representation of the pitch of the vocal in the form of a red pitch curve. The corresponding waveform is shown at the bottom of the pitch graph.

10. In the Auto-Tune window, position the cursor over the waveform at the bottom of the pitch graph. The Zoom/Select tool (magnifying glass) appears. Drag it across the waveform at the bottom of the pitch graph to zoom in on the pitch information. Adjust the scroll bars in the Auto-Tune window if necessary to center the pitch curve, as shown in Figure 12-4.

The horizontal lines in the pitch graph represent the different notes in the chromatic scale. Play the phrase again and watch as Auto-Tune scrolls through. The red pitch line represents Medusa's voice as it travels from one note to another. The pitch graph shows which notes she is singing, and whether or not they are in tune. For instance, the correct pitch for the phrase "I am" is A2. The A2 line in the graph shows the correct, or *target*, pitch and the red pitch curve shows us that the phrase is *sharp*, or above the correct pitch.

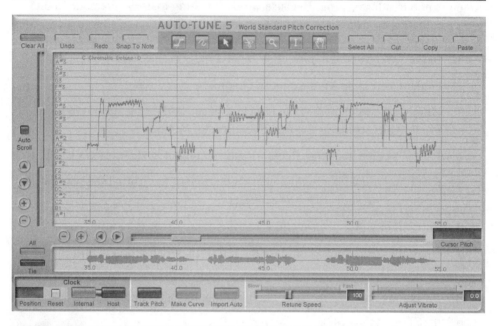

FIGURE 12-4   Zoom in on the Auto-Tune pitch pitch information

11. In the Auto-Tune window, select the Zoom/Select tool (magnifying glass) and drag a box around the phrase "I am" as shown here:

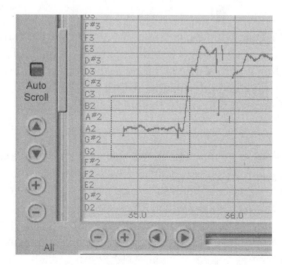

12. In the Auto-Tune window, select the Line tool, as shown here:

The Line tool

13. Click the Snap To Note button. This feature makes it easier to draw a straight line at the target pitch.

14. Click once on the A2 line at the beginning of the phrase "I am," and then double-click at the end of the note. This causes a blue pitch-correction line to be drawn between the two points, as shown here. If you make a mistake, use the Undo button in the Auto-Tune window and try again.

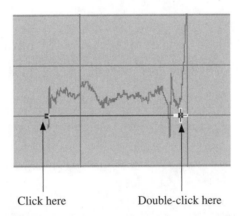

Click here   Double-click here

By drawing this line, you have instructed Auto-Tune to bring the pitch down to A2 for the duration of the phrase "I am."

15. Press Play, and listen to "I am." Now both words are on pitch.

16. Select the Hand tool in the Auto-Tune window and click in the pitch graph. Pull down and to the left to navigate to the next phrase, "a poor."

17. The target pitch for the word "a" is E3. As you can see, it's pretty sharp. The first part of the word "poor" starts at D3, and then returns to E3 a little *flat*, or below pitch, at first. Select the Line tool again and draw a line for "a" and another one for the flat part of "poor," as shown in Figure 12-5.

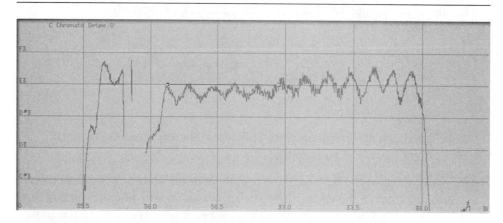

FIGURE 12-5   Pitch information for the phrase "A poor"

18. Use the Hand tool to navigate to the next word, "wayfaring."

19. Use the Line tool to draw lines to fix the pitches, as shown in Figure 12-6.

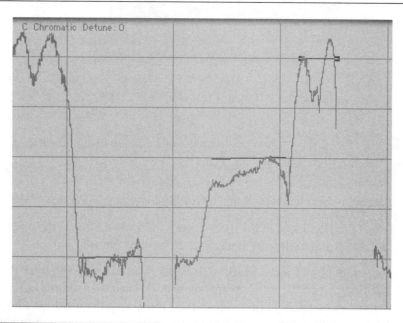

FIGURE 12-6   Pitch information for the word "Wayfaring"

20. Use the Hand tool to navigate to the next word, "stranger."

21. Use the Line tool to draw lines to fix the pitches, as shown in Figure 12-7.

22. Listen to the entire sentence, and then listen again with Auto-Tune bypassed. If you can't tell much difference, don't worry about it. Listening for pitch is a skill that usually has to be developed over time. After working with vocals for a while, you will start to hear the difference between on- and off-pitch vocals.

23. Use Auto-Tune's Hand tool to navigate to the phrase "travelin' through."

24. Go through the phrase as before, using the Line tool to draw lines for off-pitch notes. If a note is on pitch or pretty close, leave it alone.

25. On the M.tune track, select the third line of the verse, and draw pitch-correction lines for it as well.

26. When you're done, select the entire verse audio region on the Pitch track and press Record (F12) to bounce the corrected audio onto the M.tune track.

27. Click the Clear All button in the Auto-Tune window to remove the pitch data.

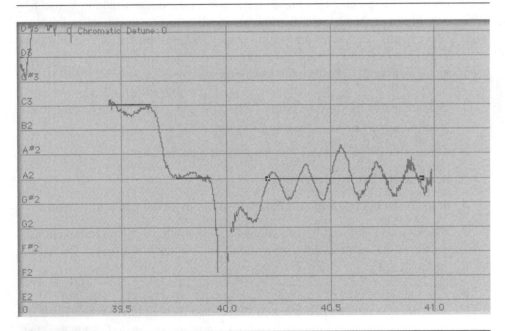

FIGURE 12-7   Pitch information for the word "Stranger"

Yes, this procedure is about as much fun as a root canal but, like editing drums, there's a pattern to it. Once you get into the rhythm, you can knock it out pretty quickly: select the phrase, track the pitch, draw the lines, bounce the track, clear the data, on to the next one. I'd like to emphasize that vocals can sound good without being *perfectly* on pitch, so use your ears to decide what should be fixed, not your eyes.

This is my preferred method of pitch correction for lead vocals because:

■ I can bounce only the parts that need fixing onto the M.tune track instead of running the whole performance through Auto-Tune.

■ I can look at the M.tune track weeks later and know exactly which phrases have been pitch-corrected, because M.tune appears in the region name.

■ The original unprocessed vocal regions are easily accessible on the Pitch track if I should need to come back and revisit them at a later date.

Using the Make Curve and Import Auto Buttons

Occasionally when I'm pressed for time and I have to do a lot of tracks, I streamline this process by using the Make Curve and Import Auto buttons in Graphic mode. This works almost as well as the previous method, and it doesn't require as much drawing. With this method, Auto-Tune automatically corrects the pitch, and then you fix the places where Auto-Tune didn't achieve the desired result. You'll inspect the pitch graph to see how the vocal was processed, make changes if necessary, and then bounce them to the M.tune track as before.

1. Select the last line of the chorus, "I'm only going over home," on the Pitch track.

2. Click Auto Tune's Track Pitch button and play the line.

3. Turn off the Track Pitch button.

4. Use the Zoom/Select tool as before to zoom in on the pitch information.

5. Click Import Auto. Auto-Tune draws an automatic pitch-correction curve. Listen to the result. It did a pretty good job, but the word "over" sounds a little strange.

6. Use the Auto-Tune Zoom/Select tool to zoom in on "over." The first syllable was sung so flat that Auto-Tune mistakenly pulled it down to B2. When the pitch rose far enough, Auto-Tune snapped it up to C3. On the "ver" syllable, the pitch wobbled quite a bit, and Auto-Tune wobbled along with it.

7. This is a situation where the vocalist was going for a bluesy effect, so the "o" needs to bend a little, eventually rising to a C. Since a straight line won't work in this situation, select the Line tool and turn off Snap To Note.

8. Draw lines for "over," like the ones shown in Figure 12-8.

As you can see, automatic pitch correction doesn't work well for bent notes (glissandos) or notes that are way off pitch.

Selecting the Key

The scale is currently set to Chromatic in the Auto mode window. With this setting, every note will appear in the pitch graph. If you know the key of the song, you can enter it in the Key field in the Auto mode window. This will prevent Auto-Tune from pulling a note toward a pitch that's not in the key of the song. Notes not in the scale are also removed from the pitch graph in Graphic mode. The following steps will demonstrate this feature:

1. Under Correction Mode, choose Auto.

2. Choose A in the Key field, and Minor in the Scale field.

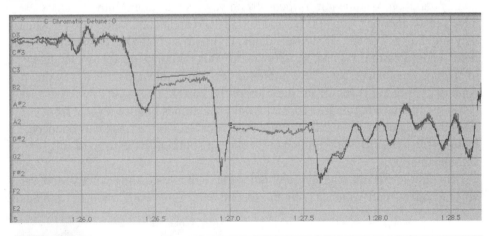

FIGURE 12-8   Pitch information for the word "Over"

3. Under Correction Mode, choose Graphic.

Note that A#, F#, and G# are no longer visible in the pitch graph, because those notes would not normally appear in a song in the key of A minor. In the case of a radically off-pitch vocal, specifying the key will make it easier for Auto-Tune to determine the correct target pitch.

4. You're on your own! Using the methods you have learned, go through the Pitch track and fix any pitch problems you find.

5. When you're done, deactivate and hide the Pitch and M.tune tracks.

6. Save the session, and then save it again as **W.Stranger 15tune**.

Incidentally, the M1 track was so off pitch because it was the first take, and Medusa's voice wasn't completely warmed up. It's a good example of why a vocalist should sing for 30 minutes or so before starting to record.

Smoothing Vocal Resonances with EQ

When recording vocalists, you will find that different people's voices resonate at different frequencies. This resonance often results in a radical change in tonal quality and a big volume jump when certain vowels are sung. Many vocalists have a resonance between 400 Hz and 1 kHz that can become quite intense when they sing an "ah" or an "oh" vowel sound. Trying to smooth the resonance with a normal compressor can make matters worse. This midrange peak has a tendency to "pump" the compressor. The compressor grabs the note and pulls it way down, slightly dulling the vocal for the duration of the vowel.

In the old days before Pro Tools, I would sometimes bounce a vocal from one track to another, manually changing the vocal EQ as the track was bounced. Pro Tools provides us with a much more elegant solution in the form of fully automatable EQ.

The first line of the chorus is a good example of a resonating vowel. Medusa's voice resonates pretty intensely on the second half of the word "mother," and again in the next line on the word "home." In fact, these resonating vowels distorted the mic preamp a bit during the recording. In the next exercise, you'll use automated EQ to smooth out the resonance. Before we start, you need to learn a little bit more about equalizers and the Zoom Toggle command.

Using the Zoom Toggle Command

The next exercise involves zooming in on certain parts of words, and then zooming back out again. When Commands Focus (the a...z button, remember?) is enabled, the Zoom Toggle command facilitates this with a single press of the E key, making the job much simpler. There are a few Preferences that control the behavior of the Zoom Toggle command, so let's take a look.

1. Open W.Stranger 15tune (if it's not open already).

2. Enable the Markers ruler (View > Rulers > Markers).

3. Unhide and unmute the Medusa.voc track. Set its Track Height to Medium.

4. Go to Setup > Preferences > Editing and set the Zoom Toggle Preferences as follows:

   ■ **Horizontal Zoom**   Selection

   ■ **Track Height**   Large

   ■ **Track View**   No change

5. Click OK to close the dialog.

What Does the Q Control Do?

Nowadays, most people understand what a graphic equalizer does. They're everywhere—boom boxes, car and home stereos, even Walkmans have them. Parametric equalizers like the EQ 3 plug-in are a little more mysterious, because most people don't understand the function of the Q, or bandwidth, control. To put it simply, the Q setting controls how much of the frequency spectrum is affected when you raise or lower the gain control. For instance, if your car stereo has a three-band graphic EQ with three little faders—Bass, Mid, and High—raising the Mid fader will boost a broad range of frequencies. This is an example of a very wide or low Q setting. A graphic representation of a midrange boost at 1 kHz with a low Q is shown here:

Although the EQ is "centered" at 1 kHz, a broad range of frequencies on either side is affected. When we were looking for the offending frequency in the squeak removal exercise in Chapter 7, we used a narrow, or high, Q setting, and swept up and down the frequency range to pinpoint the squeak's center frequency. A graphic representation of a midrange boost at 1 kHz with a high Q setting is shown here:

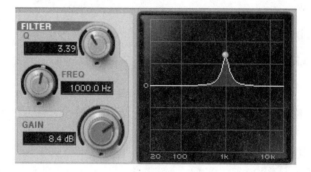

As we did in the squeak removal exercise, we are going to sweep the frequency up and down with the EQ plug-in to find the point at which the vocal is resonating.

1. The first step is to isolate the offending frequency range by sweeping the track with an EQ, as we did earlier with the guitar squeak. Insert the 1-Band EQ 3 (Mono) plug-in on the second insert (B) of the Medusa.voc track.

2. We need a fairly narrow bandwidth, or high Q, for sweeping purposes, so set the Q to 4.

3. Set the Input to −6 dB, and the Gain to +12 dB (lowering the Input will help prevent clipping the plug-in).

4. In Slip mode, select the word "mother" in the first chorus and activate Loop Playback mode.

5. Use the Frequency knob to slowly "sweep" the equalizer between 400 Hz and 1 kHz. Pay special attention to the second syllable "ther" as you sweep.

6. Things really get obnoxious around 800 Hz, so we'll use that as the center frequency. Click the Auto button in the EQ plug-in window. The Plug-in Automation dialog appears.

7. We want to automate the Gain control, so choose Gain, click Add, and then click OK to close the dialog.

8. OPTION+click (ALT+click) the Input and Gain knobs in the plug-in window to return them to 0 dB.

9. We need to widen the Q, so enter a setting of 1 in the Q field.

10. Click the vocal track's Track View selector (currently set to Waveform) and choose 1-Band EQ 3 > Gain.

11. With the word "mother" still selected, press the E key; the Zoom Toggle command zooms in and expands the Track Height automatically.

12. Use the Grabber to place four breakpoints, as shown in Figure 12-9, to pull the gain down 2 dB during the middle of the second syllable. Here's a tip: place the outside breakpoints first, and then place and adjust the ones in the middle. Use the ⌘ (CTRL) key for finer control.

13. Press the E key again to return to the previous zoom setting.

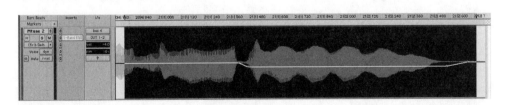

FIGURE 12-9   EQ automation for the word "Mother"

14. Play back the word and watch as the EQ automatically dips 800 Hz. You should be able to discern a difference in the way the vowel resonates. You may notice a slight drop in overall volume, which may need to be boosted slightly to compensate, but we'll save that for the mix.

15. There's a big resonant "oh" vowel on the next occurrence of the word "home." This time, use three breakpoints to pull the EQ gain down about 3 dB, with the gain slowly returning to 0 dB, as shown in Figure 12-10.

16. Select and copy the EQ Automation data for "home" and paste it over the "home" at 42|1|000 in Chorus 2.

Click the Bypass button to compare the difference in the sound of these words with and without the EQ. The goal here is to keep the sound of the vocal consistent, and the effect should be subtle. The improvement should be more noticeable on the word "home," because that word required a larger reduction in gain.

Different vowels resonate at different frequencies. An *e* vowel, for instance, may cause problems in the 2 kHz to 4 kHz range. Therefore, you may find yourself automating both the Frequency and Gain controls for a particularly problematic vocal.

17. Return the Track View selector to Waveform.

Dealing with Vocal Sibilance

Sibilance is the whistling sound your mouth makes when you sing or say a word containing an "ess" sound. Some singers exhibit more sibilance than others. It's

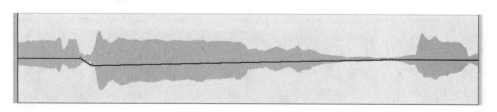

FIGURE 12-10   EQ automation for the word "Home"

always been a problem in recording, because sibilance often manifests itself as an intense burst of high-frequency information around 5 kHz to 8 kHz that has a tendency to cause distortion. In the days of vinyl record mastering, excessive sibilance could literally make the record needle jump out of the groove, so mastering engineers developed the *de-esser*, a compressor that attenuates high frequencies when triggered by overly sibilant passages.

Because sibilance doesn't come from your vocal cords, a person's voice will have about the same amount of sibilance, regardless of the volume of their performance. A whispered vocal is almost *all* sibilance, whereas a loud vocal will tend to be less sibilant.

Compression compounds the problem. While most compressors do a good job of keeping the overall volume in check, they usually let the sibilance sail right on through, increasing the ratio of sibilance to voice. Other fricative sounds, such as the *t* and *ch*, will also sneak through. In general, the more a vocal is compressed, the more sibilance you're going to hear.

Brightening a vocal will also increase sibilance. Often, an engineer will compress and brighten a vocal to help it pop out of the mix, only to find that she has to insert a de-esser before the compressor in the signal chain to keep the sibilance under control. In this exercise, we will simulate this situation and explore ways to correct it.

Medusa's vocal isn't very sibilant, so we're going to have to exaggerate the EQ and stomp the vocal track hard with the compressor to make the esses stand out.

1. Insert another 1-Band EQ 3 plug-in on the Medusa.voc track's last (E) insert, click the Librarian menu (currently labeled Factory Default), and choose the Medusa Voc setting.

2. Insert Plug-in > Dynamics > Compressor/Limiter Dyn 3 on the third plug-in insert (C) and choose Vocal Levelor from its Librarian menu.

3. Raise the Gain setting to 8 dB.

4. Play the first line in the song. The Compressor plug-in's Gain Reduction (GR) meter shows how much compression is occurring. If you listen closely, you'll notice that the Compressor is grabbing *everything but* the esses. Now some of the louder esses are starting to get a little obnoxious.

Using the DeEsser Plug-in

Listen to the first line of Chorus 1 ("I'm going home to see my mother"). The word "see" is now pretty sibilant. One solution would be to automate the EQ plug-in to pull the high frequencies down on the esses, but the DeEsser plug-in will attenuate the sibilance automatically.

1. Insert Plug-in > Dynamics > DeEsser Dyn 3 in the first (A) insert of the vocal track.

2. Select the phrase "to see my" and let it run continuously in Loop Playback mode.

3. Select the Female DeEss setting in the Librarian menu. You should notice quite a difference in ess sound.

4. Click the HF Only button. The effect is more subtle, because only the frequencies above the Frequency setting are affected.

5. Try lowering the Frequency setting to 4 kHz. Now the DeEsser attenuates everything above 4 kHz.

NOTE *When properly set, the DeEsser doesn't do much until the ess sound comes along and triggers gain reduction. The DeEsser has an extremely fast attack and release, so that (ideally) it compresses only for the duration of the sibilance, leaving the rest of the vocal unaffected.*

When the DeEsser is triggered, it attenuates the high end pretty severely, so you usually don't want it grabbing anything but sibilance, or the results can sound unnatural. Set the Range too low, and the vocalist will sound as though they have a speech impediment. It's a fun trick to play on vocalists when things get a little dull around the studio.

Piling On the Plug-ins

We now have a total of four plug-ins on the vocal track. This may seem like a lot but, remember, the DeEsser and the automated EQ aren't working all the time. If you have the screen real estate, you can view multiple plug-ins simultaneously.

1. Click the red target icon in the DeEsser plug-in. This will keep the window from closing when you open another one.

2. Open the other three plug-in windows, clicking on their targets as well. Arrange the windows so that you can see the graphic display in each one.

3. Play the first chorus and watch the show.

The Compressor is still at a pretty extreme setting. Try raising the Threshold to −20 and backing the Gain control down to 6 for a more natural sound. If the vocal is sounding too bright, back the Gain control of the Medusa Voc EQ down to a lower setting, like 2.5 dB. As you can see, having all the plug-in windows open at once can be convenient when dialing in sounds. Some Pro Tools users have a separate display for that purpose.

Choosing the Plug-in Order

When using multiple processors in a track, it's important to pay attention to the order in which they're inserted. The plug-in order on the vocal track should now be as follows: DeEsser, automated EQ, Compressor, and Medusa Voc EQ (high-end boost). There are good reasons for having them in this particular order. Processors that *attenuate* unwanted frequencies like the automated EQ and the DeEsser should be placed *before* the compressor, because they make the compressor's job easier. Because compressors exacerbate sibilance problems, it makes sense to reduce the sibilance before it reaches the compressor.

Compressors have a tendency to dull the sound somewhat, so anything you use to brighten the sound should go *after* the compressor. Similarly, any low-end boost should normally occur after the compressor, or it will make the compressor work much harder.

What about Volume Rides?

Here's an important question—should volume adjustments occur before or after these plug-ins? The plug-in inserts are pre-fader, and cannot be changed to post-fader. Therefore, volume changes written into the automation will occur *after* the plug-ins have processed the signal. However, if you have written volume data for the purpose of smoothing out a track's dynamics to keep the peaks from pumping the compressor too much, it follows that the volume changes should occur *before* they reach the compressor.

There are two ways to place plug-ins after the fader. If you have a large multichannel system with every instrument assigned to its own output and routed to a mixing console, you would create a new mono Master fader, assign it to the same output as the track in question, and move the Compressor plug-in to one of the Master fader's inserts (Master faders require no additional DSP). This would effectively place the compressor *after* the vocal track's fader in the signal chain. This won't work in a situation like ours, because we're mixing within Pro Tools.

Let's pretend for a moment that Medusa's vocal performance was very dynamic, with some whispered sections, followed by some extremely loud passages, and you were compelled to write a lot of volume changes into the automation to keep the vocal even. In that situation, it would be preferable to put the compressor after the fader in the signal chain. We can use an aux track to accomplish this.

1. Close all the plug-in windows.

2. Create a new Mono Aux Input and name it **M.aux**.

3. Assign the input of M.aux to Bus 6 (any unused bus will do). Leave the output set to OUT 1-2.

4. ⌘+click (CTRL+click) the M.aux track's Solo button to put it in Solo Safe.

5. Assign the output of Medusa.voc to Bus 6.

6. Drag the Compressor and the Medusa Voc EQ plug-ins down onto the M.aux track to place them after the fader. (The automated EQ plug-in and DeEsser are working just fine where they are.)

Now you could automate all sorts of complex volume changes on the Medusa.voc track, and use the M.aux track as a Master fader to adjust the overall vocal level.

There's one more consideration here. The reverb send is still on the Medusa.voc track. If you change the volume on the M.aux track, the reverb won't change with it unless the send is moved to the M.aux track.

7. Enable the Sends (A-E) view.

8. Go to View > Sends A-E > Assignments.

9. Drag the Bus 3 send down onto the M.aux track.

10. Your insert and send setup should now appear as shown here:

11. Save the session, and then save it again as **W.Stranger 16vocfx**.

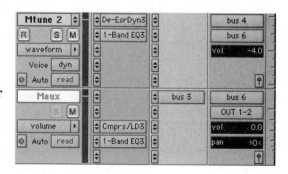

Chapter 13

Advanced Mixing Techniques

In this chapter, you'll be putting the finishing touches on the Honeywagon project. The band members have contributed additional tracks that you'll add to the mix and tweak with various plug-ins, and a final mix will be created. As the session grows in size and complexity, LE users may need to increase the Hardware Buffer Size to 512 or 1024 Samples (Setup > Playback Engine > H/W Buffer Size).

Listening for Phase Problems

Engineers must be constantly on the lookout for phase problems, especially during mixing. A "phasey" mix is fatiguing to listen to and sounds radically different in mono. Beginners will often put tracks out of phase, and pan them left and right to make them sound "wider," only to find they disappear when played in mono. The following exercise will demonstrate what this sounds like.

1. Open the session titled W.Stranger 16vocfx.

2. Show the V loop track and Solo it.

3. Make sure Inserts view is enabled, and insert the Time Adjuster plug-in on the V loop track—Multichannel Plug-in > Delay > TimeAdjuster (Short). Because this is a stereo plug-in, you will see two Phase buttons, as shown here:

Phase buttons

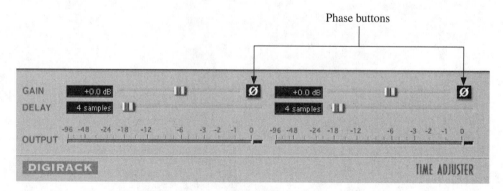

4. Play the V loop track, and click one of the Phase buttons.

The left and right channels are now 180 degrees out of phase. The low-end punch is gone, and the kick drum is mushy and indistinct. Click the Phase button on and off to hear the difference. I don't know about you, but listening to out-of-phase tracks makes me feel as if my brains were being sucked out of my head. It's exactly the same effect as switching the wires on one of your speakers.

5. Leave the V loop out of phase and pan both sides of the track to the center by OPTION+clicking (ALT+clicking) the Pan controls (beneath the volume [vol] display). Now the V loop track is in mono. Listen to the V loop. Everything that was panned to the center is almost completely canceled, leaving only the reverb and the instruments that were panned to the sides.

6. Take the V loop track out of Solo and return its Pan controls to full left and right. Remove the TimeAdjuster plug-in.

What Causes Phase Cancellation?

Now you know what it sounds like when two tracks are inverted, or 180 degrees out of phase, but what about tracks that are only partially out of phase? This type of phase problem is more common and more difficult to recognize. It's important to understand that timing problems can also cause tracks to be out of phase.

Fortunately, Pro Tools is an excellent tool for learning about phase cancellation, because it enables you to compare waveforms visually as you listen. In Chapter 10, you learned about using the Invert AudioSuite plug-in to get the drum samples in phase. Timing problems can also cause nonpercussive tracks to be out of phase. You'll usually run into this problem when combining a direct bass sound with a mic'ed bass amp. The mic'ed signal will be slightly delayed in comparison to the direct signal, because of the time it takes for the sound to travel through the air from the speaker to the microphone. This can cause phase cancellation when the two signals are combined, often resulting in a loss of low end or punch. Let's look at a couple of sine waves to see how this happens.

1. OPTION+click (ALT+click) on the Mute button of one of the tracks in the session to mute all the tracks.

2. Hide all the tracks in the session.

3. Import the LoTone A and LoTone B tracks from the WS Tracks session.

4. Set their Track Heights to Large (if they're not already set).

5. Set the Main counter to Min:Secs.

6. Select Slip mode.

7. Set the Nudge value to 1 msec.

8. CONTROL+click (right-click) the Play button (if necessary) to loop playback.

9. Hide the Tracks list and turn off the Inserts and Sends views.

10. Use the Grabber to select the LoTone B audio region.

11. Zoom in on the front of the two audio regions, both vertically and horizontally, until your Edit window looks like the one shown in Figure 13-1.

> What you are seeing is two identical 100 Hz sine waves created with the Signal Generator plug-in. They are perfect sine waves, but they don't look that much different from a bass guitar waveform. 100 Hz is close to a G# on a bass guitar.

12. Press Play to start the loop.

13. As the loop plays, press the > key three times to nudge the LoTone B audio region three milliseconds to the right.

> The drop in volume you hear is due to phase cancellation. In other words, the two tracks are starting to cancel each other out. Two or three milliseconds is about the time it takes for the sound to travel from a speaker to a close microphone.

14. Press the > key two more times, so that the waveforms are 180 degrees out of phase, as shown in Figure 13-2.

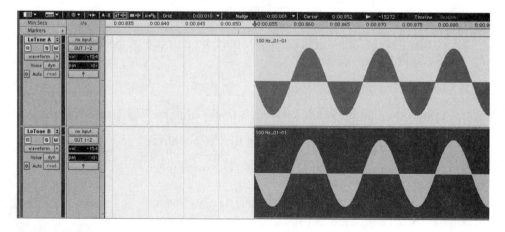

FIGURE 13-1   LoTone waveforms

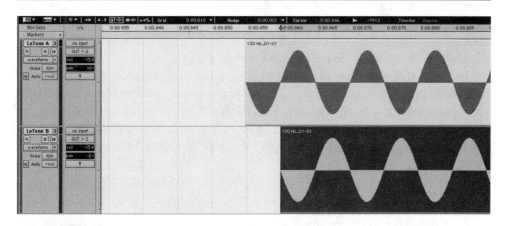

FIGURE 13-2   Waveforms 180 degrees out of phase

At this point, the two waveforms completely cancel each other. One waveform is at its peak, or highest amplitude, while the other is at the lowest amplitude. This shows that if you put a microphone in front of a bass amp at just the right spot, a G# note will be partially cancelled when the signal from the mic is combined with the direct signal from the bass. Before I started using Pro Tools, I would often record the bass direct and bass amplifier to separate tracks, and delay the direct bass track a few milliseconds with a digital delay to get them back in phase during mixdown. In Pro Tools you could just line them up visually, or you could use the TimeAdjuster plug-in to delay the direct track.

15. Delete the LoTone A and LoTone B tracks and save the session as **W.Stranger 17amp**.

Fixing Phase Issues with Virtual Guitar Amps

Otis has expressed the desire to make his steel guitar sound "fatter" in the solo sections by adding a little distortion. The tricky part is that he wants to blend the clean steel guitar sound with a distorted steel guitar sound. Uh-oh. This presents us with the same sort of timing and phase issues discussed in the 100 Hz tone exercise, plus it adds another wrinkle or two to the equation.

It's easy enough to insert a guitar amp plug-in like IK Multimedia's AmpliTube or Line 6's Amp Farm on the Otis.steel track and bounce a distorted version to a new track, but the plug-in delay will probably cause phase cancellation when the clean track is blended with the distorted one. This leaves us with a couple of choices: we can shift one of the tracks in time, or use the TimeAdjuster plug-in on the clean track to match the delay of the distorted track.

In this lesson, you'll use AmpliTube LE to create a processed Steel track and make adjustments to keep the processed and unprocessed tracks in phase. AmpliTube LE is included free with all Pro Tools LE systems. If you have not installed it yet, do so now. If you are using an HD system, or don't have access to AmpliTube LE, you can import the Otis.tube track from WS Tracks and skip Steps 3 through 11.

1. With W.Stranger17amp open, show the Otis.steel guitar track in the Edit window.

2. Change the Main counter display from Min:Secs to Bars:Beats, as shown here:

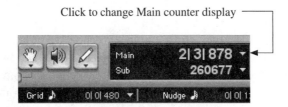

3. Rename the track **Otis.clean**, and set the track's volume to 0 dB and its output to Bus 7.

4. Create a new track named **Otis.tube**, and set its input to Bus 7.

5. Solo both tracks.

6. Enable the Inserts view (if it is inactive) and insert Plug-in > Other > AmpliTube LE (Mono) on the Otis.clean track.

7. A plug-in setting for the steel guitar has been stored in the session's Plug-in Settings Folder. Click the Librarian menu in the AmpliTube plug-in window and choose Session's Settings Folder > Otis Steel.

8. Put the Otis.tube track into Record.

9. Use the Grabber to select the entire audio region on the Otis.clean track and press Record to bounce the steel guitar through the plug-in and onto the Otis.tube track.

10. Take the Otis.tube track out of Record and set the Otis.clean track's output to OUT 1-2.

11. Close the AmpliTube plug-in window and remove the plug-in. Set the Track Height of the two tracks to Large.

At this point you should have two tracks showing in the Edit window: Otis.clean and Otis.tube. Even though they are the same instrument, the waveforms look very different. The distortion from the AmpliTube plug-in has compressed the sound, rounding off the peaks and making the quieter parts louder.

12. Turn the Otis.tube track down 3 dB and listen to the two tracks together. There is a slight hollowness to the sound due to phase cancellation.

13. Zoom in on the beginning of the first note, as shown here:

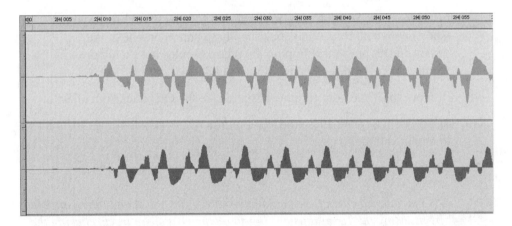

Even though the AmpliTube plug-in has altered the waveform, if you study the repeating patterns on the two tracks closely, you should be able to tell that there is a similarity between the two. The phase of the Otis.tube track has been inverted, and is also delayed slightly. Let's flip the phase.

14. Use the Grabber to select the Otis.tube audio region.

15. Under the AudioSuite menu, choose Other > Invert, and then click Process.

16. Now the phase is a better match, but the timing is still off. Zoom in closer if necessary and move the Otis.tube region slightly to the left in Slip mode so that the waveforms match as closely as possible, as shown here:

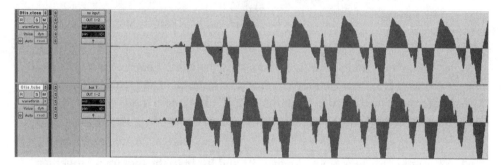

17. Play the tracks together. The sound should be fuller and louder now that the tracks are more in phase. Let's do a quick test to make sure we have made an improvement.

18. Insert the TimeAdjuster plug-in—Plug-in > Delay > TimeAdjuster (short)—on both tracks and click the Phase button on one of the TimeAdjuster plug-ins. Flipping the phase should cause a big drop in volume and a "hollowing out" of the sound.

19. Remove the TimeAdjuster plug-ins and take the Otis tracks out of Solo.

20. OPTION+click (ALT+click) the Mute button *twice* on one of the Otis tracks to unmute all the tracks.

21. Set the volume of both tracks to –10 dB. Save the session.

NOTE   *As I mentioned earlier, we could have solved the phase and timing problem by inserting the TimeAdjuster plug-in on the Otis.clean track, clicking the Phase button, and playing with the delay time to get the fullest sound, but I've found that aligning the tracks visually is faster and more accurate.*

Using the Delay Compensation Feature (Pro Tools HD Only)

In Pro Tools HD systems, every time you insert a plug-in, bounce a track, or put an aux input or Master fader in the signal chain, the signal is delayed by a certain amount. Most of the DigiRack plug-ins cause only three or four samples of delay, which is usually not enough to worry about. (In this session, 44 samples = one millisecond.) The Waves Linear Phase Multiband Compressor plug-in does some heavy-duty number crunching, and clocks in at 3531 samples.

Often these delays are so short as to be unnoticeable, but they can cause problems when inserted on one of two identical (or nearly identical) tracks, as in the previous bass guitar example, or on one side of a stereo pair.

One common example of stereo micing is to place a pair of overhead mics above a drum kit. These mics will normally be recorded to a pair of tracks, which are then panned left and right for a stereo image. Inserting a plug-in on one of these tracks will delay the track, altering the stereo image and possibly causing phase or timing problems. If the snare drum and overhead mics are carefully placed so that they are all in phase, inserting a plug-in on the snare mic can cause phase or timing problems between the snare and overhead mics. It follows that inserting a plug-in on one of several drum tracks can be problematic unless you insert the same plug-in on *all* the drum tracks, so they will all be delayed by the same amount. This is easy to do, but it can unnecessarily squander a lot of DSP.

Pro Tools HD provides the Delay Compensation feature to get around this problem. When enabled (under the Options menu), Pro Tools keeps the tracks time aligned by delaying the unprocessed tracks so that they are in time with tracks containing plug-ins. Since you don't want to be overdubbing to delayed tracks, Delay Compensation should be turned on at the beginning of the mix stage.

Compressing Time Manually

Medusa has brought in an analog tape from an old recording session, which has an organ part she wants you to fly in. The organ part is in the same key, but the tempo is different. Because the organ part is not a rhythmic loop, time compression/ expansion plug-ins won't necessarily give the best results. Our best bet is to manually line up the individual notes with the grid.

1. Mute and hide the steel guitar tracks and import the Organ track from the WS Tracks session. The organ part consists of eight short phrases. Medusa wants to try to make them fit into the solo sections.

2. Show the M.aux channel and mute it.

3. We'll use the first, second, and fourth phrases, so separate those three regions and name them **1, 2**, and **4**, as shown here:

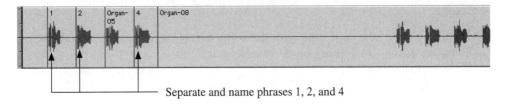

Separate and name phrases 1, 2, and 4

4. Keep these three phrases and delete everything else from the Organ track.

5. Select phrase 1 and press the E key to zoom in.

6. In Slip mode, trim the front of phrase 1 up to the attack of the first note.

7. Do the same for phrases 2 and 4.

8. Press the E key to zoom back out, and switch to Spot mode.

9. The first phrase should go to 4|1|240, so double-click with the Grabber on phrase 1 and enter that location in the Start field, and then click OK.

10. Switch to Slip mode and listen to the phrase along with the music.

The phrase is too slow for the current tempo, but it's pretty close. We can make it fit by separating the notes in the phrase and aligning them with the grid.

11. Enable the Tab to Transients function (next to the a...z button).

12. Zoom in on the second note of phrase 1, so you can easily identify its attack.

13. Click with the Selector just before the attack and press the B key to place a separation.

14. Press TAB to go to the next note, and place a separation there as well.

15. Continue through the phrase until you have separated all six notes.

16. Set the Grid pop-up to 1/16 note.

17. Switch back to Grid mode, and drag the second note to 4|1|480 (it should already be close to that spot).

18. Drag the third note to 4|1|720, the fourth to 4|2|240, the fifth to 4|2|480, and the sixth to 4|1|720, as shown here:

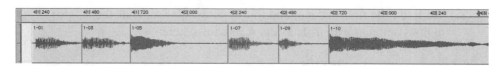

19. The phrase is now in time with the song. Select the entire phrase and press ⌘+F (CTRL+F) to bring up the Batch Fades dialog.

20. Use Equal Power fades, set the Length to 2 milliseconds, and click OK.

21. Consolidate the phrase (OPTION+SHIFT+3 / ALT+SHIFT+3).

22. Double-click the phrase and rename it **Organ 1**.

23. Switch to Spot mode, double-click phrase 2, and spot it to 6|1|240.

24. Switch to Slip mode and tab through the phrase, separating each note as in Steps 11–15.

25. Switch to Grid mode. Starting at the second note, drag the notes to the left one by one to the nearest 1/16 note.

26. Batch fade and consolidate the phrase, naming it **Organ 2**.

27. Spot phrase 4 to 10|1|240.

28. Switch to Slip mode and separate each note, as in Steps 11–13.

29. Switch to Grid mode.

30. Drag notes 2 through 6 to the left one by one to the nearest 1/16 note.

31. Batch fade, consolidate, and name the region **Organ 4**.

32. We need to put Organ 1 in a few more spots. Switch to Spot mode.

33. OPTION+click (ALT+click) Organ 1 with the Grabber to copy and spot it to the following four locations:

8|1|240

29|1|240

51|1|240

55|1|240

34. In a similar fashion, copy and spot Organ 2 to 31|1|240 and 53|1|240.

35. The Organ.comp track is now complete. You should now have a total of nine regions on the Organ track; four in the Intro, two in the Solo, and three in the Outro. To check your work, you can import Org-1 from WS Tracks.

36. Save the session, and then save it again as **W.Stranger 18org**.

Creating a Stereo Ping-Pong Delay

The band wants the organ to sound distant and ethereal, sort of floating from speaker to speaker. A popular method of achieving this effect is the Ping-Pong delay. This effect is created by feeding the output of one digital delay to the input of another, and then creating a feedback loop to keep the signal bouncing back and forth.

1. Hide all the tracks currently showing in the Edit window, except for the Organ track.

2. Enable the Sends view, add a send to the Organ track, and assign it to Bus 10, leaving the fader turned all the way down.

3. Click the red target icon on the Send window, so it will remain visible.

4. Create two new Mono Aux Input tracks, and name them **Delay.L** and **Delay.R**.

5. Pan Delay.L all the way to the left, and Delay.R all the way to the right.

6. Assign the input of Delay.L to Bus 10.

7. Assign the input of Delay.R to Bus 11.

Calculating Delay Times

It's often beneficial to calculate the delay settings, so the repeats will be in time with the music, as it helps the groove and keeps the mix from getting muddy. You can use mathematical formulas to determine the delay time according to tempo, but it's much easier to let Pro Tools do the math.

1. Enable the Inserts view (if necessary) and insert Plug-in > Delay > Long Delay II (Mono) on Delay.L

2. In the plug-in window, click the 1/8 note icon, as shown here:

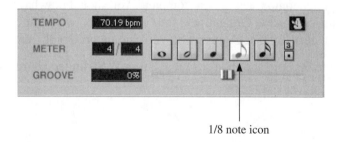

1/8 note icon

3. Pro Tools automatically calculates an 1/8 note delay for the session tempo and enters a delay time of 428.57 msec in the Delay field.

4. On Delay.R, insert Plug-in > Delay > Long Delay II (Mono) and click the 1/16 note icon (to the right of the 1/8 note icon). Pro Tools sets the delay to 214.29 msec.

5. Close the Delay plug-in window.

Now we're going to do something I've been telling you not to do throughout this book—create a feedback loop.

6. Create a send on Delay.L and assign it to Bus 11.

7. In the Send window, click the Pre button to change the send to pre-fader operation, and set the fader to 0.0 dB.

8. Create a send on Delay.R and assign it to Bus 10.

9. Set this send to pre-fader operation as well, but leave the fader turned all the way down.

10. Click the red target icon on the Send window so that it will remain visible.

11. Group the two Delay channels, naming the group Delay.

12. Put both Delay channels in Solo Safe. (You should know how to do that by now.)

13. Solo the Organ track and play the Intro.

14. Raise the Organ track's send fader to feed the signal to Delay.L.

The signal goes to the left delay, where it is sent to the right delay, causing the sound to ping-pong from left to right. Now let's get a little feedback going.

15. *Carefully* raise the Delay.R send fader to send the signal back to Delay.L, creating a feedback loop. The higher you set this fader, the more feedback you'll get, and the repeats will continue longer.

If you raise the send too far, the feedback loop will get out of control, eventually clipping everything.

This Hammond organ sound is clicky. All that clicking bouncing around the digital delays is somewhat distracting. Luckily, the Delay plug-ins have low-pass filters to cut out those high frequencies.

16. On Delay.L, set the Delay plug-in's LPF to around 1000 Hz to attenuate the frequencies above that point. Play the track and note that the delays are much darker, each repeat a little darker than the last as it cycles through the filter again and again.

17. Create another send on Delay.L and assign it to Bus 3, the D-Verb plug-in. This will enable you to send the delay back to the reverb for a more spacey sound.

18. Take the Organ track out of Solo and turn the volume down so that it's in the background. Then play with the delay sends for the desired amount of effect.

19. Now that there are a lot of effects on the organ, the sustained notes at the end of the phrases are swelling up too much. Using the Smart tool in Slip mode, fade the end of each one of the phrases, as shown here:

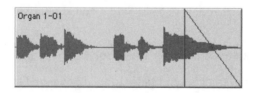

20. Otis wants to hear some of this effect on the clean steel guitar track, so unhide Otis.clean and create a Bus 10 send on his track for that purpose.

21. Close all the send and plug-in windows.

22. Save the session.

I realize that this could be one of those moments where you're thinking, "I followed the steps and it worked, but I have no idea what I just did." Hopefully the flow chart in Figure 13-3 will help you better understand the signal flow of the Ping-Pong delay.

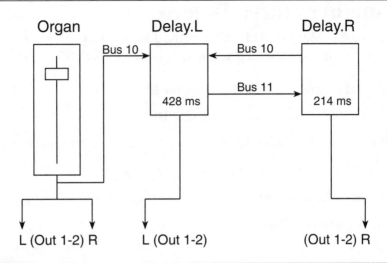

FIGURE 13-3   Ping-Pong delay flow chart

Deleting Unused Tracks and Regions

The session is getting crowded with tracks we don't need anymore. It's safe to remove them from the session—we can always import them from a previous session if we need them again.

1. Open the Tracks list and choose Show All Tracks from the Tracks List pop-up menu (click on the word Tracks).

2. Select any inactive tracks and delete them from the session.

3. Even though these tracks have been deleted, their unused audio files remain in the session. Press ⌘+SHIFT+U (CTRL+SHIFT+U) to select the unused regions.

4. Press ⌘+SHIFT+B (CTRL+SHIFT+B) to bring up the Clear Audio dialog.

5. OPTION+click (ALT+click) on Remove to clear the selected regions from the session.

Adding Another Stereo D-Verb

The band likes the Medium Hall setting on the drums, but would prefer a longer, airier reverb on the vocal and steel guitar. Let's set up a second D-Verb for Bus 4.

1. Show the current D-Verb channel in the Edit window.

2. Change the D-Verb channel's name to **Hall.verb**.

3. While the Hall.verb channel is still selected, duplicate it (Track > Duplicate).

4. Rename the new channel **Plate.verb** and assign its input to Bus 4.

5. On the Plate.verb channel, set the D-Verb plug-in to the following parameters:

- **Algorithm**   Plate
- **Size**   Large
- **Decay**   4.2 sec
- **Pre-Delay**   40 msec
- **HF Cut**   Off

6. Reassign the send on the M.aux channel to Bus 4. (Open the Send window, click Bus 3, and change it to Bus 4.)

7. On the Otis.clean track, reassign the Bus 3 send to Bus 4, and close the Send window.

Using Relative Grid Mode

Up to this point, we have been using the standard, or *Absolute*, Grid mode, where regions always snap to the nearest gridline. But what if your region needs to start between the gridlines? In those situations, you can switch to Relative Grid mode, which preserves a region's position relative to the nearest gridline.

The band would like to have a tambourine in parts of the song. Because the band members are all percussively challenged, nobody wants to play it (much to your relief), so you're going to fly in a sample instead.

The general idea is to paste the sample wherever the snare drum hits occur, and then decide later which ones should be used. However, we can't trim the tambourine sample right up to the attack, because we want to preserve the jingle that precedes the attack. The prospect of manually pasting and aligning the tambourine at every snare drum hit is not very attractive, so we'll use Relative Grid mode instead.

1. Import the Tamb track from WS Tracks.

2. Position the Tamb track directly underneath the Sn Smp track, and set its Track Height to Large. As usual, the tambourine sample region is located at the song start.

3. In Slip mode, select and copy the tambourine sample, and then delete it from the song start.

4. Paste the tambourine sample at the first snare hit after the song starts (approximately 3|4|000) and align the attack of the tambourine with the attack of the snare, as shown in Figure 13-4.

5. Press the F4 key twice to select Relative Grid mode (the Grid button turns purple).

6. Set the Grid pop-up to 1/4 note.

7. OPTION+drag (ALT+drag) the tambourine sample to the next snare hit. Note that the region start does not line up with the gridline; the region retains its *relative* position to the gridline.

8. Continue OPTION+dragging (ALT+dragging) the tambourine sample until you have placed a sample for each snare hit in the rest of the song. (Aren't you glad this song isn't ten minutes long?)

9. Lars has contributed a couple of background vocal tracks. Import Lars.1bv and Lars.2bv from the WS Tracks session.

10. Save the session, and then save it again as **W.Stranger 19bv**.

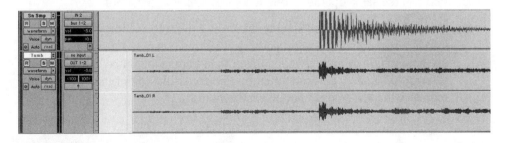

FIGURE 13-4   Aligning the tambourine

Preparing for Mixdown

The band's recording budget is about to run out, so it's time to prepare the session for mixdown. The next section will show you some ways to get things organized.

Cleaning Up the Edit Window

When preparing for mixdown, any extraneous regions or sounds that don't belong in the song should be muted or deleted.

1. The first sound you hear should be the steel guitar, so select and mute (⌘+M / CTRL+M) the V loop regions that occur in the countoff bars before Bar 3. (Hint: It's easier to do this if the tracks are in Waveform view.)

2. Mute the Shaker tracks in the first two bars.

3. Because we used the Loop Trimmer on the K Smp and Sn Smp tracks, the entire Intro is treated as a single region. Therefore, place a separation at 3|1|000 on these two tracks so that you can mute the first two bars.

4. In Slip mode, add a new marker titled **Start** at the entrance of the steel guitar.

5. Go to the end of the song and use the Smart tool to fade out the ends of the guitar and bass audio regions to get rid of any noises that may be present as the last note fades out on each instrument. For instance, the ends of the steel guitar tracks have a nice 60-cycle hum that needs to go away.

6. One of the band members has pointed out that the stops in the middle of the choruses could use an extra kick drum beat. Switch to Grid mode and change the Grid pop-up to 1/16 note.

7. Select the kick drum beat on the C loop track at 23|2|720, and press ⌘+D (CTRL+D) to duplicate the kick.

8. Perform the same operation on the kick at 43|2|720 in Chorus 2.

9. Otis only wants distorted steel guitar during the solo section. An alternative to selecting and muting regions using the Mute command would be to use automation to mute the Otis.tube track. Set the Otis.tube Track View selector to Mute. A black automation line across the top of the track indicates that the track is not currently muted.

10. Use the Grabber to place a breakpoint in the space after the steel stops playing and pull it downward to write a mute at that point, as shown here:

Click here and pull down to write a mute

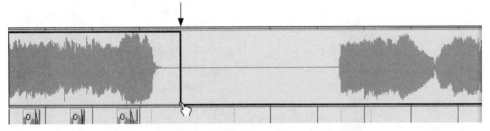

11. Go to the start of the Solo and unmute the track by placing a breakpoint and pulling up. Mute the track again after the Solo is over.

12. Unmute the track at the Outro. The track should now appear as shown here:

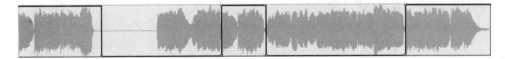

Organizing Your Tracks by Type

You should now have a total of 16 tracks and 7 aux channels in your session, and things are starting to get a little complicated with all the signal routing that's going on. This section presents some ways to make things less confusing visually.

Arranging Your Tracks in Groups

A good way to retain your sanity in the virtual world is to organize your tracks by type. The Mix window is the best place to get an overview of what's going on.

1. Go to the Mix window (⌘+= / CTRL+=).

2. Open the Tracks list and make sure all the tracks are showing. If your display isn't wide enough to see all the tracks, choose View > Narrow Mix. Arrange the tracks from left to right as shown in the following list.

1 V loop	13 Lo Synth
2 C loop	14 Organ
3 K Smp	15 M.tune
4 Sn Snp	16 M.aux
5 Shaker	17 Lars.1bv
6 Tamb	18 Lars.2bv
7 Drum bus (aux)	19 Hall.verb
8 Lars.bass	20 Plate.verb
9 Gtr	21 Pad
10 Otis.clean	22 Delay L
11 Otis.tube	23 Delay R
12 Hi Synth	

Color Coding Your Tracks

There are a variety of ways to use color coding in Pro Tools. Read through the *Reference Guide* for a complete list. Here are a few of my personal favorites:

1. Go to the Edit window (⌘+= / CTRL+=).

2. Go to Setup > Preferences > Display and choose Always Display Marker Colors. Now each section of the song is a different color in the Markers ruler.

3. If the Track Color view is enabled, you will see a vertical color bar at the left edge of each track. The default color is dark blue. Click the V loop track's color bar to bring up the Color Palette with 96 color choices. The current color is outlined.

4. Choose a new color for the color bar.

5. Triple-click with the Selector in the V loop track to select all the regions. In the Color Palette's drop-down menu next to Apply To Selected, choose Regions In Tracks. Choose a new color for the V loop regions and close the Color Palette. You can also use this method to change the color of individual regions within a track.

6. Go to Setup > Preferences > Display and choose Default Region Color Coding: Marker Locations. Now the regions in the Edit window follow the color coding in the Markers ruler, except for the regions in the V loop. That's because your Color Palette choices override the choices made in Preferences.

Creating a Stereo Master

As you learned in Chapter 5, there are two ways we can record the final mix to disk—record to a stereo track or use the Bounce to Disk command. Wayfaring Stranger is a 16-bit session because I needed it to fit on the CD-ROM. Due to the drastic difference in sound quality, I don't recommend *ever* creating 16-bit sessions unless file size is a major issue. For instructional purposes, we're going to pretend that Wayfaring Stranger is a 24-bit session. Let's say that we're planning to send this mix to a mastering house for further processing. In this case we definitely want the final mix to be at the highest possible resolution: an undithered 24-bit stereo WAV file. We also want to create a dithered 16-bit stereo WAV or AIFF file to burn onto a CD so we can listen to it in the car to check the mix (dither is automatically applied when exporting regions to a lower bit depth). The easiest way to accomplish this is to record to a stereo track, and then export the mix in two different formats.

As you may recall, recording to a stereo track requires submixing, so we'll have to reassign some of our outputs.

1.   Hide every track in the session whose output is *not* assigned to OUT 1-2.

2.   Show every track in the session whose output *is* assigned to OUT 1-2.

3.   OPTION+click (ALT+click) the output of one of the audio tracks showing in the Edit window and assign the output to Bus 15-16. The outputs of the other visible tracks will follow suit.

4.   Create a new stereo aux track named **Stereo Master**. This channel will provide a Master volume fader to control the level of the entire mix and a stereo meter with clip indicators. It's also where we will insert any plug-ins for processing the entire mix.

5.   Put the Stereo Master track in Solo Safe and assign its input to Bus 15-16 and its output to Bus 17-18.

6.   Create a new stereo audio track and name it **Mix**. Put it in Solo Safe and assign its input to Bus 17-18 and its output to OUT 1-2.

7.   Put the Mix track into Record-Ready and make sure you are in Input mode.

Labeling Your Effects Sends

Many engineers label their effects sends to make mixing more intuitive. So far, we're using four different effects sends: Bus 3 (Hall.verb), Bus 4 (Plate.verb), Bus 10 (Ping-Pong delay), and Bus 11 (Ping-Pong delay Feedback).

1. If they're not already active, enable the Sends and Inserts views in the Mix window (View > Mix Window > Inserts or Sends A-E).

2. Under Setup, choose I/O.

3. Before you change your I/O settings, you should save the current settings, so you can easily return to them. Click the Export Settings button, name your current setup **Normal**, and click Save.

4. In the I/O Setup window, click the Bus tab.

5. Click the triangle next to Bus 3-4 to view the individual mono busses.

6. Double-click Bus 3 and rename it **Hall.verb**.

7. Double-click Bus 4 and rename it **Plate.verb**.

8. Click the triangle next to Bus 9-10 to view the individual mono busses.

9. Double-click Bus 10 and rename it **Ping-Pong**.

10. Click the triangle next to Bus 11-12 to view the individual mono busses.

11. Double-click Bus 11, rename it **Feedback**, and press RETURN (ENTER).

12. Click OK to save the settings and close the I/O Setup window.

Hiding Nonessential Tracks

If you're hurting for screen space, the first tracks to hide would be the effects aux channels, because they usually don't require a lot of fader changes.

Accessing Other Essential Pro Tools Windows

Many of the more commonly used windows can be accessed by keyboard shortcuts.

NOTE   *The following commands require that the numbers be entered on the numeric keypad, located on the right side of a full-sized keyboard. With laptop computers, consult the manufacturer's documentation to access the numeric keys.*

1. Show the Transport window: ⌘+1 (CTRL+1). The Transport buttons are handy to watch while you're learning to use the numeric keypad to control the transport. If your numeric keypad is in the default Transport mode (Setup > Preferences > Operation > Numeric Keypad > Transport), the numeric keys in the following list will control the transport:

   - **0** Play
   - **1** Rewind
   - **2** Fast Forward
   - **3** Record

2. You don't need the MIDI controls anymore, so turn them off: View > Transport > MIDI Controls.

3. A counter would be helpful: View > Transport Window Shows > Counters.

4. Show the Memory Locations window: ⌘+5 (CTRL+5) or Windows > Show Memory Locations.

5. Show the Session Setup window: ⌘+2 (CTRL+2) or Setup > Session. This window displays useful information about the session format and Time Code ssettings.

What Does a Compressor Do?

In the simplest possible terms, a compressor is an audio circuit designed to even out variations in volume levels. It attempts to keep the volume constant by turning the loud passages down. Compression is something of a mystery to most novices, because, unlike reverb and delay, the effect of the various parameters is not always immediately obvious to the untrained ear. A recording of a vocal with no compression sounds rough or unnatural to most of us, probably because we grew up listening to television, radio, and pop recordings at home, where we were extremely unlikely to encounter a voice that had not been compressed. The broadcast industry has always used compressors to keep the human voice from distorting and overmodulating the signal chain.

Compression is often used to maintain a track's audibility, so it will "sit" consistently in the mix. Compression can increase the apparent sustain of an instrument like guitar or bass. When applied to drums, it can bring out the ambience, making a room sound bigger than it really is. It is often used as a creative tool to radically change the sound of an instrument. It is without a doubt one of the most important tools available to the recording engineer.

The following exercise will give you a brief overview of the functions of the DigiRack Compressor/Limiter plug-in that is bundled with all Pro Tools systems. A more in-depth explanation of its controls can be found in the *DigiRack Plug-ins Guide* under the Help menu.

1. Save and close the current session and open the session titled Compressor in the Honeywagon folder. Like the EQ plug-in, the Compressor/Limiter plug-in (from now on I'll refer to is simply as "the Compressor") includes a graph that provides a visual indication of what the plug-in is doing. The vertical axis represents output level and the horizontal axis represents input level. The orange line represents the threshold, and the white line shows how much gain reduction is applied once the threshold has been reached, and whether the knee is soft or hard (explained in Step 7).

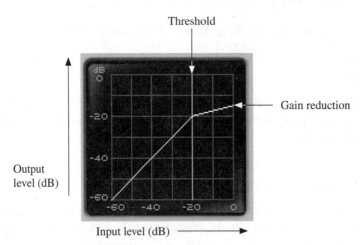

2. The Signal Generator is set up to feed a 400 Hz tone through the Compressor. You shouldn't be able to hear the tone, but turn your speakers down anyway to be on the safe side. Slowly raise and lower the Signal Generator Plug in's Level control and watch as the white square representing the signal level travels across the graph. The input and output levels are the same until the signal level reaches the threshold, which is currently set to −20 dB. When it crosses the threshold, the square turns red to indicate that gain reduction is being applied. The orange Gain Reduction meter (labeled GR) shows the amount of gain reduction in decibels (dB).

3. Pull the Signal Generator's level control all the way down and raise it up again while watching the green Input and Output meters. Note that once the input reaches the −20 dB threshold, the output increases at a much slower rate.

4. Bring the Level control up to −5 dB. The Ratio control is currently set to 4:1. This means that raising the input 4 dB will result in a 1 dB increase at the output.

5. Click the Ratio control and increase the ratio while watching the graph. You can see that increasing the ratio causes the signal to be more compressed, which will have a more drastic effect on the sound. Return the Ratio control to 4:1.

6. Click the Threshold control and raise and lower the threshold while watching the graph. Lowering the threshold causes the Compressor to kick in sooner as the level increases, resulting in more gain reduction and less output level, thereby increasing the effect. Return the threshold to −20 dB.

7. The angle of the white gain reduction line as it crosses the threshold is known as the "knee." It is currently at a "Hard Knee" setting. This means that as the signal crosses the threshold, the Compressor immediately begins reducing the gain by a *constant* 4:1 ratio. Click the Knee control and increase the knee value while watching the graph. The angle of the knee begins to soften into a curve. At the softer knee settings, the Compressor *gradually* increases the ratio as the signal level increases. This will result in smoother, more transparent sounding compression. This type of compression is often favored on vocals.

I don't expect you to swallow all this technical information in one bite. Here are the main concepts I want you to get from the exercise so far:

■ Lowering the threshold increases the amount of compression, making the effect more noticeable.

■ Raising the ratio increases the amount of compression, making the effect more noticeable.

■ Raising the knee setting creates a softer knee, making the effect less noticeable.

The Attack and Release Controls

The Attack control determines how quickly the Compressor kicks in once the threshold has been crossed. In earlier exercises we learned that vocal sibilance and consonant sounds are of such short duration that they often sneak through the Compressor before it has a chance to grab them. That's why de-essers have a very fast attack and release time. The Release control determines how quickly the Compressor "lets go" of the signal when it drops below the threshold. The Attack and Release controls don't have much effect on a 400 Hz tone, so let's try some percussive audio.

1. Mute the Tone track and put the Bounce track into Record-Ready. Close the Signal Generator plug-in window.

2. Make sure you are in Input mode (OPTION+K).

3. Click the Compressor's Librarian menu and choose Factory Default. Then turn the Attack control all the way up to the slowest setting of 300.0 msec.

4. Play the Loop track and look at the graph. The signal is well above the threshold most of the time, but there's no gain reduction. That's because the Compressor's attack is so slow, the transient peaks in the drum loop don't stay above the threshold long enough for the Compressor to react.

5. While the loop is playing, slowly reduce the attack time and listen to the change in the sound of the loop. The first thing you notice is the kick drum receding into the background at around 60 msec. By the time you get down to 1 msec, the attack of the kick is pretty much gone, as well as a good bit of the snare. Set the Attack control to its fastest setting (10 μs—ten *microseconds*—that's pretty fast when you consider that a microsecond is 1/1000 of a millisecond).

6. Turn the threshold down to around −30 dB. Listen to the difference with the Compressor turned on and off. Reducing the threshold brings out the ambience in the loop, as if you had turned up the reverb.

7. We're losing a lot of volume with this extreme setting, so bring the Compressor's Gain control up to 16.0 dB to compensate.

8. Turn the Release control all the way up to its slowest setting of 4 sec. At this slow setting, the Compressor isn't really doing much.

9. Slowly lower the Release control to speed up the release time as you listen. At around 300 msec, you start to hear the reverb rising up after the

snare hit. This effect is known as "pumping" or "breathing." It was originally considered to be undesirable, but nowadays it's often used for a creative effect.

10. Set the release time to about 160 msec and bring the Ratio control up to 6:1. At this setting, the Compressor is more or less pumping in time with the music.

11. This setting might come in handy on other songs, so let's save it to the Root Settings folder. The Root Settings folder is usually located on the startup drive, as opposed to the Plug-in Settings folder in the current session folder. You can use the Root Settings folder to build a library of your favorite presets to use in other sessions. To specify the Root Settings folder as the destination, click the Settings menu (to the left of the plug-in's Librarian menu) and choose Settings Preferences > Save Plug-in Settings To > Root Settings Folder. Then click the Settings menu again and choose Save Settings As and name the setting **Drumnuke**.

12. What's all this squashing doing to the waveform? Record the first two bar loops onto the Bounce track and zoom in for a look. As you might expect, the waveform is much denser and the transient peaks are shorter.

Limiting vs. Compression

What's the difference between limiting and compression? A compressor with a ratio of 10:1, usually combined with a fast attack time, is generally considered to be a limiter. It is not usually used to enhance sonic characteristics—it's more like a safety device to prevent levels from going above the threshold. Ratios between 50:1 and 100:1 are generally referred to as *brick wall limiting*. As you might have guessed, it sounds pretty nasty. There's an example of this in the factory presets.

1. In the Librarian menu, choose Brickwall. Note that the ratio is 100:1, and the attack and release times are very fast. This type of limiter is usually set so that it kicks in only occasionally on transient peaks. Listen to the loop and you may notice that the kick drum sounds a little distorted. Bring the threshold down to −30 dB and the gain up to 22 dB.

2. Record a couple of bars onto the Bounce track. Note that the transient peaks on the bounced region are completely leveled out.

3. We're through with this session. Save it, and then choose File > Open Recent > W.Stranger 19bv.

There's a good bit more to compression than what has been presented here. I urge you to read the section in the *DigiRack Plug-ins Guide* that deals with the Dynamics III plug-ins. Here are a few additional concepts to remember:

- An attack time that is too fast can make a track sound dull and far away.

- An attack time that is too slow on percussive material will result in the Compressor not having much effect on the sound.

- A release time that is too fast on complex material like a stereo mix can cause rapid fluctuations in gain, resulting in audible distortion.

- A release time that is too slow can cause the Compressor to continue to attenuate signals after they fall below the threshold, resulting in "pumping and breathing."

- Dynamic range isn't necessarily a bad thing. Using too much compression on a track can make it sound lifeless.

- Putting a lot of compression on every track will turn your mix to mush.

The best way to understand the subtleties of compression is to try it on different types of program material and play with the controls until you start to recognize their effect. In general, percussive material calls for shorter attack and release times, and sustained sounds like bass and steel guitar can use longer attack and release times. Vocals can contain both sustained and transient sounds and will sometimes benefit from a combination of two or more different types of compression.

Getting a Static Balance

Before we start automating volume levels, we need to establish a starting balance between the song elements. Now is the time to listen to all the instruments and think about how all the pieces of the puzzle fit together. Play the song a few times and get a rough mix going with all the major elements present, keeping an eye on the Stereo Master fader's meters (especially in the choruses). If the Stereo Master clips, back all the faders down a little (except for the Stereo Master). Here are a few suggestions:

- Don't try to make everything loud in the mix. The synth pad and organ are for atmosphere, and should be in the background.

- Try turning off the vocals and just listening to the balance of the instruments. Can you hear everything? Is there too much reverb? Is the tambourine obnoxious?

- Decide which instruments should have priority. Which instrument is the linchpin that holds everything together?

- Every instrument doesn't have to play throughout the song. Some sounds are more effective if they are heard only occasionally.

- Pan some instruments to the side to make room for the vocals. The center position is usually reserved for the bass, kick, snare, and lead vocal.

- Keep the reverb settings to a minimum.

Clearing Up the Mud

One of the biggest problems a mixer faces is masking. This is a dark, moody song, and many of the instruments are centered in the same frequency range: 150–300 Hz. This results in an overall muddiness and difficulty in picking out the individual instruments. Otis will no doubt complain that the synth pad is masking the steel guitar, and he's absolutely right. Jimbo's request to transpose them an octave down turned out to be a bad idea. This is the beauty of using virtual synths—you can make last-minute changes in the sounds. Here are a few things we can do to clear up the mud:

- Transpose the synth tracks up an octave to get them out of the frequency range of the steel guitar, and switch to a string sound like Ballad-String Pad. Keep it very low in the mix—it's just there for texture.

- The main instrument in the song is the acoustic guitar. Even though we've already taken out some low end, it's still a little dark. Try raising the high pass filter to 160 Hz, and boosting the high end a few dB at 3 kHz.

- Another major source of murk is reverb and delay. Check the steel guitar to make sure you didn't go overboard on the effects. The feedback send on the Ping-Pong delay could be a culprit if set too high. Try setting the volume of the distorted Otis.tube track 2 or 3 dB lower than Otis.clean, and pan the two tracks about 50 percent.

- On a song like this, the acoustic guitar should take priority over the bass.

Smoothing Out the Drums

Because the drums are coming from different sources, there's a bit of unevenness in the levels. Let's try some compression on the drum bus to help smooth out the drums and bring up the percussion. To make it easier to solo the drums, let's create a drum group.

1. Click the V loop track name, and then SHIFT+click the C loop, K Smp, Sn Smp, Shaker, and Tamb tracks.

2. Press ⌘+G (CTRL+G) to create a group and name it **Drums**.

3. Solo the drum tracks by clicking any drum track's Solo button.

4. Insert the Compressor/Limiter plug-in on the Drum Bus aux channel, with the parameters set as follows:

   - **Knee**   0.0 dB

   - **Attack**   42 msec

   - **Gain**   0.0 dB

   - **Ratio**   3.0:1

   - **Threshold**   −22 dB

It would be nice to use the Drumnuke preset to bring out some of the percussion and drum ambience with the Compressor, but we don't want to squash the transient peaks by inserting it on the Drum Bus channel. We can prevent that from happening by inserting Drumnuke on another aux channel and mixing it in with the Drum Bus channel.

1. Create a new stereo aux input track, put it in Solo Safe, and name it **Drumnuke**. Set its input to Bus 1-2 (Stereo).

2. Insert the Compressor/Limiter plug-in on the new aux track and choose the Drumnuke preset.

3. The idea is to mix a little of the Drumnuke aux in without overwhelming the mix, so bring its level down to −10 dB.

4. From earlier experience we know that a 1/16 note delay at this tempo is 214 msec, so set the Drumnuke release time to 214 msec.

Automation Tips

Once you have a static mix that sounds good overall, it's time to start thinking about which tracks need volume changes during the song.

The automation in Pro Tools is so flexible and comprehensive, a casual journey through the chapter on automation in the *Pro Tools Reference Guide* can leave the reader feeling completely overwhelmed. In reality, Pro Tools automation can be as simple or as complicated as you want it to be. After years of using Pro Tools on a daily basis, I would say I use about 10 percent of its capabilities, yet it does everything I need it to do.

There are two basic approaches to creating automation data in Pro Tools. Throughout this book, we have mostly been using the graphic approach, where breakpoints are manually placed in tracks and manipulated to make volume and parameter changes. I prefer this approach for most automation chores because it seems simpler to me, and it uses the minimum number of breakpoints, which, in turn, places the least amount of strain on the CPU.

Dynamic Automation

In Pro Tools, the alternative to adding breakpoints manually is known as *dynamic automation*, where the automation data is written by enabling one of the automation modes on a track and moving the faders and other controls during playback. Click any track's Auto button, and a drop-down menu presents you with a choice of automation modes. Pro Tools HD has additional modes that aren't present in the LE version. The most commonly used modes are as follows:

Off	Automation is suspended.
Read	Plays back previously written data.
Touch	Data is written as soon as you touch (or click) a control, and stops writing when the control is released.
Latch	Data is written as soon as you touch a control, and stops writing when the transport is stopped.
Write	Data is written from playback start to stop (previous data is erased).

While dynamic automation is more performance-oriented, it is ultimately more complicated, and, in the case of volume automation, results in zillions of breakpoints being generated every time you move the fader. The large amount of automation data generated can bog down smaller host-based Pro Tools systems.

I can see this approach being the preferred one for those using a control surface, such as a Pro Control or Command 8, where you can touch real, motorized faders. Let's try a simple fader move so you can see how it works.

1. Choose Window > Automation. This window is useful if you have already written some automation on a track and want to protect it from being overwritten. For instance, we have some plug-in automation in the choruses on the M.tune vocal track. If you were to put that track into Write mode and play through the chorus, the plug-in automation would be erased unless you clicked the Plug-in button to protect it. This is why I rarely use Write mode. In Touch and Latch modes, automation data is erased only for the control you are touching at the time.

2. We don't want to accidentally overwrite any plug-in data, so click the Plug-in button in the Automation window, and close the window.

3. The steel guitar tracks need to be faded down at the last note of the Intro. Select the two tracks and create a group named **Steel**.

4. Click the Automation Mode selector on the Otis.clean track and choose Touch. The other steel track will follow suit.

5. Fader automation can be written by clicking the track's volume indicator, but it's often easier to use the fader in the Output window. Click the Otis.clean track's Output Window button, as shown here:

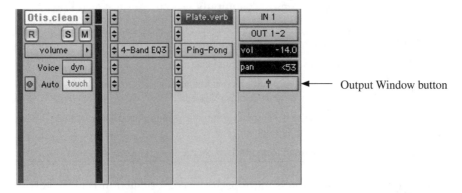

Output Window button

6. Play the end of the Intro and fade the last note. Then stop the transport.

7. Enable the Volume view on the Otis tracks. Your volume automation data should look something like Figure 13-5.

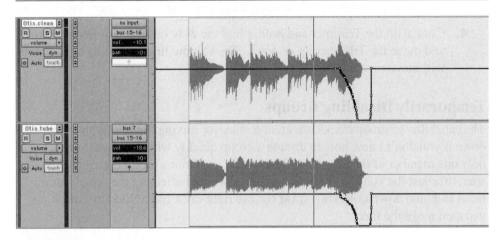

FIGURE 13-5   Volume automation data on the Otis tracks

I'd like to give you a few more automation tips, and then encourage you to go to town with the automation in this session—see if you can max out your system. This is as good a time as any to see how much automation your CPU can handle. Keep an eye on the System Usage window to see which parts of the song cause the biggest CPU load.

Toggling Track Views

Here's a real time saver: when Commands Focus is enabled (the a...z button below the Zoom presets is outlined in blue), Track views on selected tracks can be toggled between Waveform and Volume view by pressing the hyphen (-) key. Pressing OPTION (ALT) before pressing the hyphen key will toggle all the Track views.

Changing the Overall Volume of a Track

Let's say, for instance, that you want to change the overall volume of the C loop track. You can't just move the fader, because you've already put some volume automation breakpoints on the track. There are many ways to do this, but here's one that won't use any extra processing power.

1. Disable the Drums group by clicking the group name in the Edit Groups list, as shown here:

2. Use the hyphen key to change the C loop's Track view to Volume.

Click to disable Drums group

   3. Scroll out past the end of the song where there aren't any more breakpoints.

   4. Click with the Trimmer and hold, press the ⌘ (CTRL) key for finer control, and move the Trimmer up or down. The volume line and all its breakpoints will move together.

Temporarily Disabling Groups

The capability to group tracks is a great feature for mixing, but it can slow you down if you don't know how to disable a group quickly when you want to change only one member of the group. For instance, if the Drums group is enabled and you want to adjust the volume of the Shaker track without affecting the other drums, press and hold down CONTROL (START) or use right-click (on a Windows machine), and then move the fader.

Performance Tips

You can do quite a few things to squeeze more performance from your CPU when your session starts to bog down:

- The amount of RAM (Random Access Memory) installed in your computer has a huge effect on its performance. On a Mac, click the Apple icon in the upper-right corner to see how much RAM you have. On a PC, click Start > My Computer > View System Information > General. Consider installing additional RAM to bump your memory up to 2GB or more.

- Consolidate tracks with a lot of edits. Heavily edited tracks put quite a strain on the computer.

- Clear unused regions from the session. Select the unused regions (⌘+SHIFT+U / CTRL+SHIFT+U) and then use the Clear Selected command (⌘+SHIFT+B / CTRL+SHIFT+B) to clear them.

- If your session is on the startup drive, move it to an external drive instead.

- Increase the Hardware Buffer size (remember this one?). Larger buffer sizes allow more tracks and plug-ins. Go to Setup > Playback Engine > H/W Buffer Size.

- Increase the CPU Usage Limit setting (Setup > Playback Engine). This setting controls how much of the CPU's processing power is allocated to Pro Tools. Users of single-processor computers can assign up to 85 percent of their processing power to Pro Tools, and users of multiprocessor computers can choose up to 99 percent, dedicating an entire processor to Pro Tools.

- Deactivate any tracks or plug-ins you're not using.

- If your session is hanging up at the same spot every time, try reducing the automation data at that spot.

- Quit any unnecessary programs. Only Pro Tools and basic system programs, such as the Mac's Finder, should be running. On a Windows machine, pressing CTRL + ALT + DELETE will bring up a window (called the Task Manager in Windows XP) that shows which programs are running, and enables you to quit programs by selecting them and clicking End Task. Refer to your computer's documentation to find out exactly which programs need to be running on your machine.

- Bounce tracks with DSP-intensive plug-ins, such as Xpand or Auto-Tune, to a new track with the processing applied, and then deactivate the original tracks.

- Turn off Audio During Fast Forward/Rewind, located under Setup > Preferences > Operation.

- Set the Sends view to Assignments. If you're viewing the little send faders instead of the assignments, changing to Assignments will free up some processing power. Go to View > Sends A-E (or F-J) > Assignments.

- Choose fewer levels of undo. This is a RAM eater. Do you really need 32 levels of undo? If not, knock it down to six or eight (Setup > Preferences > Editing).

- Turn off Scrolling (OPTIONS > Scrolling > No Scrolling). This OPTION causes a lot of extra screen redrawing, which uses processing power.

- Set Track views to Blocks in the Edit window. It's a lot easier for the computer to draw blocks than waveforms.

Creating a Stereo Mix

When you're finished torturing your computer and you've achieved the perfect mix, it's time to capture the magic onto a stereo file. Here are a few items to consider before committing your mix to ones and zeroes:

- Make sure the mix is as loud as it can be without clipping. Go to the loudest part of the song (probably the word "home" in the chorus) and turn up the Stereo Master fader as high as it will go without lighting the clip indicators.

- Insert the Compressor/Limiter plug-in on the Stereo Master aux channel and select the Gentle Limiting preset. Tweak the Threshold control so that occasional peaks are smoothed out.

- As the instruments are fading out at the end of the song, use the Stereo Master fader to fade the overall volume down.

- You have to select the part of the session you want to bounce to disk or record, or Pro Tools will keep on recording until the end of time. In the Edit window, use the Selector to highlight the song from the first sound you want to hear to the end of the fadeout.

Exporting Your Mix

Now that you have recorded your mix, double-click the region and name it **Wayfaring Stranger**. This region may look like a stereo file, but it's actually two separate mono WAV files: Wayfaring Stranger.L and Wayfaring Stranger.R (Pro Tools does not support stereo interleaved files). For this mix to be of use to the mastering house, it must be converted to a stereo interleaved file. To accomplish this, we can use the Export Regions as Files command.

1. Select the stereo mix and press ⌘+SHIFT+K (CTRL+SHIFT+K). The Export Selected dialog appears. Set the options to create a 24-bit, Stereo WAV file at a Sample Rate of 44,100 Hz (44.1 kHz).

2. Under Destination Directory, you can specify a location for the file, or let it be stored in the Audio Files Folder for the current session. Click Export to create the file. The dialog closes.

3. Now we need a 16-bit WAV or AIFF file for a reference CD-ROM. Press ⌘+SHIFT+K (CTRL+SHIFT+K) to bring up the Export Selected dialog again.

4. Use the Export Options to create a Stereo WAV or AIFF 16-bit 44.1 kHz file, and click Export.

5. Because there is already a stereo file named Wayfaring Stranger in the Audio Files Folder, Pro Tools will prompt you to rename the file. Rename the file **Wayfaring Stranger_16** and click Save.

6. Save your session as **W.Stranger 20mix**.

Deleting Expired Plug-in Demos

Once the Auto-Tune demo expires, it'll become a nuisance during startup. Here's how to delete it.

Mac OS X   Quit Pro Tools and go to Main Startup Drive > Library > Application Support > Digidesign > Plug-ins, drag the Auto-Tune plug-in into the trashcan, and empty the Trash.

Windows XP   Quit Pro Tools and go to Start > Control Panel > Add or Remove Programs. You will see a list of currently installed programs. Scroll through the list to look for the plug-in demos. If you see them, select and uninstall them. If you don't see them, go to Start > My Computer > Local Disk (usually the C drive) > Program Files > Common Files > Digidesign > DAE > Plug-ins. Right-click the demo plug-ins and choose Delete. In the window that appears, confirm the Delete command to put them in the Recycle Bin. Then, right-click the Recycle Bin, choose Empty Recycle Bin from the pop-up menu, and confirm.

Conclusion

Congratulations on completing *The Musician's Guide to Pro Tools, Second Edition.* I hope you've learned enough about your system to be able to have fun with it. After all, that's why you bought it in the first place, isn't it?

Part IV

Appendixes

Appendix A

Changing the Monitor/Display Resolution

Your display's resolution setting will determine how many tracks can be viewed in Pro Tools, so you should experiment with different settings to find the resolution that works best for you.

Macintosh OS X

In Mac OS X, the settings are in System Preferences > Displays in the Apple menu in the upper-left corner of the screen. Just click the different resolution settings to see what they look like. If your video card or monitor does not support the higher resolutions, the monitor will go fuzzy for about 20 seconds, and then it will revert to your previous setting.

Windows XP

Right-click a blank area of the Desktop and choose Properties. In the Display Properties dialog, click the Settings tab. Adjust the screen resolution slider to view the different settings. It's usually better to select the More setting so that you can view more items in the Edit window. Then click Apply. If you're not already at the More setting, Windows will ask if you want to resize your desktop. Choose OK. Windows will then ask if you want to keep the setting. Choose Yes, and then click OK to close the Display Properties dialog.

Appendix B

Cheat Sheets and Function Key Labels

Chapters 1–5: Mac and Windows Cheat Sheets

Mac

Record & Play	⌘+SPACEBAR
Save Session	⌘+S
New Track	⌘+SHIFT+N
Zoom In	T
Zoom Out	R
Auto/Input	OPTION+K
Pre/Post-Roll	⌘+K
Crossfade	⌘+F
Separate Region	B
Heal Separation	⌘+H
Return to Start	RETURN
Zoom to Fill Window ..	OPTION+F
Green Light	Input mode

Record & Play	⌘+SPACEBAR
Save Session	⌘+S
New Track	⌘+SHIFT+N
Zoom In	T
Zoom Out	R
Auto/Input	OPTION+K
Pre/Post-Roll	⌘+K
Crossfade	⌘+F
Separate Region	B
Heal Separation	⌘+H
Return to Start	RETURN
Zoom to Fill Window .	OPTION+F
Green Light	Input mode

Windows

Record & Play	CTRL+SPACEBAR
Save Session	CTRL+S
New Track	CTRL+SHIFT+N
Zoom In	T
Zoom Out	R
Auto/Input	ALT+K
Pre/Post-Roll	CTRL+K
Crossfade	CTRL+F
Separate Region	B
Heal Separation	CTRL+H
Return to Start	ENTER
Zoom to Fill Window ..	ALT+F
Green Light	Input mode

Record & Play	CTRL+SPACEBAR
Save Session	CTRL+S
New Track	CTRL+SHIFT+N
Zoom In	T
Zoom Out	R
Auto/Input	ALT+K
Pre/Post-Roll	CTRL+K
Crossfade	CTRL+F
Separate Region	B
Heal Separation	CTRL+H
Return to Start	ENTER
Zoom to Fill Window ..	ALT+F
Green Light	Input mode

Chapters 6–13: Mac Cheat Sheet

Toggle Mix/Edit window	⌘+=
Zoom Toggle	E
Select the Smart Tool	F6+F7
Nudge Back by next Nudge Value	M
Nudge Back by Nudge Value	<
Nudge Forward by Nudge Value	>
Nudge Forward by next Nudge Value . . .	/
Create Group	⌘+G
Suspend Groups	⌘+SHIFT+G
Lock/Unlock Region	⌘+L
Zoom Vertically	⌘+OPTION+[or]
Locate Selected Region Start	LEFT ARROW
Locate Selected Region End	RIGHT ARROW
Toggle Waveform & Volume view	Dash key
Half-speed playback	⌘+SPACEBAR
Fades window	⌘+F
Fade (without Fades dialog)	F
Go to next edit point	TAB
Extend selection to end of session	OPTION+SHIFT+RETURN
Undo	Z
Cut	X
Copy	C
Paste	V
Select Unused Audio	⌘+SHIFT+U
Clear Audio window	⌘+SHIFT+B
Delete Breakpoints	OPTION+click (Grabber)

Chapters 6–13: Windows Cheat Sheet

Toggle Mix/Edit window	CTRL+=
Zoom Toggle	START+E
Select the Smart Tool	F6+F7
Nudge Back by next Nudge Value	M
Nudge Back by Nudge Value	<
Nudge Forward by Nudge Value	>
Nudge Forward by next Nudge Value	/
Create Group	CTRL+G
Suspend Groups	CTRL+SHIFT+G
Lock/Unlock Region	CTRL+L
Zoom Vertically	CTRL+ALT+[*or*]
Locate Selected Region Start	LEFT ARROW
Locate Selected Region End	RIGHT ARROW
Toggle Waveform & Volume view	Dash key
Half-speed playback	SHIFT+SPACEBAR
Fades window	CTRL+F
Fade (without Fades dialog)	F
Go to next edit point	TAB
Extend selection to end of session	CTRL+SHIFT+ENTER
Undo	Z
Cut	X
Copy	C
Paste	V
Select Unused Audio	CTRL+SHIFT+U
Clear Audio window	CTRL+SHIFT+B

Function Key Labels: Full-Size Keyboard

Cut these out and tape or glue them above the function keys at the top of your keyboard. Align "Zoomer" with the F5 key.

> **NOTE**

These function key labels will not work for the newer Mac keyboards, which have a different spacing between function keys and no longer have a convenient ledge for the label.

Print the function key labels the correct size by following these directions: On a Mac, open the Print dialog, which defaults to the Copies and Pages pop-up, then set the Page Scaling to None. On a PC, open the Print dialog, go to the Page Handling section, and set the Page Scaling to None.

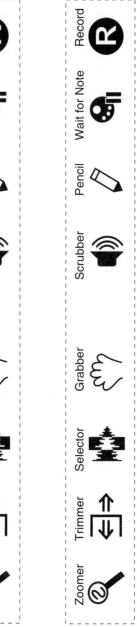

Function Key Labels: Mac Laptop

Cut these out and place them above the function keys at the top of your keyboard. Align "Shuffle" with the F1 key. Align "Zoom" with the F5 key.

Print the function key labels the correct size by opening the Print dialog, which defaults to the Copies and Pages pop-up, and then setting the Page Scaling to None.

Shuffle   Slip   Spot   Grid

Zoom   Trim   Select   Grab   Scrub   Pencil   Record

Shuffle   Slip   Spot   Grid

Zoom   Trim   Select   Grab   Scrub   Pencil   Record

Appendix C
Preventing and Troubleshooting Problems

I'm one of those people who have a real gift for crashing computers (or anything else containing a microprocessor, for that matter). Even the computer that controls the transmission in my truck crashes from time to time and refuses to go into fourth gear. When this happens I have to pull over, kill the engine, and restart it. I'm not kidding. I could crash a Casio wristwatch if I worked at it long enough. As a result of this unusual talent, I have seen many a hard drive become "totally hosed, dude," to use the vernacular of the Apple Tech Support staff (they know me well).

The first time I booted up OS X on a brand-new G4, I thought, "Great! Finally, a crash-proof operating system!" It took me nearly 15 minutes to crash it. I have no doubt that this is partially due to my penchant for fearlessly installing all sorts of third-party software on my Pro Tools computer, which is really not a good idea. I just can't help myself.

Over the years, I have developed certain steps to follow when I start having trouble with either Pro Tools or the computer's operating system. I start with the fastest and easiest, and work my way through them until the problem clears up. I use Macintosh computers for Pro Tools, but many of these steps also apply to Windows machines. These steps are meant for general troubleshooting. One could easily write an entire book on troubleshooting specific problems with Pro Tools and Macintoshes. If I found one, I would buy it immediately. The only problem is, the information would be obsolete in a very short time. Due to the constantly changing nature of any software-based system, the best place for up-to-the-minute information is the Digidesign web site. The DUC (Digidesign User Conference), **http://duc.digidesign.com/,** is a great place to go for in-depth troubleshooting. For additional information about Macintosh computers, try the following web sites:

- **Mac OS X Hints**   www.macosxhints.com
- **Accelerate Your Mac**   www.xlr8yourmac.com
- **MacInTouch**   www.macintouch.com
- **MacFixIt**   www.macfixit.com

The tips and procedures in this appendix are presented with the assumption that your Pro Tools system was originally set up and working correctly at some point, and you haven't done anything dumb, like install a bunch of dodgy cracked software. A further assumption is that you're using a supported computer and your system meets all the minimum requirements, such as RAM.

Routine Maintenance

Here are a few things you can do periodically to keep your system running smoothly.

Repair Disk Permissions (Mac)

This command can be found in the First Aid section of the Disk Utility. Repairing disk permissions is usually the first thing I do if my Mac is slowing down. According to Apple, permissions should be repaired about once per month, and after installing any new software (it's not necessary to verify the permissions first).

Rebuild the Directory

Most of the problems I have encountered with operating systems are due to directory corruption. The directory is a table of contents of sorts for the information stored on a hard drive. Whenever the operating system needs to access the data on a particular drive, it goes to the directory to determine its location. When storing information to a disk, the operating system checks the directory for available space.

The operating system is constantly updating the directory, and if it is unexpectedly interrupted by an improper shutdown, crash, or power outage, the directory can be damaged. Software bugs can also damage the directory by causing it to be updated incorrectly. Audio drives often suffer from directory damage as well. Removing a FireWire drive without first unmounting it can interrupt a directory update and cause directory damage. The effect of this damage may not be noticeable at first, but the corruption tends to spread, causing a snowball effect. Eventually it may cause the computer to crash. In my experience, if nothing is done to stop this cycle, this snowball effect will cause the computer to crash more often until it gets to the point where it won't even boot up. When a startup drive becomes so damaged that it won't boot the computer, it could mean replacing the drive and reinstalling everything. In some cases the data is rendered inaccessible and can only be retrieved by sending the drive to a data recovery company to be disassembled—a very expensive process.

There's no reason to let your drives get that far out of whack. You should use repair utilities for preventative maintenance. If you don't routinely repair your drives, you really can't expect your computer to run indefinitely without problems any more than you can expect your car to drive problem-free indefinitely without an oil change.

On a Mac, you can repair some disk problems with Apple's Disk Utility, in the First Aid section. To accomplish this you must boot the computer from the original Apple Software Install DVD, which is usually a matter of putting in the DVD and restarting while holding down the C key (be patient, this takes a while). This DVD is "bootable," which means it contains a stripped-down system folder that takes over the operation of the computer. The Disk Utility on the installer DVD can be used to repair the main startup drive, which is now idle. Select Utilities > Disk Utility. When the application opens, select your startup volume (usually titled something like Macintosh HD). Under the First Aid tab, click Repair Disk. Run the application twice; once on the startup volume (partition) and once on the drive itself. While this utility is better than nothing, it doesn't go very deep, and is often more of a band-aid than anything else.

NOTE   *Do not use the install DVD to repair permissions. That operation should be done from the Apple Disk Utility on your main startup drive.*

Fortunately, Macintosh users can completely rebuild their directory with DiskWarrior, a Mac-only program from Alsoft, Inc. (**www.alsoft.com**). Like all disk repair utilities, DiskWarrior comes on a bootable CD-ROM (it's usually not a good idea to disassemble your car's engine while it's running, and the same goes for computers). While some utilities attempt to patch a damaged directory, DiskWarrior scans the drive and builds a completely new error-free directory for it. I have seen this utility restore drives that I thought were goners. DiskWarrior is a simple and inexpensive application that requires no technical expertise. Alsoft recommends running DiskWarrior on your main startup drive every month or so. I have seen people send their ailing computers off to be repaired, only to find out that the technician just ran DiskWarrior on it. They could have bought the program for the cost of shipping the computer alone, never mind the repair fee!

In cases where a drive is too far gone for DiskWarrior, I have used a utility called Data Rescue II, a data recovery product by Prosoft Engineering, Inc. (**www.prosofteng.com**). This utility meticulously scans the damaged drive, sometimes for several hours. The recovered data is then saved to another volume.

Since booting from a CD-ROM to run diagnostic software is time consuming, I have DiskWarrior and Data Rescue installed on my laptop. When I need to run one of these programs, I start up my Pro Tools computer in Target Disk Mode (choose System Preferences > Startup Disk > Target Disk Mode, or restart and hold the T key). Once the Pro Tools computer is running in Target Disk Mode, it can be connected to the laptop (or any other Mac) with a FireWire cable, and it shows up on the laptop's desktop like any other FireWire drive. Then I use the repair utility on the laptop to fix the damaged drive.

It's worth mentioning here that *all* hard drives have directories and are therefore susceptible to directory corruption. FireWire drives in particular are prone to corruption because people often forget to unmount them before unplugging the FireWire cable.

Defragment Hard Drives

In a hard drive, fragments of computer files can become scattered willy-nilly across the spinning disks as files are added and deleted over months of normal operation. This process is known as *fragmentation,* and it can reduce drive performance, shortening the life of your hard drive. A fragmented hard drive will take much longer to seek and retrieve data. In extreme cases, it can even cause mechanical failure. Fragmentation usually starts to become a problem when a drive is around 80 percent full. As the drive fills up, the operating system has more trouble finding space for new data, so the data must be broken up into smaller pieces.

Windows XP users can periodically defragment their drives using Windows Disk Defragmenter (right-click My Computer, choose Manage, and click Disk Defragmenter under Storage or choose Start > All Programs > Accessories > System Tools > Disk Defragmenter).

Improvements in Mac OS X have made fragmentation much less of an issue than in past operating systems. Mac drives that are low on contiguous free space can still exhibit flaky behavior, however. If you think your drive might be low on free space, you can download the free demo of Coriolis Systems' iDefrag (**www.coriolis-systems.com**) and use it to check your drive. If you choose to defragment your drive, you will need to purchase the software. In addition to defragmentation, iDefrag will attempt to rearrange the files into an order that will improve the drive's performance, a process commonly referred to as *optimization*.

Another way to defragment a drive is to simply get a new drive, copy the old data to the new drive, and then erase the old drive and start over with it. This works well for audio drives, but is somewhat inconvenient for startup drives because software may have to be reauthorized. A startup drive should not be merely copied, but *cloned* with a utility such as Carbon Copy Cloner (**www.bombich.com**) to make sure that the target drive is bootable, and all hidden files are also copied. A simpler approach would be to avoid using more than 80 percent of your startup drive.

Format Your Audio Drives Periodically

Whenever you reach a point where you need to clear an audio drive for a new project, you should completely erase (or initialize) the drive. In Mac OS X, drives should be erased and partitioned using the Disk Utility (Main Startup Drive > Applications > Utilities > Disk Utility). Windows XP users can use the included disk management software. Right-click My Computer and choose Manage. Under Storage, choose Disk Management.

Check S.M.A.R.T. Status

Most modern hard drives use S.M.A.R.T. (Self-Monitoring, Analysis, and Reporting Technology), a monitoring system designed to warn the user of impending drive failure. The Mac Disk Utility shows the S.M.A.R.T. status of any internal drives (not FireWire or USB) in the drive information at the bottom of the Disk Utility window. If it reads "Verified," the drive is in good shape. If it reads "Failing," you should back the drive up immediately without powering down, if possible. SMARTReporter is a free Mac application that polls your internal drives and warns of impending failure with an icon in the Menu bar.

Clear System and User Caches (Mac)

Many experts agree that it's a good idea to occasionally clear out application-specific caches. They can be found in these two locations:

■ Main Drive > Users > (*your username*) > Library > Caches

■ Main Drive > Library > Caches

Also, your Internet browser caches should occasionally be cleared with a utility such as Tiger Cache Cleaner or Cache Out X.

Avoid Internet Pollution (Windows)

Unless you've been living under a rock, you're surely aware that surfing the Internet can pour an endless torrent of malicious garbage into your computer. Be that as it may, many people can't afford to buy a separate computer just for e-mail, and everyone has to download software updates from time to time.

Since most viruses are written for PCs, Windows machines are much more susceptible than Macs to viruses and other nasty Internet parasites. Therefore, this section provides tips for Windows users only. Windows machines are not my area of expertise, so I interviewed Dean Klear, the former Windows guru at Atlanta Pro Audio, the epicenter for Pro Tools activity in the Southeastern United States (and a great place to buy Pro Tools stuff). Dean graciously provided the following tips for recognizing and dealing with viruses and spyware on Windows machines:

1. Take a look at your System Tray. If there are a million little icons filling it up, you have too much software running in the background. Go to Start > Control Panel and double-click Add/Remove Programs. Uninstall anything you don't use, and if you seem to have a lot of programs installed that aren't familiar to you, you most likely have been infected with spyware

programs. Right-click any icons in your System Tray and look for configuration options that tell the program not to run on startup.

2. If you can't find an option to disable these programs, there's close to a 100 percent chance your computer is infected with spyware. Examples include Gator Software, WeatherBug, Kazaa (major culprit), and almost every "enhancement" that you see for Internet Explorer. If you've never heard of the company, you shouldn't trust it enough to run its programs on your computer. I recommend using Ad-Aware or Spybot Search & Destroy to remove spyware and using Norton AntiVirus to remove viruses and to immunize your operating system.

3. If your System Tray is svelte, press CTRL+ALT+DELETE to pull up the Task Manager. Click the Processes tab, and you'll see four columns: Image Name, User Name, CPU, and Mem Usage. If you click CPU twice, it should arrange all the processes to show you which items are using the most CPU power. When you first boot up, System Idle Process should be the first thing listed, usually taking up 99 percent of available CPU. Click the Applications tab. When you first boot up, the Applications tab should be empty. If any of these tabs shows you something different, you could have a virus or a piece of spyware running. Also, a good free cache-cleaning software for Windows is CCleaner.

When Pro Tools Starts Acting Up

When things start to go awry in Pro Tools, the indications may be subtle at first. When the screen redraw starts getting jerky or the controls become sluggish, something is slowing down the system. It could be that you're merely overtaxing the system, but it could point to something more serious. Or, you may get error messages. It'll take a bit of sleuthing on your part to find the source of the problem. There are plenty of things you can try before resorting to calling Digidesign Tech Support. If you suspect the Digidesign hardware, HD system users can run DigiTest, a program installed in the Digidesign folder on the startup drive. I've found that most problems with Pro Tools systems are software related, and can generally be divided into three main categories. You have to ask yourself:

■ Is it a Pro Tools software problem?

■ Is it a hard drive problem?

■ Is it an operating system problem?

The following steps can help determine the answers to these questions.

Quit Pro Tools, Then Relaunch   Sometimes this will clear up odd behavior. If you've deleted tracks to free up some DSP in your session, you have to quit Pro Tools and start it up again in order for these changes to take effect.

Disconnect All Nonessential Peripherals and Restart   Whenever you start any kind of troubleshooting procedure, you should shut down the computer and disconnect any external hard drives, MIDI interfaces, CD burners, nonessential USB items, and so forth. If you have any extra IDE drives installed in your computer, disconnect them as well. If the problem goes away, reconnect them one by one to isolate the troublemaker.

Increase the Hardware Buffer Size   If Pro Tools starts exhibiting sluggish or erratic behavior, the Pro Tools software isn't necessarily the source of the problem. Often the problem is the audio drive or the operating system. If you use FireWire drives, you've probably seen error messages like "DAE can't get audio from the drives fast enough." This message often results from trying to play too many tracks off a FireWire drive. If you get this message, try increasing the Hardware Buffer Size setting: Setup > Playback Engine > H/W Buffer Size. Bumping this up to a higher setting will sometimes clear up the problem, especially when you're attempting to bounce to disk. If this doesn't help, you can copy the session and its audio files onto an extra internal drive (*not* the drive containing the operating system). Internal audio drives will usually play more tracks than a FireWire drive. If you transfer a session from a FireWire drive to an internal drive, you should then unmount the FireWire drive to prevent Pro Tools from trying to access it. This will force Pro Tools to reference the copied audio files on the internal drive instead.

Add More RAM (Random Access Memory)   You've probably heard this one before. All types of computers will benefit from having additional RAM installed. New computers rarely come from the factory with enough RAM for Pro Tools. Fortunately, RAM is relatively inexpensive and easy to install. Adding more RAM can make a huge difference in large sessions. A Pro Tools rig with 2GB or more of RAM is the norm these days.

Keep Your Computer Clean   Pro Tools places a heavy demand on your computer. The more programs you have installed on your computer, the more likely you are to encounter software conflicts. Any programs that scan or index your computer in the background should be avoided.

Turn Off the Calculate Folder Size Option (Mac OS)   When this option is enabled, the computer constantly scans a drive or partition to determine the size of each of its folders. With a Finder window open, go to View > Show View Options, check All Windows, and uncheck Calculate All Sizes.

Turn Off Hardware Acceleration   In some Windows computers, the hardware acceleration for the video card can cause odd behavior in Pro Tools. Because various video cards in PCs have different control panels, check the computer (or video hardware) manufacturer's manual for directions on either reducing or switching off hardware acceleration.

Keep Your Desktop Clear   Having too many items on your desktop can impact performance. Create a folder on your startup drive titled "Old Desktop Items" and use it to store any extraneous desktop files. Remember that aliases (Macintosh) or shortcuts (Windows) can be deleted without affecting the underlying file or application.

Turn Off File Sharing (Mac OS)   If you have your computers on a network, you should turn File Sharing off when running Pro Tools. Go to System Preferences > Sharing.

Close Unnecessary Windows   Any windows that are open on the desktop behind the Pro Tools windows should be closed. Even though you can't see them, the computer is still wasting time redrawing them.

Make Sure Classic Mode Is Not Running (OS X)   Classic Mode is OS X's way of running older, non-OS X applications (only on an older dual-boot Mac with OS 9 installed). It uses memory and should be turned off when using Pro Tools (System Preferences > Classic).

Streamline Your Session

Maxing out the computer with a lot of tracks, plug-ins, and automation is a common source of sluggish behavior in Pro Tools, especially for LE users. If you suspect that performance problems may be due to the complexity of your session, try opening a less complex session to see if the problem goes away. Or, save the session as a test session and delete a bunch of tracks to see if the problem clears up. If one session has problems and others don't, try the following tips, which suggest ways to streamline the session. You may recall reading this information in Chapter 13.

■ Consolidate tracks with a lot of edits. Heavily edited tracks put quite a strain on the computer.

■ Clear unused regions from the session. Select unused regions by pressing ⌘+SHIFT+U (CTRL+SHIFT+U) and then clear them with ⌘+SHIFT+B (CTRL+SHIFT+B).

■ If your session is on the startup drive, move it to an external drive instead.

- Increase the CPU Usage Limit. This setting controls how much of the CPU's processing power is allocated to Pro Tools. Users of single-processor computers can assign up to 85 percent of their processing power to Pro Tools, and users of multiprocessor computer can choose up to 99 percent, dedicating an entire processor to Pro Tools.

- Deactivate any tracks or plug-ins you're not using.

- If your session is hanging up at the same spot every time, try reducing the automation data at that spot.

- Quit any unnecessary programs. Only Pro Tools and basic system programs, such as the Mac's Finder, should be running. On a Windows machine, pressing CTRL+ALT+DELETE will bring up a window (called the Task Manager in Windows XP) that shows which programs are running, and enables you to quit programs by selecting them and clicking End Task. Refer to your computer's documentation to find out exactly which programs need to be running on your machine.

- Bounce tracks with DSP-intensive plug-ins, such as Xpand or Auto-Tune, to a new track with the processing applied, and then deactivate the original tracks.

- Turn off Audio During Fast Forward/Rewind, located under Setup > Preferences > Operation.

- Set the Sends view to Assignments. If you're viewing the little send faders instead of the assignments, changing to Assignments will free up some processing power. Go to View > Sends A-E (or F-J) > Assignments.

- Choose fewer levels of undo. This is a RAM eater. Do you really need 32 levels of undo? If not, knock it down to 16 or 8 (Setup > Preferences > Editing).

- Turn off Scrolling (Options > Scrolling > No Scrolling). This option causes extra screen redrawing, which uses processing power.

- Set Track views to Blocks in the Edit window. It's easier for the computer to draw blocks than waveforms.

Split Your Session across Two Hard Drives

If your session has grown to the maximum number of tracks for your system and/or contains a lot of edits, you may need to move some of your audio files to another hard drive to split up the work load. (Note: I said another *drive*, not another partition on the same drive.) Merely changing the disk allocation won't do the trick, however. You'll have to copy the audio files to the new drive, and make sure Pro Tools knows where they are. The easiest way to accomplish this is as follows:

1. Go to Setup > Disk Allocation. In the Disk Allocation dialog, you will see a list of your current session's tracks, and a second column showing the drive where the audio files for that track are located.

2. SHIFT+click to select about half the tracks in the session, and then click the pop-up menu of one of the selected tracks. You will see a list of available hard drives.

3. Choose another hard drive to switch the disk allocation for the selected tracks. Now, any *additional* material recorded on the selected tracks will go to the new drive, but the existing tracks will still be playing from the original drive. Click OK to close the dialog.

4. Select and consolidate the audio regions on the tracks you have reallocated. Pro Tools will automatically create a new folder on the new drive containing the newly consolidated audio files. The change in disk allocation will tell Pro Tools to access the newly copied files for playback.

When Pro Tools Crashes

It's difficult to determine the cause of a crash. Before you can do any sleuthing however, you need to find a way to quit the program. If Pro Tools is not responding to any commands, it may be possible to force quit the application without powering down the computer. In any case, you should trash the Preferences before attempting to restart Pro Tools.

Force Quitting Pro Tools (Mac)

On a Mac, pressing OPTION+⌘+ESCAPE brings up the Force Quit window, which shows a list of currently running applications. Choose Pro Tools from the list, and click Force Quit. This usually gets you out of a Pro Tools crash without bringing down the whole computer. If the entire computer is frozen, as in a kernel panic, you can restart the computer by holding down the Power button for several seconds. Whenever Pro Tools crashes, the Pro Tools Preference files may have been corrupted and should be deleted. This is not a big deal, as these files will be regenerated when you reboot. The procedure for this is outlined in Chapter 2. Be sure to delete *all* Preference files that have to do with Pro Tools (these will vary

What Is a Kernel Panic? (Mac OS X)

A *kernel panic* is a crash at the core of the operating system, and is usually caused by damaged or incompatible software. Kernel panics manifest themselves in different ways. The most common kind is a gray screen accompanied by the following message in four different languages: "You need to restart your computer. Hold down the Power Button for several seconds or press the Restart button." Sometimes updating to the latest version of Mac OS X that is compatible with your system will resolve issues with unexpected quits. Check the Digidesign web site first to make sure that the latest version of Mac OS X is supported. Deleting corrupt .plist files for whichever application was open at the time of the crash is always a good thing to try. You can try deleting these two, which are sometimes implicated in unexpected quits:

- Com.apple.ATS.plist
- Com.apple.BezelServices.plist

Automatic virus protection software such as Symantec's Norton Auto-Protect scans your system constantly and should be turned off when using Pro Tools. Cache-clearing utilities such as Cocktail, Tiger Cache Cleaner, or Mac Pilot can sometimes resolve issues in the operating system.

according to which system you have; some examples are DAE Prefs, DigiSetup Prefs, Pro Tools Prefs, and com.digidesign.ProTools.plist) and then empty the Trash or Recycle Bin. Pro Tools also places on each audio drive a Digidesign Databases Folder that should be trashed as well. The files will be regenerated on relaunch. If Pro Tools won't relaunch, try logging out and logging back in, or restart the computer.

Force Quitting Pro Tools (Windows)

On a Windows system, pressing CTRL+ALT+DELETE brings up the Task Manager window. Choose Pro Tools from the list of currently running applications, and click End Task. If the computer will not quit, hold down the Power button until the computer shuts down. Trash the Pro Tools Preferences as discussed in Chapter 2, reboot the computer, and relaunch Pro Tools to see if the problem persists. If it does, this would be a good time to run a disk utility such as Norton Disk Doctor on the startup and audio drives to look for file corruption.

Windows XP has a program located in Accessories called System Restore. It is listed under System Tools along with other utilities. It allows the operator to create restore points when the computer is running well and then reinstate the system to that point if something later goes wrong. This can be very useful, and it's a good idea to set a restore point before you experience problems. This is done by going to Start > Programs > Accessories > System Tools > System Restore > Create Restore Point.

Repair Session Corruption

On rare occasions, the session file itself will become corrupted. This could be the problem if you're having trouble with one session but the others are working fine. In this case, reinstalling the Pro Tools software won't fix the problem. Sometimes you can get out of this pickle by opening a new session with the same start time, sample rate, and bit rate as the old one, and then importing all the tracks from the corrupted session into the new session.

Reinstall the Pro Tools Software

Corruption in the Pro Tools application can sometimes cause crashes. Third-party plug-ins are more often the culprit. If the Pro Tools software or third-party plug-ins are suspect, reinstalling Pro Tools will usually fix the problem. If you go this route, be sure to trash the Pro Tools Prefs again beforehand. Then pop in the Pro Tools Installation Disk and select Uninstall under the Custom Install pop-up menu. Then install the program again. (This is the main reason you should guard your installation disk and serial number with your life, and take it everywhere you take your Pro Tools rig.) Any third-party plug-ins will be removed as well. It's possible to remove these from the Plug-ins folder ahead of time and then drag them back into the current Plug-ins folder, but they may be the source of your problem. It's safer to reinstall fresh copies of the third-party plug-ins one at a time, rebooting each time to see if the problem recurs.

Also, be aware that any Pro Tools upgrades you may have downloaded and installed since you first installed the program will be wiped out, and will have to be reinstalled. Therefore, it behooves you to save any update installers you download from Digidesign in case you need them again.

Troubleshoot Your Operating System

If the Pro Tools software has been ruled out, you may have a problem with your operating system or hardware. The following sections provide a few troubleshooting tips that I have learned over the years.

Remove Third-Party RAM

Having the wrong kind of RAM can cause your computer to do all kinds of weird stuff, and the problem may not manifest itself for weeks or months. If you or someone else has added any RAM to your computer, try pulling it out to see if the problem goes away.

Remove Third-Party PCI Cards

Sometimes a bad Pro Tools or SCSI PCI (or PCE) card will cause problems, even preventing a computer from booting. Occasionally, a PCI card will need to be "reseated" by taking it out and putting it back in. Make sure the cards are installed in the correct slot order (consult the Digidesign documentation for correct placement).

Reset Parameter RAM (Mac OS)

Your computer stores information in an area of memory called Parameter Ram. If this RAM becomes corrupt, your computer may behave erratically. Anytime you remove or replace a PCI card, you should reset the Parameter RAM:

1. Restart the computer and immediately press and hold OPTION+⌘+R+P.

2. Hold the keys down until you hear the startup chime three times.

3. Release the keys.

Reinstall the System Software

If all else fails, you may need to reinstall the system software. This involves booting from the Software Install disc and following the instructions. When reinstalling the system software on a Mac, you can click an Options button that presents a choice between two types of installation:

- ■ **Archive and Install**   Preserves your Users and Network Settings, as well as any other applications, and their Preferences, you have installed on the disk.

- ■ **Erase and Install**   Completely wipes the drive clean and starts over from scratch. Choosing this option (formerly referred to on Macs as "Clean Install") means every single bit of software on the drive will have to be reinstalled and reauthorized.

It's a tough choice, but I have to say that the more convenient Archive and Install option has *never once* fixed a serious operating system problem on any of my computers—possibly because this option does not remove Preferences files that may have been causing the problem in the first place. In my experience, it usually comes down to using the Erase and Install option, which means wiping the drive clean and starting over. A clean install is a real pain, but it's the only way to be sure you've removed any corrupted files. I end up having to do this on my main Pro Tools computer, an average of twice a year.

Replace the Internal Hard Drive

Hard drives have a limited life span, which is getting shorter all the time due to the corner-cutting practices that hard drive manufacturers use to make them cheaper. Most of the wear and tear on a drive occurs when it is starting up or shutting down, so drives actually last longer if you just leave them running. I have two identical hard drives in my main Pro Tools computer, with identical information on each. If I start having problems during a recording session, I just boot off the other drive and continue. I'll go back when I have time and try to figure out what's wrong with the drive in question. If I don't feel like tinkering with it, I just wipe the drive and use Carbon Copy Cloner (**www.bombich.com**) to copy all the data over from the good drive. This may seem extreme, but it can prevent the loss of days of studio time. It's the next best thing to having a spare Pro Tools computer.

Appendix D

About the Session Disc

The Session Disc is a CD-ROM containing the following items:

- Pro Tools session files and plug-in demos for use with the lessons in the book

- Academic versions of Chapters 1 through 4 (in PDF format) for classroom/ lab applications

- A PDF file titled "Cheat Sheets" with printable function key labels and keyboard shortcut charts. This file can be opened in Adobe Reader or Adobe Acrobat. If you don't have either, you can download Adobe Reader for free from **www.adobe.com**. If you don't have access to a printer, cutout versions are provided in Appendix B.

NOTE   *It is recommended that you label your keyboard's function keys and tape a cheat sheet to your monitor before you start the exercises.*

The Pro Tools session files on this disc cannot be played in a music CD player. They can only be opened in Pro Tools and are specifically for use in certain exercises. The best course of action is to copy the entire contents of the CD-ROM to your audio drive from the beginning to save yourself the trouble of inserting the Session Disc more than once. Once you have copied the files, per the following instructions, you can place the Session Disc back in the sleeve in the back of the book.

Copying the Session Disc to Your Hard Drive (Mac)

Remove the Session Disc CD-ROM from the back of the book and insert it into your computer's CD-ROM drive. When the Session Disc icon appears on the desktop, OPTION-drag the icon to your audio drive or main startup drive to copy the files and create a Session Disk folder at that location.

Copying the Session Disc to Your Hard Drive (Windows)

Remove the Session Disc CD-ROM from the back of the book and insert it into your computer's CD-ROM drive. Then go to Start > My Computer and locate the Session Disc on your CD-ROM drive (usually the D drive). Right-click the Session Disc icon and choose Copy from the pop-up menu that appears. Right-click your audio drive or Desktop and select Paste to copy the files and create a Session Disk folder at that location.

Index